5

The Asia-Pacific, Regionalism and the Global System

The Asia-Pacific, Regionalism and the Global System

Edited by

Christopher M. Dent

Professor of East Asia's International Political Economy, University of Leeds, UK

Jörn Dosch

Professor of Asia Pacific Studies, University of Leeds, UK and Professor of International Relations, Monash University, Sunway Campus, Malaysia

WUN
Worldwide Universities Network
IN ASSOCIATION WITH THE WORLD UNIVERSITY NETWORK (WUN)

Edward Elgar
Cheltenham, UK • Northampton, MA, USA

Published by
Edward Elgar Publishing Limited
The Lypiatts
15 Lansdown Road
Cheltenham
Glos GL50 2JA
UK

Edward Elgar Publishing, Inc.
William Pratt House
9 Dewey Court
Northampton
Massachusetts 01060
USA

A catalogue record for this book
is available from the British Library

Library of Congress Control Number: 2012930624

ISBN 978 1 78100 446 3

Typeset by Servis Filmsetting Ltd, Stockport, Cheshire
Printed and bound by MPG Books Group, UK

Contents

Figures and tables

FIGURES

TABLES

Contributors

Richard P. Appelbaum is MacArthur Chair in Sociology and Global and International Studies at the University of California, Santa Barbara. His main research interests are the globalization of low-wage production and its impact on workers, and the role of emerging technologies in fostering more equitable and sustainable economic development.

Minglu Chen is Lecturer of China Studies at the University of Sydney. Her main research interests are the institutions of China's local politics, private entrepreneurship and governance in China, class and social stratum in China, and China–Latin America Relations.

Christopher M. Dent is Professor of East Asia's International Political Economy at the University of Leeds. His main research interests are East Asian regionalism, free trade agreements, Asia–Europe relations, energy diplomacy and renewable energy development in East Asia.

Hugo Dobson is Professor of Japan's International Relations at the National Institute of Japanese Studies and the School of East Asian Studies, University of Sheffield. His main research interests are global governance, the G8 and G20, and Japan's role therein.

Jörn Dosch is Professor of Asia-Pacific Studies at the University of Leeds and Professor of International Relations, Monash University, Sunway Campus, Malaysia. His main research interests are International Politics of the Asia-Pacific, regionalism and domestic change in Southeast Asia, EU–Asia relations and relations between Asia and Latin America.

Melba Falck Reyes is Professor of International Political Economy at the University of Guadalajara. Her main research interests are economic Transpacific relations, Japan–Mexico historical and contemporary economic relations, processes of integration in East Asia and Latin America.

Fang Qing is a PhD candidate at Nanjing University. Her main research interests are European Union studies, global governance, and postmodern theory of international relations.

David S.G. Goodman is Professor of Chinese Politics and a member of the China Studies Centre at the University of Sydney. His main research interests are social and political change in China.

Jeffrey Henderson is Professor of International Development in the School of Sociology, Politics and International Studies and Director of the Centre of East Asian Studies at the University of Bristol. His main research interests are concerned with the political economy and sociology of global transformation with particular reference to the East Asian region. He is part of a global network involved in analysing the implications of the rise of China for other parts of the developing world.

Hong Yousheng is Professor at Nanjing University. His main research interests are European international relations, Europe–US relations, and China's foreign policy.

José Luis León-Manríquez is Professor at the Metropolitan Autonomous University, Mexico City. His main research interests are regional economic integration, and the international political economy of Mexico, Latin America and Asia.

Simen Andersen Øyen is a PhD candidate at the University of Bergen. His main research interests are political philosophy, theories of democracy and modernity, and China and political processes.

Cheol Hee Park is Professor and Associate Dean at the Graduate School of International Studies, Seoul National University. His main research interests are Korea's external relations, Japanese politics and diplomacy, Korea–Japan relations, and international relations in East Asia.

Rachel Parker is a Research Staff Member at the Science and Technology Policy Institute, Washington DC. Her main research interests are economic sociology, public policy, and international development as well as the intersection of science and technology with research capacity development

John Ravenhill is Professor and Head of the School of Politics and International Relations, Research School of Social Sciences, at the Australia National University. His main research interests are in global political economy, especially trade and production in the Asia-Pacific region.

James Reilly is Senior Lecturer in Northeast Asian Politics at the University of Sydney. His main research interests are in Chinese foreign policy, the international relations of East Asia, and the role of public opinion in authoritarian states.

Arturo Santa-Cruz is Professor at the Pacific Studies Department, and Director of the Centre for North American Studies at the University of Guadalajara. His main research interests are Mexico–United States relations, security, and identity politics in North America.

Yao Chaocheng is Professor at Shanxi University. His main research interests are regional integration in Europe and Asia.

Preface

Writing about Asia-Pacific regionalism and its interface with the global system does not only require a comprehensive, multidimensional and multidisciplinary perspective but also an international network of researchers if the goal is a holistic and balanced analysis. While everyone involved in this book project looks back on long-standing experiences and achievements in investigating the Asia-Pacific region in all its facets, the immediate origins of the *The Asia-Pacific, Regionalism and the Global System* lie in two grants provided by the World University Network (WUN). In January 2010, with the generous support of WUN, colleagues from the Universities of Leeds, Sydney, Alberta and Guadalajara met in Mexico to set up the 'WUN Asia-Pacific International Relations Network' which has rapidly expanded since then and now comprises 19 universities from five continents. The first network conference ('Asia-Pacific: Shaping the World') took place in Leeds on 12–13 May 2011. Funded by a WUN grant from the Fund for International Research Collaborations (FIRC), this event brought together key experts on Asia-Pacific affairs from around the world to particularly explore the relationship between different forms of regionalism (economic, business, politico-security, socio-cultural) within the Asia-Pacific and issues of global governance. Over the following months the papers presented at the conference were extensively revised and edited and now form the chapters of this book. We wish to thank all contributing authors for their strong commitment to this project, and Laura Elgar, Jo Betteridge and everyone at Edward Elgar Publishing for their hard work and professional guidance.

We would like to express our gratitude to the WUN office at Leeds and particularly Kirsty Mattinson for the continuous support of our network activities and the funding that has made this project possible. We are also thankful to the School of Modern Languages and Cultures (SMLC) at Leeds and the White Rose East Asia Centre (WREAC), an international Centre of Excellence on China and Japan managed collaboratively by the Universities of Leeds and Sheffield, for providing a fruitful and conducive research environment without which this book project and many related research activities would never have flourished.

Jörn Dosch would like to thank his parents, Gisela and Roland Dosch, for their lifelong support of his academic and other activities, as well as his mentor and friend Manfred Mols who first introduced him to the many faces of Asia-Pacific politics and international relations more than two decades ago. As always he is grateful to his wife Ana Lucía and his children Nils-Mateo and Amelie for their love, patience and encouragement. Christopher M. Dent too would like to thank all his family for their love and support over the years, and for having great faith in him, even though his school qualifications were not that impressive! We hope that you, the reader, will find many new and interesting things from reading this book.

Christopher M. Dent and **Jörn Dosch**

PART I

Introduction

1. The Asia-Pacific, regionalism and the global system: an introduction

Jörn Dosch and Christopher M. Dent

1. THE ASIA-PACIFIC IN THE WORLD

Ever since the Asia-Pacific transformed from an 'institutional desert' into one of the most networked areas in the world, questions of the region's future and the future of the global system have become closely intertwined. The Asia-Pacific area, the world's largest 'trans-region', comprises three main regional constituents: East Asia, Pacific America (North and Latin American nations with a Pacific coast) and Oceania, for example Australia and New Zealand. It hosts around a half of the world's population and accounts for a similar proportion of the global economy. Individual countries from the region have significant global impact. The Asia-Pacific contains the world's three biggest economies (the United States, China and Japan), the world's largest military power (the US) and the world's most populous nation (China). The region is also home to eight of the world's ten largest military forces. Meetings between the 21 member economies of the Asia-Pacific Economic Cooperation (APEC) forum – the world's largest regional grouping – represent an important global constituency in a world increasingly defined and structured around regions, regional communities and regional powers. Recent and future endeavours to build a 'Pacific Community' could have a profound effect on all countries.

In fact, it was the founding of APEC in 1989 that triggered a novel process of institution-building and regionalism in the Asia-Pacific that was distinctly different from European experiences[1] and seemed to provide answers for the then emerging 'new world order', a term coined by George W.H. Bush. Even without the US president's magic and vague words, an international debate about the basic structures of the post-Cold War world was necessary and inevitable at a time when an end-of-history spirit proved to be prevalent, with Fukuyama's position as shibboleth among the Western powers and elsewhere (Fukuyama 1992). This discourse was embedded in a widespread feeling of relief because a cluster of totalitarian and authoritarian states and their claim of a world revolution seemed to be fading away. The Soviet Empire simply dissolved, and this offered hope that a new and lasting peace, based on peoples' consent, would prosper worldwide on a basis of a consensual political order, shared values, free markets, and large economic networks. While contemporary observers might smile at this somewhat naïve neo-Wilsonian preposition of two decades ago, it would be wrong to conclude that the optimism and promises of the early 1990s went entirely unfulfilled. Structural features of the Cold War order, such as hegemony and unilateralism, still feature prominently in the Asia-Pacific, but in parallel the ongoing multilateralisation of international relations in the region has contributed to a sustained situation of relative peace and stability. At the same time this process has opened new windows for regional governance that have started to challenge the very foundations of the existing global system – for better or worse. As a recent high-level meeting of political practitioners and academics on the future of the international system, held under the Chatham House rule, concluded,

> The rise of Asia and a rebalancing of global governance – with more power flowing to Asia – has created anxiety in the West about the future of that system. There are fears that 'the rise of the rest' will result in new global norms, new operating principles for global institutions, and different outcomes in international decision-making.

In addition to the ever-growing economic might of some East Asian nations, first and foremost China, and the potential implications for the prevailing balance of power in global organisations like the World Trade Organisation (WTO), International Monetary System (IMF) and World Bank, much of the discourse on the promises and challenges of 'Asia's rise' is driven by the uniqueness of the approaches to regional governance in the Asia-Pacific. First, contrary to transatlantic experiences and maybe for the first time in modern history, in the Asia-Pacific a multilateral system of interstate relations was initiated and continues to be significantly influenced by medium powers (ASEAN – Association of Southeast Asian Nations, South Korea, Japan, and to some extent Australia) and not by the dominant actors, particularly the United States. China has only recently begun to take a stronger interest in regional organisations but has increasingly put its mark on the shaping of regionalism. At the same time it is important to note that the role of the United States cannot be ignored in the process of regionalisation and multilateralisation, even though Washington did not spearhead the process and is excluded from some regional forums. Second, and equally if not more important, regionalism in the Asia-Pacific as manifested not only by APEC but also a growing number of other organisations and co-operation mechanisms such as

ASEAN Plus Three (APT), East Asian Summit (EAS), ASEAN Regional Forum (ARF) and the China–Japan–Korea trilateral summit, stands for a model of regional co-operation that has emerged as an alternative to the European approach.

2. REGIONALISM AND GLOBALISATION IN FOCUS

While the European integration process is characterised by treaties and legally binding commitments, the Asia-Pacific has followed a non-legalistic approach to inter-governmental co-operation based on the so-called 'ASEAN way' of soft institutions, open regionalism, co-operative security, non-binding decision-making, convention and consensus-building. The ASEAN way is based on the premise that the moral power of informal procedures can determine relations between actors as effectively as legally binding rules. The former – so the argument goes – has allowed for more flexibility in dealing with specific policy challenges of regional governance than the latter. Empirically sound or not, the realities of intergovernmental co-operation in the Asia-Pacific have markedly shaped general discourses on regionalisation and regionalism.

The idea of the regionalisation of international relations refers to the underlying, often undirected, processes bringing adjoining states, societies and economies into intensified interaction. Through this interaction a particular cluster of states may be said to have a distinctive orientation to each other and may be said to constitute a region. The term regionalism is more complex. According to Joseph Nye, 'in the descriptive sense [it means] . . . the formation of interstate associations or groupings on the basis of regions; and in the doctrinal sense, the advocacy of such formations' (Nye 1968: vii). Thus, while regionalisation is what happens, regionalism can be understood as a conscious orientation by actors to bring about specific forms of regionalisation. In other words, 'we may refer to regionalism as the structures, processes and arrangements that are working towards greater coherence within a specific international region in terms of economic, political, security, socio-cultural and other kinds of linkages' (Dent 2008: 7).

In the debate on regionalism it has become commonplace to distinguish between an older generation of regionalism (under the label of 'regional integration' these were studies that mainly focused on the process of European integration) in the 1950s and 1960s, and a more recent new 'wave' of regionalism (the 'new regionalism') starting in the latter half of the 1980s. Traditional theories of regionalism (or 'old regionalism') are closely associated with scholarly work of the 1950s and 1960s, with Europe being the principal basis for empirical studies. David Mitrany (1943) and Jacob Viner (1950) are acknowledged as two of the most influential pioneers in this area. While Mitrany is considered the father of functionalism – that focuses on the common interests and needs shared by states and postulates a gradual transfer of authority and sovereignty from the state to a supranational level (that is, new regional agencies above the traditional nation states) in functional, technical and economic areas – Viner made ground-breaking contributions to the analysis of international trade. His work was later refined and built upon by many other scholars like Béla Balassa (1961) who described regional economic integration a linear process over five different levels.

Apart from their focus on economic integration, 'old' theories or approaches to regionalism were predominately concerned with peace, and tended to see the nation-state as the problem rather than the solution. 'New regionalism' considers novel aspects, particularly those focused on conditions related to globalisation and is prominently linked to aspects of economic governance (Hettne 2005). As Harrison (2006) contended, 'New regionalists go so far as to claim that contemporary capitalism and its territorial configuration are best regulated and governed in and through the decentralisation of socioeconomic decision-making and associated policy implementation to sub-national institutional frameworks and supports' (p. 22). According to Hettne (1999), one of the main proponents of new regionalism, 'the two processes of globalisation and regionalisation are articulated within the same larger process of global structural change' (p. 2). Väyrynen (2003) further adds that 'national actors may . . . perceive regionalism as a defence mechanism against the competitive pressures arising from the globalisation process' (p. 32). The Inter-American Development Bank (2002) has meanwhile observed that 'an increasing number of countries are relying on formal regional integration to mediate the forces of globalisation' (p. 24).

In addition to the strong linkages between the 'new regionalism' debate and discourses in international political economy, social constructivists have also discovered regionalism as a preferred empirical focus. There can be little doubt that a sense of regional consciousness has emerged in many world regions and that states have actively promoted the idea of mutual co-operation. Regardless of whether regions need to be defined in geographical terms or can also be thought of as socially constructed 'imagined or cognitive regions' (Väyrynen 2003: 37), identity is one of the most important and solid pillars of regionalism, no matter whether this pillar is based on a geographical concepts or has a foundation driven by norms and values.

It is the regional–global nexus combined with the notion of cognitive regions that bears particular relevance to the Asia-Pacific. Little more than a decade ago, the East Asian developmental state and, linked to it, governance models and work ethics based on a crude understanding of political Confucianism, almost emerged as the gold standard for the efficient management of opportunities and challenges in the dawning, globalised 21st century and strongly contributed to the formation of an East Asian identity. The 'Asian values' debate served as a central piece in the explanatory puzzle as to why East Asian economies enjoyed tremendous economic growth and success. Nowhere else did the three main pillars of globalisation in the mainstream understanding of the concept – economic integration, domestic economic deregulation and rapid advances in technology – manifest themselves more clearly than in the post-World War II economic history of Northeast and Southeast Asia (Coclanis and Doshi 2000). East Asian self-confidence and a 'them versus us' mentality was the order of the day, with prominent political voices proclaiming the 'demise of European modernism' (Mahathir and Ishihara 1995) and academic observers discussing the dawn of the 'Pacific century' (Borthwick 1992) as well as a potentially looming 'obsoleteness of the West' (Elegant 1990). However, when the East Asian financial crisis of 1997/98 shattered the dream of globalisation as a never-ending profit-generating phenomenon and forced the region into an economic downturn that also had far-reaching political, social and ecological ramifications, the self-perception quickly changed, from being the champion of globalisation to being the first victim of the borderless, information-driven world. To many, the 1997/98 crisis, often dubbed the first crisis of globalisation (Higgott 1998), demonstrated in great clarity the link between national and regional corporate activities, and global economic organisations such as the World Bank and the IMF. Even those who did not subscribe to the idea of predatory global integration as the main factor behind the economic turmoil agreed that the 1997/98 East Asian financial crisis has had a fundamental impact on the perception of globalisation. The discourse shifted from the confrontational mode to a more sober analysis of the sovereignty of the state, centred on the argument that the manifold and simultaneous processes of globalisation were undermining the foundations of national sovereignty and reducing the capacity of policymakers to act autonomously or effectively within national jurisdictions (Beeson 2009). This, in turn, led to a new – and the most recent – phase in Asia-Pacific regionalism which has seen the rise of new institutional mechanisms to mitigate the regional impact of any future global crises, to deal more effectively with regional challenges and to foster the idea of community-building. The Chang Mai Initiative currency swap system (first a network of bilateral agreements, then multilateralised in 2010) and related attempts at strengthening monetary and financial co-operation largely through ASEAN Plus Three diplomacy, as well as initiatives to extend transpacific relations beyond APEC, such as in the case of the Forum for East Asia–Latin America Co-operation (FEALC) inaugurated in 2003, are clear manifestations of this new wave in Asia-Pacific regionalism (Beeson 2009, Dosch and Jacob 2010, Volz 2010). As Dieter (2009) argued, 'Overall, the Asian crisis has had a lasting influence on the region's institutional development . . . After the traumatic experience . . ., the desire for greater independence required the exclusion of those countries that had done little to solve the problems created by the crisis' (p. 81).

The second and increasingly expanding pillar of region-wide (but not necessarily coherently regional) co-operation in the Asia-Pacific is bilateralism, particularly in the form of bilateral free trade agreements (FTAs) that have mushroomed since the late 1990s. The simultaneous intensification of economic bilateralism and multilateralism in the Asia-Pacific, which is constituent to the broader integrational trend of globalisation, has posed questions as to the compatibility of these two processes – a discourse that builds on the 'lattice regionalism' hypothesis: to what extent is trade bilateralism precursory to Asia-Pacific regionalism (Dent 2006)?

Studies on Asia-Pacific regionalism and its interface with globalisation are not new. However, the Asia-Pacific is such a fluid and dynamic region that it demands continual reappraisal and reconsideration. Communist, democratic and authoritarian regimes cohabit and coexist within the region, if not always peacefully. Many Cold War relics remain scattered throughout the Asia-Pacific. Taiwan remains a point of friction between the USA and China; the People's Republic of China remains a communist state, albeit one with many of the trappings of a capitalist market economy; the 1953 division of the two Korea states at the 38th parallel persists; and US military pre-eminence in the region continues. But can it co-exist with China's growing assertiveness in the region and indeed the world? We should not blind ourselves to the fact that the soft institutionalised Asia-Pacific regionalism is no safeguard against assertive hegemony and that the existing multilateral architecture is not immune to hegemonic co-operation (Dosch 2006), which is dominated by a state that 'holds a sufficiently decisive share of power assets to impose the distribution of benefits and costs it desires and international arrangements which make for that distribution' (Bobrow 1999: 175). However, there is a fine line between regional hegemony and leadership. It can be argued that it is precisely the lack of the latter that has hindered the Asia-Pacific from making more rapid progress towards a working system of regional governance. Any development towards a form of 'regulatory regionalism' (Jayasuriya

2003; Hameiri and Jayasuriya 2011) in East Asia remains nascent. There is a growing gap between political rhetoric and actual policy implementation at the national level with regards to the emerging system of regional multilevel regulation as evidenced, for example, by the ASEAN regional surveillance process (ASP), which was endorsed by ASEAN Financial Ministers in 1998. Similar observations apply to regionalism in the realm of security. Political and public expectations vis-à-vis the steering capabilities of existing multilateral forums are often unrealistically high. The ASEAN Regional Forum, for instance, provides a valuable framework for communication in international relations which increases transparency and contributes to trust building; but the ARF has struggled to agree on any specific norms or even rules and procedures that go beyond the general interest of keeping the region peaceful and stable. The forum's institutional design has not allowed for the implementation of preventive diplomacy in the Asia-Pacific or any serious contribution to the long-term resolution of the Korean crisis or conflict-resolution in the case of the disputes in the South China Sea.

3. STRUCTURE AND SUMMARY OF THE BOOK

This volume sheds critical light on these and many other developments and delves into the key issues of regional governance, integration and international affairs within and across the Asia-Pacific. We ask how these developments are impacting on the global system, in particular on emerging forms of global governance. In short, this book looks at how the Asia-Pacific region is shaping the world. Unlike many other publications on similar topics our discussion is not limited to East Asia but takes Latin America prominently into the equation.

The book is structured along the following lines. After this introductory chapter in Part I, Part II examines different aspects of economic integration in the Asia-Pacific from regional and global perspectives. In Chapter 2, Melba Falck Reyes analyses Japanese manufacturing FDI in Mexico and the extent to which it has fostered international production network (IPN) activity in this part of Latin America, and thereby helped incorporate Mexico into broader regional and global business networks. In 2005, Mexico and Japan signed their landmark Economic Partnership Agreement (EPA), for each country their first trans-Pacific free trade agreement. Japan's motive was largely investment driven, its aim being to recover the privileged position that Japanese firms had under the Mexico's *maquiladora* policy, a privilege lost in 2001 when a special clause implemented under the North American Free Trade Agreement (NAFTA) eliminated the tariff-free import of parts and components outside the NAFTA region. The Japan–Mexico EPA helped restore the advantages of Japanese investors and led to a new spurt in Japanese manufacturing investment in Mexico. Decades before, Japanese companies had pioneered the development of international production networks in East Asia, these being embedded in larger global networks and supply chains. One consequence, then, of Japan's post-EPA increase in investment was to extend Japanese firms' IPN activity deeper into Mexico, and thereby bring the country into deeper cross-border integration with Japanese business networks in the United States and East Asia. This bilateral investment relationship thus had regional and cross-regional dimensions, this too being indicative of how global capital is organised.

Links between Latin America and East Asia are considered by José Luis León-Manríquez in Chapter 3, who discusses the different approaches that South Korea and Mexico have taken to dealing with the challenges of global trade, integration and economic crises. Special attention is paid to the 2008/09 global economic crisis. South Korea and Mexico are two similar sized economies, both notably dependent on manufacturing exports, and have had their own experiences with accommodating neo-liberal reforms as well as significant financial crises – Mexico in 1994/95 and South Korea in 1997/98. Yet their responses to the 2008/09 global economic crisis were markedly different. León-Manríquez attributes this primarily to the contrasting political economies of each country that in turn are representative of broader regional political economy differences between East Asia and Latin America. He argues that South Korea's revitalised developmental state – centring on the substantial public funded new 'Green Growth' development strategy and associated 5-Year Plans – have proved more effective at navigating the economy through the crisis than the passive market-liberal approach pursued by Mexico. The South Korean state's response to the crisis is moreover indicative of a wider revitalisation of East Asian developmental statism and other forms of state capacity. Meanwhile, Mexico's entrenched market-liberalism is consistent with the dominance of US-led neo-liberal thinking that still pervades most of Latin America.

In Chapter 4, Arturo Santa-Cruz focuses on how the North America region was 'constructed' in the contexts of globalisation and region-building. He asks the fundamental question of whether North America exists as a meaningful region: that is, do Canada, Mexico and the United States share perceptions regarding interests, threats and values. Furthermore, what does North America's regionalism and regionalisation experience tell us about globalisation and the regionalisation experience in the Asia-Pacific? In addressing these questions, Santa-Cruz discusses the twin concepts and processes of globalisation and regionalisation in some detail, and argues that while both processes are complementary, the latter remains a second-best outcome. He then considers these questions in relation to North America's, and thereby NAFTA's, engagement with APEC, providing insights on comparative region-building.

Part III of the book shifts the focus to key issues of regional and global multilateralism relating to the Asia-Pacific. In Chapter 5, John Ravenhill considers the 'numbers game' in Asia-Pacific co-operation. He observes that over the last few years an increasing discontent has been expressed about the effectiveness of existing regional institutions in the Asia-Pacific region. These criticisms have equally targeted institutions primarily concerned with security matters (for example ARF) and those primarily focused on economic issues, such as APEC. Criticisms have come not just from academics but also from government leaders and from think-tanks closely associated with governments, for example Indonesia's Centre for Strategic and International Studies. The depth of concern about existing regional institutions was evident in the 'regional community' proposals in the late 2000s from Japanese Prime Minister Yukio Hatoyama and Australian PM Kevin Rudd for a radical departure from the status quo. Both proposals, at least implicitly, attacked the ASEAN-centric character of existing regional institutions and proposed instead either that leadership be exercised by or membership be confined to 'regionally significant states'. Meanwhile at the global level the G20 of 'systemically significant economies' has been elevated to the status of the premier forum for managing the global economy. Through an examination of the recent experience of regional institutions, the fate of the Hatoyama and Rudd proposals, and the experience of the G20, Ravenhill explores the question of the relationship between selective membership and governability.

In Chapter 6, Yao Chaocheng applies the 'subsidiarity' principle, long associated with the European integration experience to that of Asia's own. He notes that a top-down, inter-governmental approach to driving forward Asian regionalism can only achieve so much. What is required is a mass, multi-level engagement of civil society and other non-state actors in a more bottom-up process where more localised support for regional integration projects can be more effectively mobilised. Yao argues that governments can take various measures to encourage and promote this, and that the greater socialisation of East Asian peoples will also improve relations between them and make valuable contributions to dealing with historic animosities that persist in the region. This, he contends, is consistent with the Subsidiarity principle of empowering localised actors to take greater ownership over regionalist initiatives and thereby underpin the macro-regionalism projects (for example free trade areas) proposed at the inter-state level.

Hugo Dobson in Chapter 7 takes a close look at how Asian nations are engaging in the new G20 global-multilateral grouping. He notes that with the rise of the G20 as the premier forum for international economic co-operation as a result of the G8 group's expanded membership, a debate has begun over whether this will encourage greater co-operation between the six Asian group members of the G20, the so-called 'A6': Australia, China, India, Indonesia, Japan and South Korea. Dobson explores these prospects based on trends emerging from the five G20 summits held by May 2011. He also discusses the extent to which Asian countries are shaping the ongoing evolution of the G20, its agenda and its relationship to other mechanisms of global governance. In reviewing the position of each A6 country, Dobson observes that Australia has been one of the most proactive countries in advocating revision of the architecture of global governance and co-ordinating an Asian response therein. However, there are questions as regards how far it will promote these changes, in what form and to what end? In the case of China, it probably means more to the G20 than the G20 means to China. Dobson contends that what the G20 means to China can be understood mostly in terms of recognition rather than as an opportunity to provide global, let alone regional, leadership. Meanwhile, he notes that India has shown little inclination to lead or contribute to the G20's work, and Indonesia's concerns revolve around moving from the regional to global level but it continues to suffer from domestic problems that have the potential to undermine this ambition. For Japan, Dobson contends that the emergence of the G20 has presented a challenge rather than an opportunity. It has worked towards the success of the G20 as the 'premier forum for international economic cooperation', even demonstrating a leadership role on occasions, whilst displaying a reactionary preference for the G8 and the status that goes with membership of this more select grouping. Finally, South Korea's participation in the G20 is an opportunity to demonstrate its ability to provide leadership in global governance, particularly in the face of a number of doubters before the November 2010 Seoul Summit, and burnish President Lee Myun-bak's domestic legacy. Overall, Dobson argues that national interests have predominantly shaped the participation of the A6 members of the G20 thus far. There is no apparent common A6 agenda or caucus. Rather, fragmentation amongst the A6 can be seen both in participation, which has been largely unilateral, uncoordinated and driven by national interest and status anxiety, and in the issue of the evolving architecture of global governance.

The Asia-Pacific's position regarding the G8 and G20 relationship is further discussed by Hong Yousheng and Fang Qing in Chapter 8, who specifically consider how the expanded G20 will bring about shifts in the dynamics of global economic governance. Hong and Fang contend that if the G8 has been one key mechanism of global economic governance since it was formed by Western advanced countries in 1975, then its influence is declining nowadays due to the rise of new economic powers which are playing an increasingly important role in the world's economic growth, resulting in the appearance of the G20. While academia is focused on the debate of whether G8 could be replaced by G20 as a more effective mechanism of world governance, the concept of G2 or 'Chimerica' has also been proposed as the key axis of global economic governance in the early 21st century. Both the consolidation of the G20 over recent years and the idea of a G2 have been indicative of the global shift in economic and geopolitical power from the Atlantic to the Pacific. The Asia-Pacific accounts for half the G20's membership, hence this raises important questions for Hong and Fang concerning how the region will shape the future dynamics and structures of global governance.

This is followed in Chapter 9 by Jörn Dosch's analysis of how multilateral organisations in the Asia-Pacific responded to the 2008/09 global economic crisis. He analyses and compares the specific actions discussed, taken and implemented by two regional organisations – ASEAN and MERCOSUR (Southern Common Market) – and two inter-regional fora – APEC and FEALAC (Forum for Asia–Latin America Co-operation) – in response to the crisis. He compares the four organisations from two different angles. First, which of the two regional organisations, ASEAN or MERCOSUR, has been more efficient and effective in responding to the crisis and why? Second, which of the two multilateral co-operation structures, regionalism or inter-regionalism, has made the more significant contributions to countering the crisis? Dosch uses the theoretical discourse on regional integration and inter-regionalism as the analytical backdrop and challenges some of the existing mainstream arguments in this debate. In particular he argues that the academic literature almost completely neglects the role and influence of extra-regional actors, including foreign donors, in regional co-operation processes in both Asia and Latin America. However, as the chapter tries to demonstrate, regional and inter-regional responses to the crisis have been most successful when policy efforts were promoted, (financially) supported or even driven by extra-regional actors, such as European Union and US stakeholders.

In Chapter 10, Cheol Hee Park focuses in on the intra-regional geopolitical dynamics of Northeast Asia (China, Japan and Korea). He discusses the various issues relating to how a rising China presents both numerous opportunities and challenges its regional neighbours in Northeast Asia and the wider Asia-Pacific. Park discusses the contending perspectives regarding international responses to China's ascendance, ranging from balancing strategies to band-wagoning strategies. More specifically concerning Northeast Asia, South Korean and Japanese approaches have converging as well as diverging elements. As he observes, there is no difference in that China is a number one trading partner for both South Korea and Japan. Also, the two countries do not disagree to the point that functional co-operation among Northeast Asian countries should be advanced. However, when it comes to security-related issues, Park contends the two countries do not necessarily share the same approach. Several issues are involved in this dynamics such as historical controversy, the North Korean problem and regional integration. Park addresses the question of meeting the challenge of rising China in the eyes of South Korea and Japan for the purpose of finding implications for regional and global governance.

Part IV of the book examines how East Asian countries, especially China, are impacting on important aspects of global development. It begins with Jeffrey Henderson in Chapter 11 reflecting on the implications of the re-emergence of China as a global economic and political power for the nature of globalisation. As such, this chapter takes 'the global' seriously as a political–economic and socio–spatial formation that has real, semi-autonomous consequences for the lives and livelihoods of humanity. Henderson begins by arguing that globalisation is not a product of abstract, disembodied rules and practices that emanate from an idealised notion of capitalism, as much of the 'globalisation' literature implies. Rather, it can be traced – through various forms and phases – to the concrete nature of the capitalisms that have dominated the given historical period. Globalisation, in other words, represents an attempt to forge the world in the image of its principal driving force. Having briefly demonstrated the link between the dominant form of capitalism and the form of globalisation in recent history, Henderson argues that with the rise of China and perhaps other Asian powers in its wake, we may be witnessing the emergence of a new form of globalisation, presaging perhaps, a 'Global Asian Era' (GAE). If this is the case, then we may expect that many of its defining characteristics will be shaped, at least initially, by its currently principal driving force, namely the Chinese form of capitalism. Henderson identifies what might be the key features of Chinese capitalism, as a political economy and social formation, which are likely to give an emergent GAE its particular character. With this in mind, and critically engaging with 'development' and 'transition' discourses of various stripes, he concludes that we need to re-conceptualise and theorise global change around the dialectics of 'transformation'.

Following in a related vein in Chapter 12, Minglu Chen and David S.G. Goodman examine China's recent developmental experience and discuss what have been its lessons for other Asia-Pacific countries. They propose that in many ways China's economic growth and transformation since 1978 seems to have directly challenged theories of economic development. The key challenge to theories of modernisation, as previously understood, is that China's experience seems to suggest that authoritarian politics and economic restructuring can co-exist. Chen and Goodman note that China's economic reform process has shown that the most remarkable feature of the country's development is not simply the continuation of Chinese Communist Party rule but rather its adaptability. While, they argue, China's rise has furthermore posed serious challenges to ideas of modernisation and economic development, the international influence of the 'China model' rests on the extent to which China's experience is seen to be presenting an alternative path that others may follow, and not simply seen to be the result of unique circumstances. From that perspective the China model rapidly becomes of little use to the developing Asia-Pacific. Goodman and Chen propose there are essentially three problems. First, there is very little agreement about what constitutes the China model. Second, China's development of the last three decades is for the most part the result of highly specific circumstances. Third and last, where there are lessons to be learnt there is little in the experience of the developing Asia-Pacific to suggest that those lessons can readily and generally be begun to be replicated.

In Chapter 13, Richard P. Appelbaum and Rachel Parker make a close examination of China's move to high-tech innovation, and what the policy implications of this are for other Asia-Pacific nations, especially the United States. High-tech industry development has long involved debates concerning the extent to which states should be a proactive agent in the process, and what forms of involvement this may or should take. Appelbaum and Parker examine the steps that China has recently taken to 'leapfrog development' through a series of government programmes intended to foster indigenous innovation. They examine the implemented programmes that serve this purpose and form the basis of China's high-tech industrial policies, comparing this with the US's approach both generally and regarding key emerging sectors such as nanotechnology. Appelbaum and Parker then critically examine the claim that China is becoming a political as well as economic superpower, before turning to a discussion of China's global and regional future. With regard to the former, they focus on US–China relations, in particular the reaction of the US government and leading businesses to what is often perceived as the Chinese threat. Concerning the regional dimension to this, they examine some of the tensions between China and its neighbours in East Asia and the Asia-Pacific.

Turning to important issues of development assistance and poverty alleviation globally, James Reilly considers in Chapter 14 whether a Northeast Asian model of foreign aid is becoming apparent given the well established importance of Japanese aid donorship, and the growing importance of emerging Asian donors such as China and South Korea. He notes that in the realm of official development assistance (ODA) there is a growing pluralism among aid donors and approaches that has emerged, representing the most significant challenge to Western aid orthodoxy in decades. In response, the still very Western-dominated Organisation for Economic Co-operation and Development's Development Assistance Committee (OECD-DAC) is striving to reshape international norms defining effective and appropriate ODA. Yet the DAC process faces a contradiction between being more inclusive by welcoming new members, collaborating with aid recipients and collaborating with non-DAC members, while also being more exclusive by codifying and promulgating selective norms on ODA. In this context, Reilly discusses to what extent are Northeast Asian aid donors challenging Western orthodoxies and prevailing norms of aid behaviour, especially given the distinctly different nature of their developmental political economies (see Chapter 3). For example, he cites that when having finally secured entry into the DAC in January 2010, South Korea pledged that it would formulate its own original model of development assistance that drew upon the country's own development experience and lessons learned, and that moreover would be aligned to its current national development strategies. Furthermore, in the same year, Chinese Premier Wen Jiabao remarked that a demonstratively successful model of Chinese development aid had now emerged, again like South Korea that derived largely from its own development path. Reilly explores the commonalties and contrasts between Japanese, Chinese and Korean approaches to ODA, thereby considering the extent to which a Northeast Asian model of development aid has formed. He discusses how such a model may impact on international norms of aid policy and practice.

Finally, Part V examines different societal perspectives on the Asia-Pacific and the global system. In Chapter 15, Simen Andersen Øyen analyses the Chinese modernisation process – both its soft power potential and its tensions – through the experience of Shanghai's hosting of the 2010 World Exhibition (EXPO). He argues that China seeks to portray its path to modernity, wealth and stability as an alternative to the Western approach. Øyen contends that the 2010 Shanghai EXPO typified how the Chinese government would like to present itself and the 'modern face' of China. At the same time, the event revealed processes of political contestation and tension, new forms of disciplinarian process, and new shifting patterns of dominance and power relations in Chinese society. He argues that taken together with corresponding recent socio-political changes in China, the 2010 EXPO experience was indicative of broader shifts from 'hard' authoritarianism to a new and 'softer' authoritarianism in the country, this being particularly relevant in an international comparative sense to other developing countries in the Asia-Pacific and elsewhere. Protest movements and protest actions, as well as social civilising campaigns initiated by the authorities before and during the Shanghai EXPO, are expressions and indications of deep underlying processes of modernisation and civilising. Øyen contends that this corresponds to complex transnational socio-political and socio-cultural influences amongst nations in a deeper globalising world where China's own 'soft power' influences are being, and will be, increasingly felt.

Lastly, in Chapter 16, Christopher M. Dent broadens out the debate of Asia's international societal influences by considering how various recent developments in East Asian regionalism will impact on the formation of global or world society. He first notes that there remains much speculation concerning whether the 21st century will 'belong' to Asia. Dent argues that while there is value in considering Asia's future in the world system, ascribing 'ownership' of a future world epoch to any particular geopolitical power or construct may distract us from pursuing more crucial paths of scholarly enquiry. Given the escalating global-level challenges and problems that confront all humanity, Dent contends that it is more important to consider how Asia, and particularly East Asia – the Asia continent's most geopolitically significant and coherent regional entity – may contribute to resolving these challenges. He argues that they are best addressed by a formative world society, and that deepening regionalism in East Asia is in some way inter-constitutive to world society formation. How the world's different nations, peoples and civilisations peacefully co-exist and co-operate with each other to deal with increasingly serious global-level challenges (for example environmental, poverty, and energy related) may be thought of prime meta-level issues of 21st-century international relations. These challenges are best addressed, according to Dent, by a collective worldwide response, and one that derives from a coherent association and unity of purpose between various forms of agency in the global system. The creation of different forms and structures of global governance represent an endeavour towards this end but something deeper is required. As a general principle, it is when society as a whole takes ownership and responsibility for problems affecting all its members, even though the impact of these problems is asymmetric, that they are most successfully resolved. Dent proposes that we should therefore work, at least in ideal terms, on the core premise that the 21st century belongs to us all rather than a certain geopolitical power or powers. He argues that inherent to East Asia's deepening regionalism are particular forms of coherence – associative, integrational, organisational – that are also inherent to processes of world society formation. As such, regional community or society-building in East Asia may make potentially important contributions to the development of world society, and thereby concomitantly address global-level challenges. The same applies to the Asia-Pacific region as a whole, and this is one of many crucially important dimensions of the regionalism–globalisation relationship examined in this book.

NOTE

1. See, for example, Mack and Ravenhill (1994), McGrew and Brook (1998), and Aggarwal and Morrison (1998) for some of the most influential early assessments of Asia-Pacific institution-building; and Rüland et al. (2002), Feinberg (2003) and Ravenhill (2001) for comprehensive analyses of APEC's decisive contribution to Asia-Pacific regionalism.

REFERENCES

Aggarwal, V. and C. Morrison (eds) (1998), *Asia–Pacific Crossroads. Regime Creation and the Future of APEC*, New York: St. Martin's Press.
Balassa, B. (1961), *The Theory of Economic Integration*, Homewood, IL: Richard D. Irwin.
Beeson, M. (2009), *Institutions of the Asia-Pacific: ASEAN, APEC and Beyond*, London: Routledge.
Bobrow, D.B. (1999), 'Hegemonic Management: the US in the Asia–Pacific', *The Pacific Review*, **12**(2), 173–97.
Borthwick, M. (1992), *Pacific Century: The Emergence of Modern Pacific Asia*, Sydney, NSW: Allen & Unwin.
Coclanis, P. and T. Doshi (2000), 'Globalization in Southeast Asia', *Annals of the American Academy of Political and Social Science*, **570**, 49–64.
Dent, C.M. (2006), *New Free Trade Agreements in the Asia-Pacific*, Basingstoke: Palgrave Macmillan.
Dent, C.M. (2008), *East Asian Regionalism*, Routledge: London.
Dieter, H. (2009), 'Changing patterns of regional governance: from security to political economy?', *The Pacific Review*, **22**(1), 73–90.
Dosch, J. (2006), 'Does multilateralism work? European and American approaches to multilateral peace-building on the Korean peninsula', *The Journal of Unification Studies*, **28**(1), 43–86.
Dosch, J. and O. Jacob (eds) (2010), *Asia and Latin America. Economic, Political and Multilateral Relations*, London: Routledge.
Elegant, R. (1990), *Pacific Destiny: Inside Asia Today*, New York: Crown Publishers.
Feinberg, R.E. (ed.) (2003), *APEC as an Institution: Multilateral Governance in the Asia-Pacific*, Singapore: Institute of Southeast Asian Studies.
Fukuyama, F. (1992), *The End of History and the Last Man*, New York: Free Press.

Hameiri, S. and K. Jayasuriya (2011), 'Regulatory regionalism and the dynamics of territorial politics: the case of the Asia-Pacific region', *Political Studies*, **59**(1), 20–37.
Harrison, J. (2006), 'Re-reading the new regionalism: a sympathetic critique', *Space and Polity*, **10**(1), 21–46.
Hettne, B. (1999), 'Globalization and the new regionalism: the second great transformation', in B. Hettne, A. Inotai and O. Sunkel (eds), *Globalism and the New Regionalism*, London: Macmillan/New York: St Martin's Press, pp. 1–24.
Hettne, B. (2005), 'Beyond the "new" regionalism', *New Political Economy*, **10**(4), 543–71.
Higgott, R. (1998), 'The Asian economic crisis: a study in the politics of resentment', *New Political Economy*, **3**(3), 333–56.
Inter-American Development Bank (IDB) (2002), *Beyond Borders: The New Regionalism in Latin America: Economic and Social Progress in Latin America*, Washington, DC: IDB.
Jayasuriya, K. (2003), 'Introduction: governing the Asia-Pacific: beyond the "new regionalism"', *Third World Quarterly*, **24**(2), 199–215.
Mack, A. and J. Ravenhill (eds) (1994), *Pacific Co-operation: Building Economic and Security Regimes in the Asia–Pacific Region*, Sydney, NSW: Allen and Unwin.
Mahathir, M. and S. Ishihara (1995), *The Voice of Asia: Two Leaders Discuss the Coming Century*, Tokyo: Kodansha International.
McGrew, A. and C. Brook (eds) (1998), *Asia-Pacific in the New World Order*, London: Routledge.
Mitrany, D.A. (1943), *A Working Peace System*, London: Royal Institute of International Affairs.
Nye, J.S. (ed.) (1968), *International Regionalism: Readings*, Boston, MA: Little Brown.
Ravenhill, J. (2001), *APEC and the Construction of Pacific Rim Regionalism*, New York: Cambridge University Press.
Rüland, J., E. Manske and W. Draguhn (eds) (2002), *Asia-Pacific Economic Co-operation (APEC): The First Decade*, London: Routledge Curzon.
Väyrynen, R. (2003), 'Regionalism: Old and New', *International Studies Review*, **5**(1), 25–51.
Viner, J. (1950), *The Customs Union Issue*, New York: Carnegie Endowment for International Peace.
Volz, U. (2010), *Prospects for Monetary Co-operation and Integration in East Asia*, Cambridge, MA: MIT Press.

PART II

Economic integration: Asia-Pacific and global perspectives

2. Is Japanese foreign direct investment fostering production networks in Mexico?

Melba Falck Reyes[1]

1. INTRODUCTION

In 2005, Mexico and Japan signed an Economic Partnership Agreement (EPA) that constituted for both countries their first trans-Pacific bilateral trade agreement. With the EPA both countries looked to increase their global competitiveness that had been lost in the past decades. Mexico's main objective was to attract more foreign direct investment (FDI) from Japan and to have a better market access in some specific sectors. For Japan, the aim was to recover the privileged position that the Japanese firms had lost in 2001, when a special clause inserted in the North American Free Trade Agreement (NAFTA) eliminated free imports of parts and components outside the NAFTA region. Japanese FDI had a long tradition in Mexico, attracted since the 1960s by the then newly established *maquiladora* system. As some authors have pointed out, this was maybe the first example of regional production-sharing where parts and components were assembled in Mexico and then sent back, as finished products, to the United States. Nonetheless, it was when NAFTA came into being in 1994 that more Japanese firms were interested in locating their production plants in Mexico.

Nowadays, with the development of advanced telecommunications and transport systems, the globalization of corporate activities has become increasingly developed. Technology and FDI have played an important role in the 'fragmentation' of production processes. Today, transnational firms are involved in more sophisticated schemes than the *maquiladora* arrangements on the Mexico–US border, fragmenting their production both at the domestic and cross-border level. Now webs of intra-firm and inter-firm transactions across borders are engaged in a growing trade in intermediate goods. Among the world's regions, East Asia has developed the most sophisticated and comprehensive regional production networks and other forms of supply chains, making 'Factory Asia' the world's most important manufacturing zone. The chapter will study the role played by Japanese FDI in fostering new types of production networks in Mexico. It considers new developments in the fragmentation theory, especially the model developed by Kimura and Ando (2005) based on empirical evidence from Asia. The chapter is divided into three main sections. It begins by discussing fragmentation production theory with reference to East Asia's case. This is followed by an examination of Japan's role in the formation of East Asia's international production networks (IPNs), as well as the role of Japanese FDI in Latin America's regional integration. Third and last, we discuss the evolution of Japanese FDI in Mexico since NAFTA and the extent to which Japanese firms have fostered production networks specifically in Mexico.

2. FRAGMENTATION OF PRODUCTION: THEORY AND REFERENCE FROM EAST ASIA

In the last two decades, advances in information and communications technology (ICT), transportation systems, and increased flows of Japanese FDI in East Asia helped spark the development of manufacturing networks that have made this region the 'factory of the world'. These networks are characterized by a high intensity in intermediate goods trade, especially in parts and components, and a high degree of sophistication in the exchange of goods between countries, where intra-firm trade has been declining in favour of arm's-length trade. This dynamism in trade in parts and components has had a positive impact on the development of local supply in less developed countries in East Asia, in their role as recipients of FDI from more developed economy firms both inside and outside the region and in which Japan has played a leading role from the 1980s onwards.

These new developments in international trade, which offer new possibilities of integration for less developed countries, have aroused the interest of scholars of international economics. There is now a vast literature and theoretical models that attempt to explain the determinants of new trade flows in intermediate products (Jones et al. 2005; Kimura and Ando 2005; Baldwin and Robert-Nicoud 2006; Helpman 2006). In this regard, Kimura and Ando (2005), based on the new theory of fragmentation of production and the East Asian experience, have provided a broader conceptual basis and empirical evidence that explains the causes of emerging trends in international trade as a reflection of the activities of transnational corporations and their affiliates in the global economy. According to these authors, firms' decisions on how to implement their production processes (in-house production, local and/or international outsourcing, subcontracting or foreign direct investment) depend on the impact that their activities have on production costs in relation to two key variables: distance and controllability. Kimura and Ando further state that when a firm decides to fragment production into blocks of value-added activity, placing them in different locations, this incurs higher transportation, telecommunication and co-ordination costs. Conversely, fragmentation can reduce costs due to lower wage levels, availability of cheaper resources and components/parts, and access to more efficient infrastructure in other geographical locations. It follows that firms will develop and extend production networks as long as there are net benefits generated by fragmentation. Based on this conceptual framework, Kimura and Ando (2005) used a database to analyse firm-level production networks in East Asia and found that Japan has played a leading role in their development. Moreover, intra-firm trade has given way to arm's-length trade, displacing purchases from Japan, and subsequently host economies have benefited from gradually involving an increasing number of local firms into regional production networks and indirectly participating in wider global value chains in which they are embedded.

3. JAPAN'S ROLE IN THE ECONOMIC INTEGRATION OF EAST ASIA AND LATIN AMERICA[2]

From the mid-1980s, Japanese FDI has become an important source of investment flows in the world, totalling US$830 billion by the end of 2010 (Table 2.1). Average annual Japanese FDI flows increased from US$24 billion between 1985 and 1999 to US$54 billion in the 2000s.[3] In the second half of the 1980s, the United States was the largest recipient of Japanese FDI, but since the 1990s East Asia had become a major recipient of such investment too. Among East Asian countries, China has been increasing its relative share. The dynamic performance of Japanese FDI has been based on the development of more than 4,000 transnational companies (UNCTAD 2008) and their 18,201 overseas affiliates, 46 percent of them in manufacturing industries. By region, 60 percent of the affiliates are in Asia (half of them in China), 16 percent in North America and 14 percent in Europe (METI 2010).[4]

The strong growth of Japanese FDI in the world and in East Asia in particular in the late 1980s can be largely explained by the 1985 yen revaluation that consequently made Japanese exports less price competitive.

Table 2.1 Evolution of Japanese FDI stocks at the end of selected years (US$ million)

	1996		2000		2005		2010	
	Value	Participation in total FDI (%)	Value	Participation in total FDI (%)	Value	Participation in total FDI (%)	Value	Participation in total FDI (%)
World	258,653	100.0	278,445	100.0	388,197	100.0	830,464	100.0
Asia	79,151	30.6	49,311	17.7	88,187	22.7	212,708	25.6
China	8,098	3.1	8,699	3.1	24,655	6.4	66,478	8.0
NIE's	28,328	11.0	23,153	8.3	32,708	8.4	68,438	8.2
ASEAN-4	41,558	16.1	15,568	5.6	27,657	7.1	58,394	7.0
North America	97,881	37.8	138,455	49.7	156,189	40.2	262,339	31.6
USA	94,336	36.5	132,222	47.5	150,152	38.7	251,805	30.3
Canada	3,545	1.4	6,233	2.2	6,037	1.6	10,533	1.3
Europe	47,719	18.4	56,789	20.4	94,277	24.3	193,499	23.3
Latin America	4,276	1.7	6,178	2.2	9,636	2.5	29,793	3.6
Mexico	520	0.2	2,193	0.8	3,635	0.9	2,755	0.3
Brazil	3,756	1.5	3,985	1.4	6,001	1.5	27,038	3.3
Others	29,626	11.5	27,712	10.0	39,909	10.3	132,125	15.9

Note: Stocks of FDI (accumulated) refers to International Investment position.

Source: JETRO database.

This, coupled with the rising cost structures of the Japanese economy, forced many companies to look for other locations of production. In addition, trade frictions with the United States in the late 1980s encouraged Japanese companies to relocate their production to that country to avoid new barriers on trade. In the 1990s, Japan's economy faced with stagnation went through a series of reforms. At the end of the decade, its FDI policy was liberalized and the mobility of capital in and outside the country was deregulated (Solis 2005).

During the 2000s, dynamic changes in East Asia's business environment compelled Japanese companies to develop new investment strategies. First, technological advances supported the formation of production networks based on the fragmentation of production, the modularization in the design of products and the formation of clusters. In fragmenting production, companies developed strong flows of parts and components with plants performing multiple tasks of processing and assembly before shipping these products to their final destinations. This system led to vertical integration and grew very rapidly in East Asia especially (METI 2007). At the same time, East Asia's middle class strata rapidly expanded and represented an attractive market for new investment and trade. Moreover, the boom over the signing of free trade agreements (FTAs) amongst the region's states helped further reduce trade and investment barriers, and consequently lowering distribution costs of intermediate goods between plants in different countries, albeit largely on a bilateral basis.

In seeking to optimize the fragmentation of production at the regional level, Japanese companies formed production networks based on specialization of labour and competences amongst plants and countries, as reflected in 'triangular trade' patterns (METI 2007). The first stage of development of the production network is represented on the left side of Figure 2.1. According to this model, both Japan and the new industrialized economies (NIEs) specialized in the manufacture of parts and components with high value added and whose production is capital-intensive. These intermediate goods were exported to China and Association of Southeast Asian Nations (ASEAN) countries, which assembled the parts and components under intensive production processes in the use of labour, then exporting those final goods to the EU, US and Japan. This process resulted in an intensive intra-regional trade of intermediate goods and extra-regional trade on final products, thus inserting the region into global markets.

In the second phase of the triangular trade model, the mutual supply of intermediate goods was incorporated. While Japan and the NIEs specialize in parts with advanced features and high-tech materials, the countries of ASEAN and China continue not only to play a role in processing and

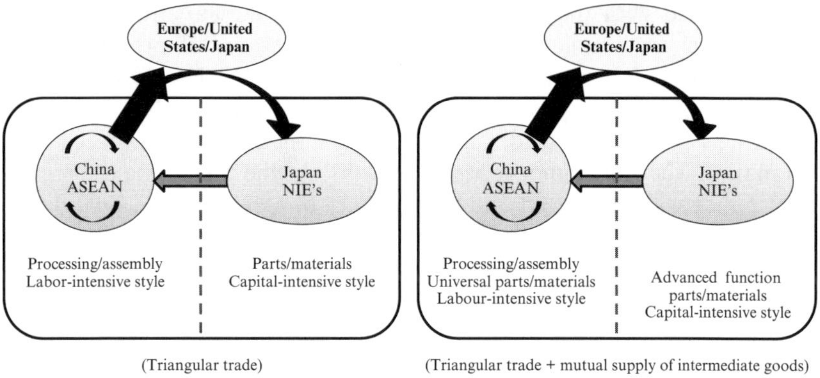

Source: Own elaboration based on METI (2007), Figure 2-2-19, p. 189.

Figure 2.1 Triangular trade in East Asia

assembly activities but nowadays they also produce generic parts and materials, helping further develop production networks and other supply chains in the region. In this phase, the region continued to be linked to the rest of the world by selling not only final products but also intermediate goods to global chains.

As noted above, China has become a major recipient of Japanese investment. Inward FDI in China has played a major role in promoting its successful exporting sector (Tao 2005). In the past decade, China also has upgraded its industrial production based on transfer of technology from foreign sources. This has led some authors to consider a new model of integration in East Asia – the so called 'East Asian Bicycle' – in which Japan and China are the axis that relate to other countries (the radius) with different intensities in their trade relations, and at the same time the axes have strong relations between them (Chen and De Lombaerde 2011). Though China still has a long way to go to develop the same kind of technological base as Japan's, it has undoubtedly played a major role in East Asia's regional economic integration, as well as in the region's integration into the wider Asia-Pacific and global economies.

Main Features of Intra-Regional Trade in East Asia

The process of economic integration described above has been reflected in the structure of East Asia's intra-regional trade relations. As is shown in Table 2.2, intra-regional trade in intermediate goods in Asia has increased substantially from 1980 to 2005, going from 42 percent to 60 percent of

Table 2.2 Evolution of intra-regional trade structure in East Asia, European Union and North America (percent)

Category of Goods	East Asia		European Union (25)		North America (3)	
	1980	2005	1980	2005	1980	2005
Final	25	31	41	45	33	38
Intermediate	42	60	50	49	46	48
Raw materials	31	7	7	5	19	13

Source: METI (2007: 167).

goods traded in the area. In the three regions presented in Table 2.2, East Asia showed the highest degree of integration in this category of goods. The intra-regional trade in final goods has also increased from 25 to 31 percent. However, this lower percentage compared to trade in intermediate goods indicates that most of the final goods trade is with countries outside the area. In contrast, in the other two regions (European Union and North America), intra-regional trade in final goods is more intense. Finally, the East Asia region sources its raw materials mainly outside the region.

In East Asia, the greater intensity in intra-regional trade in intermediate goods is evident in the electrical machinery, general machinery and chemicals sectors. Another important feature is the new sourcing strategy of Japanese affiliates. Although these companies have bases in China and ASEAN, sourcing from local suppliers has increased. This is due, among other causes, to the fact that local companies nowadays produce parts and components of general standard use for the electrical industry. Besides, the development of manufacturing parts for the automobile industry has been fostered by the FDI coming not only from Japan but also from NIEs and Western countries. The development of local suppliers in East Asia has helped the companies from those countries to construct a comparative advantage in the production of specific parts and components, hence facilitating their engagement in global supply chains, typically in higher value-added activities (METI 2007). Finally, the recent proliferation of FTAs and EPAs – especially in the Asia-Pacific – has helped intensify such trade (Kawai and Wignaraja 2009).

Japanese FDI in Latin America

Japan has been the major East Asian source of foreign investment in Latin America. In fact, Latin America has been the major recipient of accumulated Japanese FDI outside Asia (CEPAL 2010). However, in Japanese outward flows of FDI, Latin America has received a much lower share compared to East Asia. Notwithstanding the several sub-regional formal integrating processes in contrast with East Asia market-driven processes of integration, Latin America has not shown the same development of production networks throughout the region. This may be generally explained by higher import tariff levels, higher costs of link services, lack of a critical mass of agglomerations, and a comparative lack of investment from foreign small and medium enterprises (SMEs). Hence, the intensity of trade in intermediate goods has been lower in Latin America compared to East Asia. In 2008, only three countries had significantly concentrated intra-regional trade in parts and components: Brazil, Mexico and Argentina (Chen and De Lombaerde 2011). This is a main reason why these countries have attracted high levels of Japanese FDI.

Brazil is at the centre of the Southern Common Market (MERCOSUR) and has close economic links with Argentina and five other southern countries plus Mexico, which is not only Latin America's second largest economy but also has close economic relations with Central America and is integrated closely to the US economy through NAFTA. Indeed, regional production networks in Mexico have been hitherto limited primarily to NAFTA, and hence North America. Brazil, for its part, has depended more on the domestic market for its industrialization and less on the US market. While Mexico has managed to integrate into higher value-added activities in the automotive and electronics industries, Brazil has developed a strong aeronautical industry based on high value-added services. Hence, Japanese investment in Mexico has concentrated on the aforementioned sectors where it has developed a competitive advantage (CEPAL 2010).

Latin America has also recently attracted more investment to the region because of the high growth rates of the majority of its economies. Japanese companies are now considering the region as a strategic base for their world operations. Moreover, since 2008, Japan has implemented a new strategy to utilize the bilateral investment treaties (BIT) and EPAs to promote new investment projects in the region. It has EPAs with Mexico and Chile, and a BIT with Peru. Among the new projects that are attracting Japanese investment are those related to mining, infrastructure and agriculture (CEPAL 2010). After the EPA with Mexico, Japanese companies have been consolidating their production bases there. In addition, Mexico has most recently developed more intense economic relations with some countries in East Asia as they are becoming important suppliers of intermediate goods for Japanese and South Korean affiliates established in Mexico.

4. JAPANESE FDI IN MEXICO SINCE NAFTA AND ITS ROLE IN FOSTERING PRODUCTION NETWORKS

Japan has been traditionally the most important economic partner of Mexico in East Asia. First attracted by the *maquiladora* programme[5] that was introduced in the 1960s, Japanese companies began to establish themselves in Mexico from this time onwards (Almaraz 2007). Since then, Japan's FDI has had a major presence in the country and has been closely linked to the Mexican export sector and therefore to the US market, the main market for Mexican exports. In the 1990s, the signing of NAFTA between Mexico, the United States and Canada was the catalyst that prompted the arrival of more Japanese affiliates in Mexico, mostly located in the electronics and automotive sectors. In this decade, with the arrival of foreign investment in Mexico seeking an export platform to the world's largest market, Mexico's international trade became buoyant, making this country the tenth largest exporter in the world and the eleventh largest importer. Thus, total trade went from representing 20 percent of the GDP in the 1980s to 64 percent by the late 2000s (Dussell-Peters 2007; Falck Reyes 2009; Falck Reyes and León Manríquez 2010).

However, in the 2000s, both the Japanese and the Mexican economy were losing competitiveness, compelling both nations to address this by the signing of their EPA. As part of this agreement, Japanese companies sought to avoid the application of tariffs on imported inputs outside the North American region; a measure that had a negative impact on Japanese firms' competitiveness compared to their American counterparts.[6] Consequently, the Japan–Mexico EPA came into force in 2005, and thereafter a significant number of new Japanese companies have demonstrated interest in starting operations in Mexico. Those already operating in the country have announced the establishment of new plants or expansion of existing ones (Solis and Katada 2007; Falck Reyes 2009).

One of the main features of the economic relationship between Mexico and Japan has been the close relationship between Japanese FDI and the growing trend of Mexican imports from Japan as well as the active participation of Japanese companies in Mexican exports to the US. This triangular relationship has been strengthened by the presence of Japanese affiliates in the US, thus forming a cross-regional arrangement within the Asia-Pacific. The question then is whether the Japanese FDI has been promoting the formation of international production networks in Mexico, as it has done in East Asia, with similar impacts on the development of local supply, intra-firm trade, arm's-length trade and close ties to the regional production clusters.

Mexico attracted increasingly high levels of FDI during the 2000s. According to the Ministry of Economy, FDI flows averaged an annual US$19 billion, with 51 percent of them coming from the US while Japan contributed officially only 1 percent. However, this latter figure leaves out inward investment by Japanese affiliates established in the US. If those flows are counted in, Japan's share rises significantly, to 20 percent (JETRO).[7] One of the main characteristics of Japanese FDI in Mexico is its high concentration in the manufacturing sector (76 percent). It was from the 1980s when the establishment of new Japanese companies operating under the *maquiladora* programme accelerated: 26 in the 1980s, 45 in the 1990s, and 37 between 2000 and 2007 (Yamazaki 2008). During the 1990s, NAFTA exerted a major attraction on Japanese investment, concentrating activities in the two most dynamic manufacturing sectors of Mexico: electronics and automotive. Many plants that operated in the US transferred their activities to the northern states of Mexico (Contreras and Evans 2003; Carrillo and Hualde 2007). By 2003, eight Japanese plants were final assemblers of TV sets in the northern border: Matsuhita, Sanyo, Sony, Hitachi, JVC, Mitsubishi, Sharp and Toshiba (Carrillo and Hualde 2007: 109–10). Moreover, among the 100 largest exporters in Mexico, 13 are Japanese companies. In the automotive sector, three Japanese assemblers, Nissan, Honda and Toyota, participate with 27 percent of automobile production in Mexico. Their share on sales on the domestic market has risen to 39 percent and they participate with 24 percent of the automobile exports of Mexico. Moreover, in this sector, the industry of harness has shown a rapid development in the northern Ciudad Juárez, Chihuahua where Yazaki Corporation has played a major role (Carrillo and Hinojosa 2003).

Related to the close relationship between Japanese FDI and trade, it must be noticed that the total trade between the two countries has tripled between 1993 and 2010 reaching a level of US$18.5 billion of which imports accounted for 80 percent (Table 2.3). However the trade balance between the two countries has presented a chronic deficit. The latter has been the result of increasing imports from Japan that are concentrated in intermediate manufactured and capital goods with high technological content (electrical machinery, non-electrical and transport equipment). Meanwhile, Mexican exports to Japan are concentrated in three groups of products: food, minerals and manufactured goods. Among the latter, auto parts and accessories, mobile phones and cars have recently become increasingly important, noting that back and forth transactions with Japan may be increasing.

Data published by Kimura and Ando (2005) constitute a valuable source to analyse the destination of sales and origin of purchases made by

Table 2.3 Evolution of Mexico's trade with Japan, 1993–2010

Period	Exports		Imports		Total Trade (US$m)	Balance (US$m)
	Value US$m	Growth %	Value US$m	Growth %		
1993–1994	1,210	24.7	4,354	21.7	5,564	−3,145
1995–1999	1,575	6.8	4,408	1.8	5,983	−2,832
2000–2004	2,028	7.9	8,429	17.8	10,457	−6,402
2005–2007	2,842	13.3	14,911	15.7	17,753	−12,069
2008–2009	3,293	−3	13,862	−15.2	17,155	−10,568
2010	3,473	24.1	15,015	31.7	18,488	−11,542

Note: Average annual values are shown for each period.

Source: Ministry of Economy and JETRO databases.

Japanese manufacturing affiliates. The years available in this source (1995 and 1998) correspond to the immediate period after the entry into force of NAFTA. Since in Latin America, Brazil and Mexico are the two countries receiving the bulk of FDI from Japan, the authors reported statistical information broken down for these two countries.

Figure 2.2 presents the types of relationships established by Japanese affiliates in Mexico and their markets of destination. First, the main targets for sales are the local and the North American market followed by sales to Japan and far behind those to Latin America. Second, the local market share increased from 47 percent to 63 percent while the North America market participation decreased from 43 percent to 29 percent. Moreover, in these two main destination markets, the arms-length trade tends to gain importance while the intra-firm loses its relative relevance. Third, sales to Japan are intra-firm sales. Fourth, sales to Latin America are barely important. Hence, unlike East Asia, sales of Japanese affiliates in Mexico involved a smaller number of regional players. However, in the two main markets arms length trade was gaining more importance against the relative share of intra-firm sales, thus engaging more local actors.

Figure 2.3 shows that the important role of the local market as supplier of inputs (41 percent) for Japanese affiliates operating in Mexico, followed by suppliers from Japan (33 percent), North America (16 percent) and East Asia excluding Japan (11 percent). It is noteworthy that between 1995 and 1998, arm's-length trade increased significantly and intra-firm trade declined in importance in all markets except North America. Second, North America had been losing its share as supplier of Japanese affiliates and trade had fallen in both arm's-length trade and intra-firm

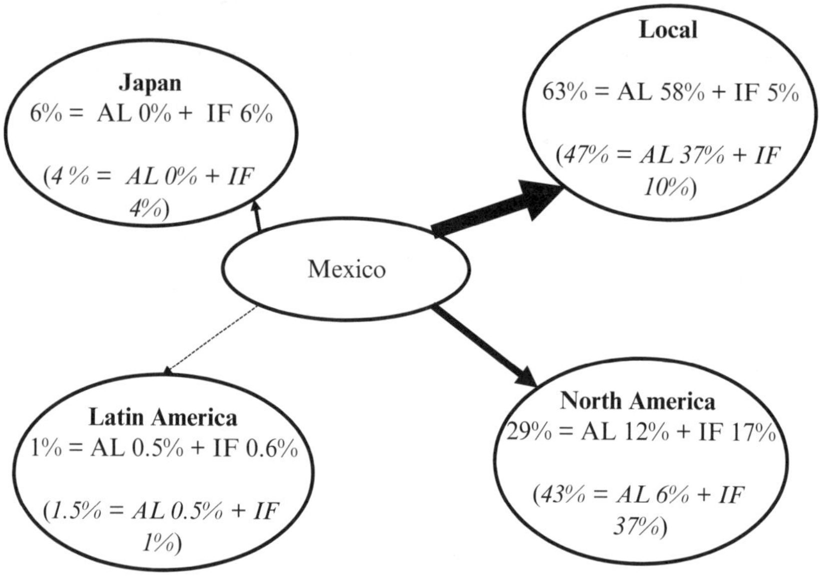

Note: Kimura and Ando based their information on the METI database.

Source: Own elaboration with data from Kimura and Ando (2005), Table 9, p. 337.

Figure 2.2 Japanese affiliates operating in Mexico: manufacturing sector (sales destination), 1998 (1995)

trade. Third, the share lost by North America has been won by East Asia (excluding Japan) in the two types of trade: arm's-length and intra-firm. These trends are also validated by the general statistics of Mexico's trade with its main partners.[8] There was thus a diversification of this supply chain trade for Japanese affiliates in Mexico during this period, with firms from more Asia-Pacific countries becoming involved, including from non-Japan East Asia.

If we now turn to the 2000s, Figure 2.4 shows the sales trends to all markets by the main manufacturing sectors from 1985 to 2005.[9] The exponential growth of sales of machinery in general from 1994 on is noteworthy, and also that the transport machinery sector is the one with the highest growth followed by electronics, denoting the dynamic role of Japanese affiliates in Mexico.[10]

Moreover, the trend shown by employment in the machinery industry also indicates a growing pattern up to the year 2000 (Figure 2.5). From that year on, the US recession (2001–2003) affected negatively the export sectors in Mexico. Japanese affiliates in the electronics industry seemed

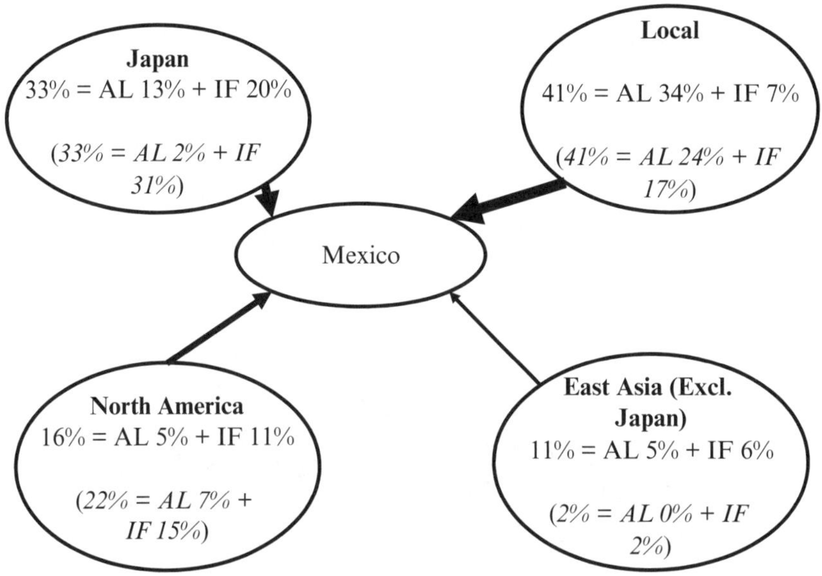

Note: Kimura and Ando based their information on the METI database.

Source: Own elaboration with data from (2005) Kimura and Ando, Table 9, p. 337.

Figure 2.3 Japanese affiliates operating in Mexico: manufacturing sector (procurement origin), 1998 (1995)

to be restructuring, while in the automotive sector, employment tended to remain stable. The figures also highlight that the levels of employment in the automotive industry are higher than in electronics. These trends, based on firm-level data, confirm on the one hand, the growing presence of Japanese firms in Mexico and, on the other hand, they highlight the growing importance of the automotive sector.

In addition to the above trends, Japanese investment in the electronics and automotive sectors has been acquiring even more relevance since the signing of the Mexico–Japan EPA in 2005 according to FDI announcements made by Japanese firms (Table 2.4). Of a total of US$6.3 billion announced as new investments, 83 percent corresponded to those two sectors – automotive 39 percent and electronics 44 percent. The already established Japanese companies in Mexico are attracting suppliers of parts and components for these industries both from Japan and the US.[11]

On a par with new investment announcements, imports from Japan showed two-digit levels of growth annually during the decade up to 2010, indicating the dynamic activities of Japanese affiliates, taking into account

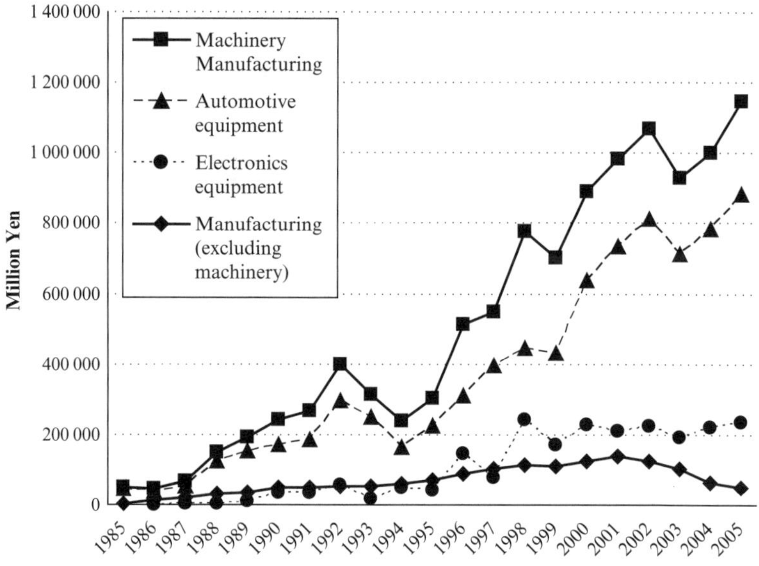

Source: Own elaboration with RIETI database.

Figure 2.4 Japanese affiliates operating in Mexico: sales trend in selected sectors, 1985–2005

the high share of parts and components in those imports. Also imports from other countries in East Asia (South Korea, Taiwan and China among others) had increased and have started to displace North America as the main supplier of Mexico in intermediate goods. Given that Japan is the main investor from East Asia in Mexico, this is indicative that East Asia is engaging as another partner in the triangular relationship among Mexico, Japan and the US, further cementing cross-regional production networks within the Asia-Pacific.

5. CONCLUSION

Japan is one of the main sources of foreign investment in the world. East Asia has received an important share of Japanese FDI, which has played a major role in fostering international production networks in the region. Since Mexico started liberalizing its economy back in the mid-1980s, Japanese investment started flowing into Mexico in that decade and since it has become a major player in the automotive and electronic

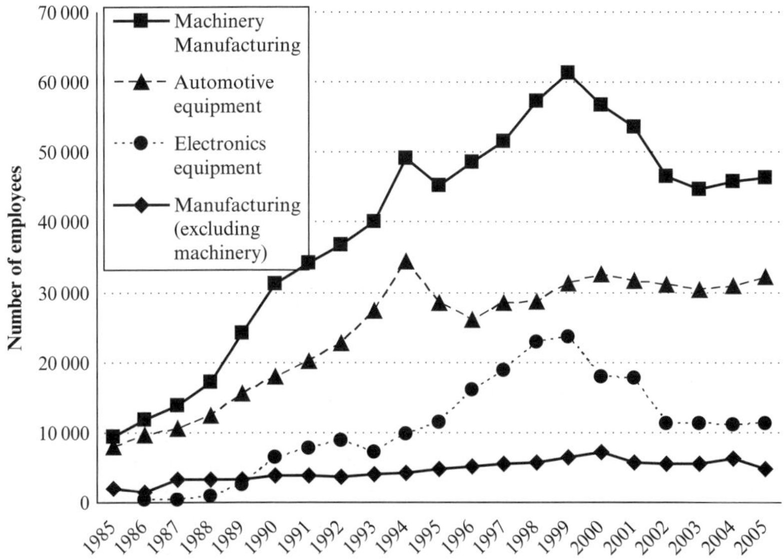

Source: RIETI Database.

Figure 2.5 Employment levels of Japanese affiliates operating in Mexico, 1985–2005

Table 2.4 Announced FDI by Japanese companies in Mexico by main sectors, 2005–2010

Period	Announced investment by sector	Value (US$ thousands)
2005–2007 Post EPA Mexico–Japan	Automotive sector	2,539,600
	Electronic sector	211,300
	Other sectors	675,200
	Total	3,426,100
2008–2009 Global Crisis	Automotive sector	94,700
	Electronic sector	66,500
	Total	161,200
2010 Post-crisis	Automotive sector	211,000
	Electronic sector	2,500,000
	Total	2,711,000
2005–2010	Total investment	6,298,300

Source: Databases of the Ministry of Economy, Office of Mexico–Japan EPA; JETRO–Mexico.

sectors, which in turn are the most dynamic sectors of Mexican exports. This chapter has shown that in the early 2000s Japanese firms operating in Mexico were playing a key role in cultivating international production network development, especially through their supply procurement activities where more networked firms on a broader geographic scale within the Asia-Pacific were being engaged. The increase of arm's-length trade as a general trend reinforced those tendencies. Therefore, one of the salient features of the activities by Japanese affiliates in Mexico nowadays is that they have gone beyond the original triangular relationship among Japanese firms established in Mexico, the US and Japan, extending their networks to firms in other East Asian nations. In this sense, Japanese firms in Mexico have to some extent linked the regional production network elements in North America and East Asia together.

Evidence provided by the patterns of trade between Japan and Mexico and the growing intensity on imports and their composition, the increasing interest shown by Japanese firms that have announced plans for new investment and/or expansion of the existing plants and the growing patterns shown by sales and employment of Japanese firm-level database, are all indirect indicators of the strengthening activities by Japanese firms in Mexico. Finally, the experience of the benefits received by host countries of Japanese investment in East Asia is of relevance for public policymakers in Mexico, especially to introduce measures that help foreign investors reduce production network services costs.

NOTES

1. The author wishes to thank Laura Navarro for her assistance in preparing the statistical data, and Takako Nakasone for translating some Japanese reports.
2. This section draws heavily on Falck Reyes (2011).
3. The source of this data is Japan External Trade Organization (JETRO), http://www.jetro.go.jp/en/reports/statistics.
4. The Survey of Overseas Business Activities conducted by METI has as its targets: a) parent companies: Japanese corporations that own or have owned overseas affiliates in the past, excluding financial, insurance and real estate industry; b) overseas affiliates: i) foreign affiliate in which a Japanese corporation has invested capital of 10 percent or more; ii) foreign affiliate in which a 'subsidiary' funded by more than 50 percent by a Japanese corporation has invested capital of more than 50 percent in the affiliate; iii) foreign affiliate in which a Japanese corporation and a subsidiary funded by more than 50 percent by a Japanese corporation have invested capital of more than 50 percent in the affiliate. http://www.meti.go.jp/english/statistics/tyo/kaigaizi/index.html.
5. Mexico's Export Maquiladora Industry Programme was introduced to develop the northern border states of Mexico by attracting investment in labour-intensive industries. Under this programme, companies were granted tariff exemptions for imported equipment and components to produce export goods. The *maquiladora* industry has evolved from simple and manual assembling production processes to more complex

and automatic ones. At the same time it has developed a network of close relations with direct and indirect suppliers and with local and public institutions (Villacencio 2004).

6. NAFTA Article 303 came into effect in Mexico in 2001 and it restricted the ability of NAFTA countries to provide export incentives in the form of waivers, refunds or reductions of import duties in connection with exports to other NAFTA countries. Since these are features of the *maquiladora* programme, it meant that producers in Mexico will no longer have duty-free access to imports from non-NAFTA countries which are used in exports to the USA.
7. According to the office of the Japan External Trade Organization (JETRO) in Mexico, the ratio of Japanese FDI coming from the US and that originated in Japan is 3.4:1 (JETRO 2004a).
8. Author's own analysis of data from JETRO and the Ministry of Economy, Mexico.
9. I use as an indirect indicator a database prepared by the Research Institute of Economy, Trade and Industry (RIETI) of Japan. To make these estimates, RIETI adjusts the information from the Survey of Overseas Business Activities of Japanese Enterprises of METI.
10. The METI database at the level of firm data can be accessed only in Japan. Therefore, at this point of my research, I am using indirect sources to look at the tendencies in the first decade of this century.
11. Interview with a representative of JETRO–Mexico, July 13, 2011.

REFERENCES

Almaraz, A. (2007), 'La Relevancia Económica y el Perfil de las Maquiladoras Electrónicas y de Autopartes en Tres Ciudades del Norte de México (1990–2003)', in J. Carrillo and M.R. Barajas (eds), *Maquiladoras Fronterizas. Evolución y Heterogeneidad en los Sectores Electrónico y Automotriz*, México City: El Colegio de la Frontera Norte and Miguel Ángel Porrua.

Baldwin, R. and F. Robert-Nicoud (2006), 'Offshoring and globalisation: what is new about the new paradigm?', mimeo, Geneva: Graduate Institute of International Studies.

Carrillo, J. and R. Hinojosa (2003), 'Cableando a Norteamérica: la Industria de los Arneses Automotrices', in O. Contreras and J. Carrillo (eds), *Hecho en Norteamérica. Cinco Estudios sobre la Integración Industrial de México en América del Norte*, México City: Cal y Arena and El Colegio de Sonora.

Carrillo, J. and A. Hualde (2007), 'Presente y Futuro de la Manufactura de Televisores en la Frontera Norte de México: de la Tecnología Análoga a la Digital', in J. Carrillo and M.R. Barajas (eds), *Maquiladoras Fronterizas. Evolución y Heterogeneidad en los Sectores Electrónico y Automotriz*, México City: El Colegio de la Frontera Norte and Miguel Ángel Porrua.

CEPAL (United Nations Economic Commission for Latin America and the Caribbean) (2010), 'Co-operación y relaciones económicas entre el Japón y América Latina', in O. Rosales (ed.), *Panorama de la inserción internacional de América Latina y el Caribe 2009–2010: Crisis originada en el Centro y recuperación impulsada por las economías emergentes*, Santiago: División de Comercio Internacional e Integración.

Chen, L. and P. De Lombaerde (2011), 'Redes de distribución regional de la producción y organización en ejes en América Latina y en el Este Asiático: una perspectiva de largo plazo', *Integración y Comercio*, **15**(32), 21–38.

Contreras, O. and R. Evans (2003), 'Más allá de las Maquiladoras: el Complejo Manufacturero del Televisor en el Norte de México', in O. Contreras and J. Carrillo (eds), *Hecho en Norteamérica. Cinco Estudios sobre la Integración Industrial de México en América del Norte*, México City: Cal y Arena and El Colegio de Sonora.

Dussel-Peters, E. (ed.) (2007), *La Inversión Extranjera Directa en México: Desempeño Potencial. Una Perspectiva Macro, Meso, Micro y Territorial*, México City: Siglo XXI Editores.

Falck Reyes, M. (2009), 'El Acuerdo de Asociación Económica México–Japón. Evolución del Comercio y la Inversión 1993–2008', in M. Falck Reyes and C. Uscanga (eds), *Las Relaciones Comerciales y Financieras entre México y Japón en el Marco del Acuerdo de Asociación Económica*, México City: Facultad de Ciencias Políticas y Sociales, Universidad Nacional Autónoma de México.

Falck Reyes, M.E. (2011), 'El Papel de Japón en la Integración Económica de Asia del Este', in Juan José Ramírez Bonilla, Daniel Toledo Beltrán and Carlos Uscanga Prieto (eds), *Japón ante la nueva configuración de Asia del Pacifico. Proactividad y reactividad ante un orden internacional fluido*, México City: EL Colegio de México.

Falck Reyes, M.E. and J.L. Leon-Manriquez (2010), 'Mexico's East Asia strategy', in J. Dosch and O. Jacob (eds), *Asia and Latin America. Political, Economic and Multilateral Relations*, London: Routledge Contemporary Asia Series.

Helpman, E. (2006), 'Trade, FDI, and the Organisation of Firms', National Bureau of Economic Research working chapter series, no. 12091, Washington, DC: NBER.

JETRO–México (2004), 'Inversión Japonesa en México', México City: Japan External Trade Organization (México).

Jones, R., H. Kierzkowski and L. Chen (2005), 'What does evidence tell us about fragmentation and outsourcing?', *International Review of Economics and Finance*, **14**(3), 377–90.

Kawai, M. and G. Wignaraja (2009), 'La Integración Económica Global y Regional: una Perspectiva desde Asia', *Instituto para la Integración de América Latina y el Caribe (BID-INTAL)*, **13**(29), January–June.

Kimura, F. and M. Ando (2005), 'Two-dimensional fragmentation in East Asia: conceptual framework and empirics', *International Review of Economics and Finance*, **14**(3), 317–48.

Ministry of Economy and Industry (METI) (2007), *White Chapter on International Economy and Trade 2007*, Tokyo: METI.

Ministry of Economy and Industry (METI) (2010), *Summary of The 2010 (40th) Survey of Overseas Business Activities*, Tokyo: METI.

Solis, M. (2005), 'From iron doors to chapter screens: the Japanese state and multinational investment', in S.M. Pekkanen and K.S. Tsai (eds), *Japan and China in the World Political Economy*, London: Routledge.

Solis, M. and S. Katada (2007), 'The Japan–Mexico FTA: a cross-regional step in the path towards Asian regionalism', *Pacific Affairs*, **80**(2), 279–302.

Tao, Y. (2005), 'A catch-up strategy? China's policy toward foreign direct investment', in S.M. Pekkanen and K.S. Tsai (eds), *Japan and China in the World Political Economy*, London: Routledge.

United Nations Conference on Trade and Development (UNCTAD) (2008), *World Investment Report: Transnational Corporations and the Infrastructure Challenge*, Geneva: UNCTAD.

Villacencio, D. (2004), 'La configuración del entorno institucional de las maquiladoras y las nuevas formas de interacción binacional', in J. Carrillo and R. Partida (eds), *La industria maquiladora mexicana. Aprendizaje tecnológico, impacto regional y entornos institucionales*, Guadalajara, Mexico: El Colegio de la Frontera Norte and Universidad de Guadalajara.
Yamazaki, B. (2008), *México y Japón: Crónica de 400 años de relaciones amistosas y económicas y 50 años de vínculos empresariales*, México City: Private edition.

DATABASES

Japan External Trade Organization (JETRO), Japanese trade and investment statistics: www.jetro.go.jp/en/reports/statistics.
Mexican Automotive Manufacturers Association (AMIA) statistics: www.amia.com.mx/index.php.
Ministry of Economy of Mexico (Secretaría de Economía), Directorate General of Foreign Investment (DGIE), Investment Flow Reporter: www.economia.gob.mx/swb/es/economia/Tablas_Reporteador_de_IED.
Ministry of Economy of Mexico (Secretaria de Economía), international trade statistics: www.economia.gob.mx/swb/es/economia/p_Estadistica.
Ministry of Economy of Mexico Office of Mexico–Japan Economic Partnership Agreement, www.mexicotradeandinvestment.com.
Research Institute of Economy, Trade and Industry Foreign (RIETI), direct investment database: www.rieti.go.jp/en/database/d08.html?stylesheet=print.
World Trade Organization, statistics database: http://stat.wto.org/Home/WSDBHome.aspx?Language=E.

3. Managing the Great Recession in South Korea and Mexico: economic institutions, domestic market and regional trade

José Luis León-Manríquez*

1. INTRODUCTION

Due to globalisation of production and financial exchanges, the 2008/09 global financial crisis (the 'Great Recession') spread across the planet with extraordinary swiftness. The mechanisms of contagion of this crisis were at least as diverse as the responses from different countries. For the sake of analytical simplicity, *The Economist* (10 March 2009) summarized these responses by stating that 'we are all Keynesians now'. However convincing this statement might seem, it is still worth analysing the mechanisms of transmission as well as the specific answers to the global crisis undertaken by different Asia-Pacific Rim countries. Two interesting comparative cases are South Korea and Mexico, both being manufacturing-export economies of similar size with parallel experiences of trade liberalisation, privatisation and productive restructuring in the 1980s and the 1990s. In terms of gross domestic product (GDP), they ranked as the 14th (Mexico) and the 15th (South Korea) largest economies in the world in 2010 (World Bank 2011). In 2008, both countries experienced a rapid devaluation of their currencies, falling levels of exports and sharp falls in their stock exchange indices. Forecasts made by the International Monetary Fund (IMF) and the Organisation for Economic Co-operation and Development (OECD) foresaw moderate declines in their GDPs by the end of 2009. Yet, at the end of that period, Mexico recorded a 6.5 percent contraction in GDP and South Korea a modest growth of 0.2 percent.

This chapter argues that the diverging economic performances of South Korea and Mexico during the global crisis can be explained by three main factors. The first concerns the orientation of each country's economic policy-making institutions, shaped in turn by path-dependent trajectories. The second is linked to the different degrees of state support conferred to the domestic market as part of wider economic recovery strategies. While Mexico was unwilling to move away from the neoliberal economic orthodoxy that had prevailed in the country since the 1980s, South Korea quickly implemented counter-cyclical measures. The third factor is linked to the broader contexts of regional economic integration. Despite the USA's plummeting demand for imports, East Asian markets remained relatively stable for South Korean exports. In contrast, Mexico was disadvantaged by the nation's high level of export dependence on the United States.

The first part of the chapter deals with the historic configuration of economic institutions in both countries, which shaped the way each nation dealt with the Great Recession. The second section discusses the crisis transmission mechanisms affecting the countries through the real economy and the financial sector, and addresses the evolution of the South Korean and Mexican economies in 2008–2009. The third part examines Mexico's and South Korea's strategies for dealing with the global financial crisis, highlighting the role of monetary and fiscal policies. The fourth part analyses to what extent formal or informal regional integration affected national economic performance.

2. INSTITUTIONS AND ECONOMIC POLICY-MAKING IN MEXICO AND KOREA: A BRIEF HISTORIC REVIEW

In order to understand the diverging reactions of Mexico and South Korea to the Great Recession, it is worth analysing, even if briefly, the institutional evolution of economic policy-making institutions in both countries. For several decades after the Revolution (1910–1920), the Mexican state enjoyed an ample degree of autonomy. Through the reorganisation of the political system in the 1930s, most social sectors were clustered under the aegis of presidency, the bureaucracy and the official party, in a peculiar corporatist arrangement. These institutional arrangements bred quite an autonomous state. Taking advantage of this autonomy, in the 1950s and 1960s Mexico developed a central guidance cluster in the economic branch of the state. That cluster was integrated by the Ministry of Treasury (Secretaría de Hacienda y Crédito Público, SHCP), the Bank of Mexico (Banco de México, Banxico) and the development bank known as Nacional Financiera (Nafinsa). There was a close co-ordination and a clear division of labour between the members of this 'triangle of efficiency'. The SHCP assigned resources and checked the fiscal deficit, Banxico guaranteed monetary stability and Nafinsa supported new industries. Since the late 1950s, these institutions agreed that SHCP would manage their relationship with the president (León-Manríquez 2001).

This institutional cluster could have been the nucleus of a developmental state. Unfortunately, in the 1970s the presidency ravaged the financial bureaucracy in order to enhance its control over economic policy-making. The populist administration of Luis Echeverría (1970–1976) systematically undermined the 'triangle of efficiency', which was clearly dysfunctional for the expansionary, distributive, state-led economic policy he had in mind. His successor, José López Portillo (1976–1982) also distrusted the SHCP. Once in office, he created the new Ministry of Programming and Budget (Secretaría de Programación y Presupuesto, SPP) which was a powerful agency that would fuse the state's planning and budget management functions; two areas of traditional bureaucratic contention. Moreover, the SPP seized some relevant political functions from the Ministry of the Interior.

This organisational change triggered fierce inter-ministerial disputes between SPP and SHCP that undermined the coherence of Mexico's economic policy-making between 1976 and 1985. Later on, a group of monetarist economists secured policy-making leadership through their control of the SPP. Its leader, Carlos Salinas, eventually became Mexican president (1988–1994) and staffed most of the ministries with his neoliberal allies. Salinas became very powerful and launched an ambitious 'technocratic revolution' that also meant the dismantling or neutralization of the surviving developmental-oriented agencies.

The new elite of political technocrats mostly belonged to the upper-middle and high income classes. Unlike the previous developmental elite, they attended graduate, private and foreign schools, where they majored in economics. Additionally, these technocrats entered the bureaucracy at lower ages and higher entry levels. Mexican elites in the technocratic era became smaller and less inclusionary. Economic policy-making in Mexico subsequently became a virtual monopoly of this new political technocratic elite that fervently believed in free markets, low inflation, fiscal discipline, trade liberalisation and closer economic integration with the United States. Despite the defeat of the Institutional Revolutionary Party (PRI) in 2000, after more than 70 years in office, orthodox technocrats have been able to keep control of the main economic institutions. Decisions taken by this technocratic core had a key impact on how Mexico dealt with the 2008/09 global financial crisis.

In South Korea, the establishment of the Economic Planning Board (EPB) by President Park Chung-hee in 1961 created a very effective pilot agency of the developmental state that oversaw three decades of consistently high economic growth until the early 1990s. Among its functions, the EPB was the key architect and co-ordinator of South Korea's Five-Year Plan, exercising control over subsidies, import licenses, export incentives, the preparation of the governmental budget and the co-ordination of economic policy-making generally. After being hitherto dominated by Japanese educated, developmental-minded technocrats, the EPB's ranks were gradually filled with US-educated and hence more neoliberal-inclined personnel during the 1980s, causing some ideological tensions within the agency and South Korea's economic-related ministries generally. Consequently, over time the preoccupation for price stability replaced the emphasis on growth as the central objective of South Korean economic policy. Running parallel to this were important political changes, with the rise to power of democratically elected presidents Kim Young-Sam (1993–1998) and Kim Dae Jung (1998–2003) who precipitated the transformation of the South Korean developmental state into a kind of post-developmental bureaucracy.

Political and economic transformations brought notable institutional changes, the most relevant being the dismantling of the EPB and the consequent dispersion of the economic policy-making functions among various ministries. In 1994, the EPB's divisions were subsumed into the newly formed Ministry of Finance of Economy (MOFE), which had oversight over tax collection, designing fiscal policy and undertaking certain planning activities. The new Ministry of Foreign Affairs and Trade (MOFAT) meanwhile was conferred responsibility for trade policy, and the Ministry of Commerce and Industry managed most functions of foreign investment policy. The 1997/98 financial crisis brought further significant institutional and policy-making change within the South Korean state, this being somewhat imposed upon the nation by the conditions attached by the IMF's bailout package. New neoliberal measures were introduced under Kim Dae-jung's presidency, thus bringing about some degree of economic ideological convergence with Mexico by the early 2000s.

In 1999, the Kim Dae-jung administration created the Ministry of Planning and Budget (MPB) which was merged with MOFE in 2008 to create the Ministry of Strategy and Finance (MOSF) as part of the new institutional arrangements introduced under new President Lee Myung-bak. Lee worked previously as a high-ranking executive in Hyundai and possesses strong pro-business, neoliberal credentials. Notwithstanding these developments, the Lee administration's policy response to the 2008/09 financial crisis demonstrated the resilience of South Korea's developmental statism, as we examine below.

3. THE GLOBAL CRISIS AND ITS CONTAGION TO MEXICO AND SOUTH KOREA

Both Mexico and South Korea have experienced notable economic crises since the early 1990s. As Figure 3.1 indicates, Mexico had a deep crisis in 1994/95, while South Korea was seriously affected by the 1997/98 East Asian financial crisis. Despite this similarity, there are still some key differences between Mexico and South Korea with regards to their economic growth pattern over the period. While South Korea's growth averaged 5.6 percent per annum between 1990 and 2010, Mexico averaged only 2.7 percent.

Mexico and South Korea were affected by the 2008/09 global financial crisis through various external shocks. In Mexico's case, this primarily concerned decreasing imports from the United States, by far its largest trading partner. Since late 2007, US imports from Mexico had been faltering, and the external sector came under stress. In 2007, its current account deficit was US$8.4 billion but in 2008 this almost doubled, reaching US$15.9 billion or 1.5 percent of the nation's GDP. In the first quarter of 2009, many external factors affected Mexican economic performance. Non-oil exports fell 24.3 percent, oil exports plummeted almost 50 percent, international tourist visitor numbers decreased by 17 percent, and remittances from Mexicans abroad diminished by 11 percent. To make things worse, Mexican currency devalued by around half in value, from 9.98 pesos per US dollar in early August 2008 to 15.21 pesos by early

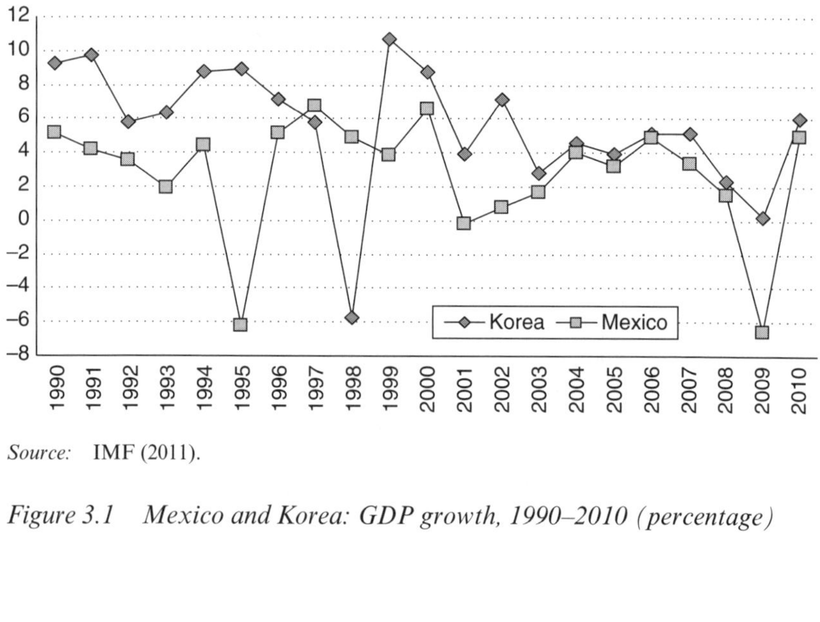

Source: IMF (2011).

Figure 3.1 Mexico and Korea: GDP growth, 1990–2010 (percentage)

March 2009 (Banxico 2009: 8). The Mexican Stock Exchange (BMV) also experienced a sustained fall, from 31,975 points on 2 May 2008 to 17,752 points by 2 February 2009.

South Korea was also deeply affected by the 2008/09 global financial crisis on many fronts. As the crisis deepened, non-performing loans of banks soared, further complicating the situation of financial institutions (Park 2009). In February 2009, the Economist Intelligence Unit's forecast for South Korea's GDP was −5.9 percent, while the IMF predicted a 4 percent contraction by the end of the year.[1] Meanwhile, the Korean won depreciated by 50 percent between early 2008 and the first quarter of 2009 on the currency markets. This was despite the bulky stock of foreign exchange reserves South Korea had at its disposal. In addition, levels of inward foreign direct investment (FDI) fell back sharply from early 2008, and the country's main stock exchange index, the KOSPI-100, fell from its historic high of 1,917.84 points in October 2007 to just 950.88 points on 25 November 2008. The stampede of capital out of South Korea was exacerbated by the deregulation of capital account transactions, implemented in 2008. To make matters worse, the nation's financial institutions and major companies had been incurring heavy foreign debt up to this time. South Korean banks' debt climbed from US$83.4 billion in 2005 to US$194 billion by late 2007. In turn, the foreign debt of public and private firms increased from US$88.9 billion to US$134.8 billion in the same period. By late 2008, foreign debt amounted to 97 percent of South Korea's foreign exchange reserves.

4. RESCUING THE DOMESTIC MARKETS: MONETARY AND FISCAL POLICIES

Initially, the Mexican government downplayed the crisis, arguing that it had started overseas and that its national impacts would be limited. In February 2008, Minister of SHCP, Agustín Carstens, remarked on the difference between the looming crisis from previous downturns, stating that Mexico would only have 'a slight cold, and not pneumonia as before'.[2] This relaxed attitude was shown in the handling of monetary policy in 2008. For much of the first half-year, Mexico's interest rate stayed at 7.5 percent then rose to 7.75 percent in June, 8 percent in July, and then 8.25 percent by August 2008. Despite the full-blown development of the global final crisis by September, the central bank did not order any interest rate reduction in the final months of the year. In the first half of 2009, the monetary authorities changed their mind. In January the Bank of Mexico reduced the interest rate to 7.75 percent, in April to 6.75 percent, and then in July down to 4.5 percent. Interest rates would remain unchanged throughout 2009 and 2010.

The Mexican government reacted more quickly on fiscal policy. Between March 2008 and January 2009, it issued three stimulus packages to deal with the effects of the global financial crisis and ensuing Great Recession (Villagómez and Navarro 2010). In March 2008, the Mexican government announced a programme to support economic growth and employment, providing provisional discounts on taxes to personal income and only scant resources to reduce unemployment. The month before, President Felipe Calderón had announced the creation of a National Infrastructure Fund with an initial US$4 billion endowment. In October 2008, the government then announced the second stimulus package. Among other measures, the package foresaw the enlargement and more efficient exercise of public spending, the construction of a new refinery for the state oil company Petróleos Mexicanos (PEMEX) worth US$1.2 billion, and the launch of a special programme to support small and medium enterprises (SMEs). In January 2009, the Mexican government launched its third stimulus package. The main measures were a reduction of the cost of gas for domestic use, a freeze on electricity and fuel prices, and credit disbursements of some US$150 million for industries hit by financial restrictions. These stimulus measures, as well as some international forecasts on the Mexican economy, seemed to validate the 'slight cold' thesis. Some international consultancy firms forecasted that Mexican GDP would be flat by the end of the year.

However, in the following months these not so unfavourable expectations were virtually shattered. Mexico suffered from the collapse of oil prices (the country being a significant oil producer), a sharp decline of its exports to the United States, a drop in remittances from US-based Mexican workers, and a substantial contraction of domestic demand. To exacerbate matters, in April 2009 the H1N1 flu appeared, stalling the economy for several weeks. As 2009 progressed, the Mexican government spoke less about stimulus packages and more about its protracted fiscal crisis, with fiscal policy shifting from increasing expenditure to budgetary cuts and tax collection. Mexican technocrats argued that there would be a fiscal gap of US$25 billion by the end of 2009 if fiscal discipline was not undertaken. In May 2009, the government started its first wave of budgetary cuts, which were deepened in July. In October 2009, the President proposed and the Congress approved an increase to the value added tax from 15 percent to 16 percent. In turn, the main income tax rate was increased from 28 percent to 30 percent. At the same time, significant government budget cuts were introduced. By the end of the year, Mexico's GDP contracted by 6.5 percent, the worst annual regression since 1932. The decline was also one of the most pronounced in Latin America.[3] Unemployment climbed from 4.6 percent of the economically active population in January 2009 to 6.4 percent by September 2009, the highest unemployment rate in 14 years. Out of Mexico's 106 million people, those in extreme poverty soared from 14 to 20 million over the same period.[4]

Despite the Mexican government's early indications of an assertive response, neoliberal orthodoxy prevailed. Unlike South Korea, which drew on its reserves and implemented a bold fiscal policy to alleviate the crisis as we later discuss, the Mexican government decided that it was more important to keep inflation under control, and the fiscal deficit close to zero. Global crisis notwithstanding, the main goal of Mexico's policy-makers was, as it had been since the 1980s, achieving a low to zero inflation even if that meant lower growth (Banxico 2009: 1). Under these imperatives, Mexico's reserves, which in July 2008 approached US$87 billion, remained virtually intact during the crisis. If some funds were taken from these reserves, it was to prevent further devaluation of the Mexican peso against the US dollar, and thus avert 'imported inflation' pressures, that is rising prices of US imports. Between March and June 2009, the Bank of Mexico implemented daily auctions of US dollars without a minimum price for US$100 million, and sales with a fixed price for US$300 million a day. In the first half of 2009, these auctions amounted to US$11.7 billion (Banxico 2009: 1). This intervention in the foreign currency market helped to control currency volatility and the depreciation of the Mexican peso.

Contrary to a more or less worldwide implicit Keynesian consensus, Mexico responded to the crisis with massive cuts to public spending and new tax hikes. Rather than being countercyclical, Mexican economic policy became pro-cyclical, thus deepening the scope of the Great Recession. The stimulus packages and the infrastructure fund were hesitantly implemented, if at all. For instance, the construction of the oil refinery foreseen in the October 2008 stimulus package has been so slow that, in the best of the cases, it will only become operational in 2015.[5] The awkward handling of the Mexican crisis was not lost on international economic analysts. In November 2009, Joseph Stiglitz (Nobel Prizewinner in Economics in 2001) remarked that Mexico's management of the crisis had been among the worst in the world. Stiglitz warned that, instead of waiting for an economic recovery of the USA, Mexico should consider other strategic alternatives for its own revitalization. In response, Ernesto Cordero, Minister of Social Development (later appointed Minister of SHCP) declared: 'I think that Stiglitz does not know in detail the countercyclical policies implemented by the Mexican government; he does not know the reality of Mexican public finances. I think he should read a little more about Mexico.'[6] Another warning of economic decay came from Carlos Slim, the owner of telecom giant Teléfonos de México. Slim's criticisms sparked a heated reaction from key policy-makers, including President Calderón.[7]

Despite international turmoil, by mid-2008 no disaster loomed on the economic horizon of South Korea. By September 2008 it seemed that the country would not be substantially affected by a global crisis that had been triggered by the subprime mortgage debacle in the USA. However, this was soon to change. The crisis was transmitted to South Korea via two main mechanisms. The first was through the financial sector due primarily to the aforementioned significant exposure of South Korean firms to foreign loans. The second was through the trade sector, South Korea's export-driven economy being hit hard by substantial falls in demand in US and EU markets.

Despite the apparent retreat of the developmental state and the increasing neoliberal orientation of South Korean policy-makers, the government crafted a textbook countercyclical Keynesian response, structured around a rapid expansion of public spending. Its main elements comprised a comprehensive fiscal policy aimed at rescuing firms, investing in infrastructure, and avoiding massive job losses, and additionally new policy measures to promote and diversify exports. On the one hand, the South Korean case highlighted how fast international turmoil can affect a national economy. On the other, it illustrates how a state's response to a crisis can either deepen or hinder the most deleterious effects of a systemic turmoil.

To further stimulate the economy, the Bank of Korea reacted swiftly by enacting a rapid decline in interest rates during the latter months of 2008. As the crisis deepened, the rate was reduced accordingly, falling below 5 percent in October and less than 4 percent in December. This continued into 2009, by March reaching just 1.77 percent. Thereafter, interest rates started to increase again but only to 2.5 percent by December 2010. More specifically on fiscal policy, President Lee Myung-bak instructed his economic team in October 2008 to increase public expenditure and set tax cuts aimed at avoiding the spread of financial crisis that could affect the real economy. At the same time, the National Assembly approved a generous increase in the government budget which totalled US$207 billion in 2009, in real terms this being a supplementary increase of 10.6 percent on 2008.[8] This was following by an additional increase of US$20.7 billion in April 2009.

Given its impact on economic recovery, it is worth analysing stimulus measures at the sector level. A key activity in the expansion of public expenditure was construction, which accounts for almost 20 percent of South Korea's GDP. In October 2008, the government announced it would spend US$3.8 billion to buy land and houses still unsold because of 'toxic' credits. South Korea's economic leaders also reduced certain regulations on mortgages and eased the restrictions previously imposed on real estate transactions in some expensive urban zones (Lowe-Lee 2008). SMEs also received considerable support from South Korean economic policy-makers. The government offered guarantees for loans to SMEs and invested US$3.6 billion to rescue them. The BOK, meanwhile, decided to raise the ceiling for loans at preferential interest rates that banks could grant to these firms. SMEs facing losses from so-called 'knock-in, knock-out' investments were given the option to either extend their due dates or get extra loans (OECD 2010).

One of the most favoured sectors of expansionary policies was the ambitious project to position South Korea as a global model of environmentally sustainable economic development. In what could be contrived as the reconstitution of the South Korean developmental state, the government launched in 2009 a comprehensive Five-Year Plan under the title of the 'National Strategy for Green Growth'. President Lee Myung-bak announced that between 2009 and 2013, the South Korean state would invest US$84 billion in this project, equivalent to 2 percent of GDP in each of those years. The strategy includes measures for mitigating climate change, creating new engines of 'clean' industry growth, and improving the quality of life of the Korean population. Specifically, the plan includes 600 projects of different scales and seeks the transformation of South Korea by 2020 into one of the world's seven leading 'green growth' economies and in the world top five by 2050, creating at the same time between 1.6 and 1.8 million new jobs (Jones and Yoo 2010; Moon 2010). This demonstrated the politico-economic resilience of South Korea's developmental statism and predilection for state capacity solutions generally, despite the aforementioned neoliberal osmosis that had occurred in recent decades within the nation's economic ministries, and also despite the strong neoliberal credentials of President Lee Myung-bak.

Within a short period, South Korea experienced a rapid recovery from the negative effects of the 2008 crisis. In the first quarter of 2009, the economy recorded 0.1 percent growth and continued to show positive figures in the subsequent quarters thereafter. Against IMF and Economist Intelligence Unit's forecasts, South Korea managed to avoid negative economic growth, its GDP rising 0.2 percent in 2009 and 5.8 percent in 2010, the highest growth rate yet recorded in the OECD group for that year. The effects of the government's fiscal stimulus measures are thought to have created 300,000 temporary positions, thus curbing unemployment and helping to revive domestic consumption (OECD 2010). With this V-shaped recovery, South Korea was recognised as the fastest country to surmount the crisis within OECD.

5. THE ROLE OF INTERNATIONAL TRADE AND REGIONAL INTEGRATION

To what extent did international trade links, either formal or informal, amplify or hinder the global crisis? In the case of Mexico, regional integration was far from an asset during the Great Recession. One prominent shortcoming, entrenched since NAFTA's inception in 1994, is Mexico's high level trade dependence on the United States. Figure 3.2 shows that in 1990 Mexico sent 70.2 percent of its exports to its northern neighbour. As Figure 3.2 shows, by 2009 this amount had increased to 80.7 percent, after reaching the peak of 88.2 percent in 2000 (ECLAC 2011). Concurrently, Mexico's share of the US market has been climbing in absolute terms, reaching 12.2 percent by mid-2010. By contrast, other traditional US trade partners such as Canada, Germany and Japan have been losing market shares.[9]

However, too much concentration on a singular market creates risks. Figure 3.3 shows the close cyclical relationship between the Mexican and US economies. When the US grows, Mexico rumbles. But, as the old saying goes, when the US sneezes, Mexico gets pneumonia. A relevant case in point is the automobile industry, the Mexican champion of exports in the manufacturing sector. Mexico's automobile industry has gained high penetration in the US market. But the demand for cars fell dramatically in the US during 2008 and 2009, the country's imports of cars made in Mexico also fell dramatically. According to data of the Mexican

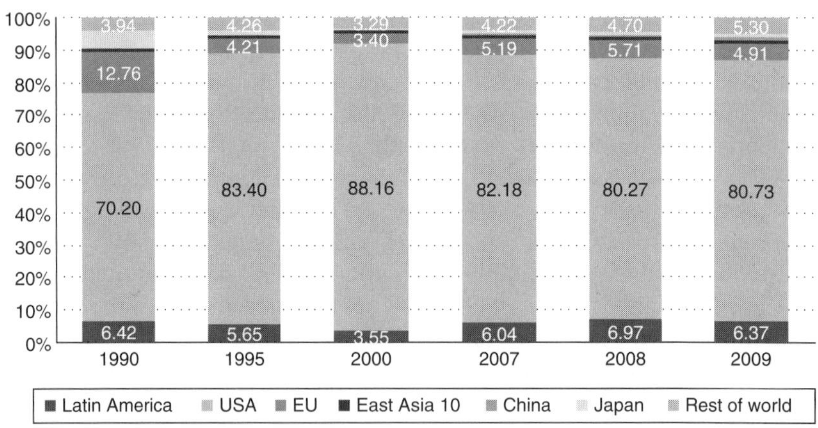

Source: ECLAC (2011).

Figure 3.2 Evolution of Mexico's exports by geographic area, 1990–2009

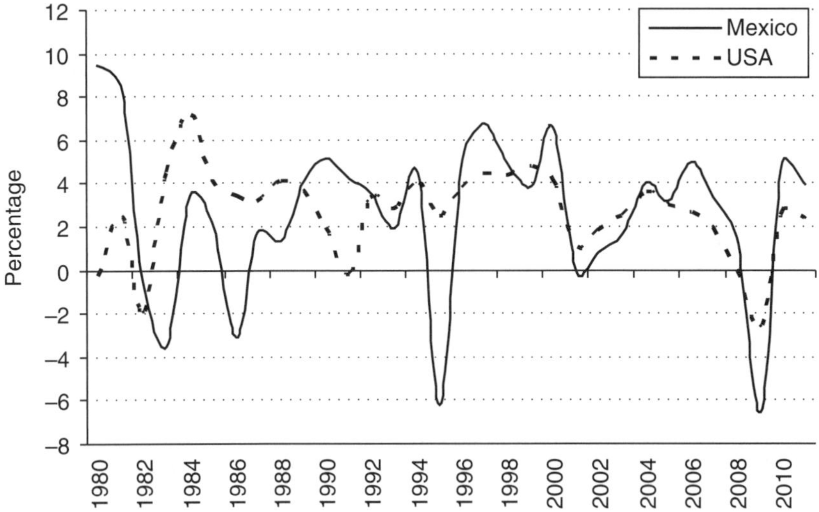

Source: IMF (2011).

Figure 3.3 GDP percent changes, Mexico and the US, 1980–2010

Automotive Industry Association (AMIA), between 2008 and 2009, Mexican car exports to the US almost halved in number.

Given the negligible diversification of that industry's exports, the Mexican automobile industry underwent a crisis within the crisis. Unemployment skyrocketed and GDP plummeted in the Northern Mexican states, where most of automobile assemblers are located (BBVA Research 2011). As shown in Figure 3.4, once the US economy returned to growth, Mexican automobile exports bloomed again in 2010, surpassing their levels prior to the crisis. By January 2011, 14 out of every 100 vehicles sold in the US were made in Mexico.[10]

Due largely to Mexico's neoliberal political economy, the nation is amongst the world's most active protagonists of bilateral and regional free trade agreements (FTAs). However, these agreements have had limited effect at diversifying the nation's trade dependence away from the United States. Although the agreement with the EU took effect in 2000, a higher percentage of Mexican exports were sent to Europe in 1990. Despite Mexico's FTAs with East Asian countries such as Japan, exports to that region have also been declining. A diversification strategy can only succeed if supported by an effective industrial policy aimed at generating exports, rewarding productive actors and incentivizing the diversification of Mexico's trade basket. Nevertheless, the expressions 'diversification'

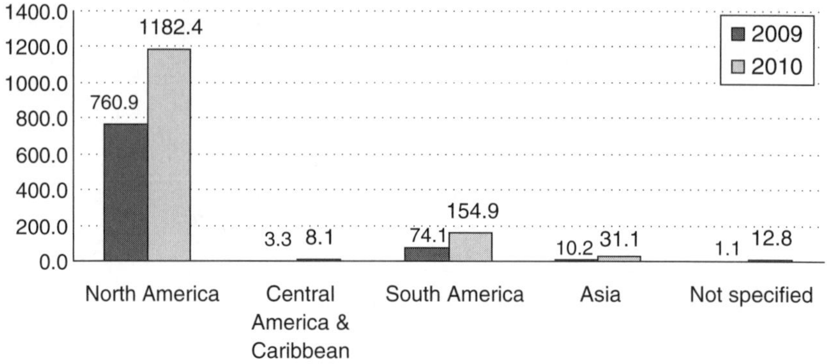

Source: AMIA (2011).

Figure 3.4 Mexico: automobile exports by market of destination, 2009–2010 (thousands of units)

and 'industrial policy' have become almost taboo amongst Mexican economic policy-makers. Increasing concern about the lack of competitiveness policies in Mexico is evident in the transformation of the ideas of Jaime Serra, Minister of Trade and Industrial Development in the government of Carlos Salinas. An enthusiastic advocate of free trade, Serra was the Mexican negotiator-in-chief of NAFTA. During his ministerial tenure he declared that the best industrial policy is the one that does not exist. In June 2010, however, Serra remarked on the inadequate support that Mexican development banks had given to the export sector and how this had eroded the country's chances of finding new international markets.[11]

For South Korea, foreign trade and regional integration are at least as relevant as in the Mexican case. In November 2008, South Korean exports shrank 19 percent *vis à vis* the same month in 2007, and in December 2008 they fell a further 18 percent (Park 2009). Between May and September 2008, South Korea's current account deficit stood at US$7 billion. By the end of the year, though, its current account reverted to a surplus, with export diversification a key explanation of this development. As shown in Figure 3.5, China began to replace the US as the largest trading partner of South Korea from the early 2000s. The United States is now South Korea's fourth largest trade partner, slipping also behind Japan and the EU. This is a general trend that applies to almost all East Asian nations, and East Asia's intra-regional trade ratio has grown substantially over the last few decades, at 55 percent second only to the European Union's. In 2000, East Asia accounted for 49 percent of South Korea's exports and by 2008 this had risen to 60 percent. Over time, these have become increasingly

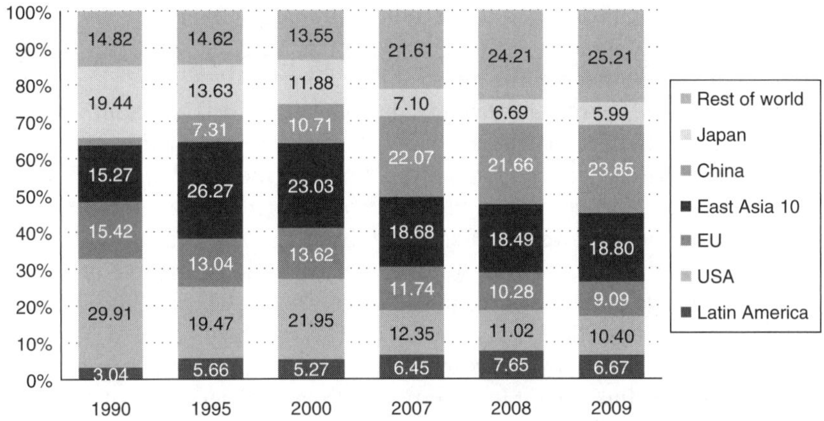

Source: ECLAC (2011).

Figure 3.5 Evolution of South Korea's exports by geographic area, 1990–2009

directed to China, from 2.1 percent of South Korea's total exports in 1990, to 10.7 percent in 2000 and to around 24 percent by 2009. The diversification of South Korea's exports towards East Asian markets over time was fortunate to the extent that other countries from the region – as in South Korea – embarked on similar developmental-oriented stimulus packages in response to the crisis (for example Japan's New Growth Strategy), helping to keep regional demand for South Korean goods stable and even grow.

6. CONCLUSION

While the 2008/09 global financial crisis and ensuing Great Recession affected most countries, governments around the Asia-Pacific and other parts of the world responded in markedly different ways. Both Mexico and South Korea were affected primarily through transmission mechanisms in the finance and international trade sectors. However, their government's responses to the crisis can be viewed from three main perspectives. The first concerns the orientation of economic policy-making institutions and the nature of the policies they introduced during 2008 to 2010. The second perspective concerns the pace and scope of monetary and fiscal policies enacted by each country. Both from quantitative and qualitative viewpoints, South Korea crafted a much more dynamic response to global crisis than Mexico. While public spending in Mexico was sluggish in order to avoid inflation, South Korea introduced a huge budget for 2009. While South Korea cut taxes to stimulate economic activity, Mexican policy-makers increased them in the midst of a sinking GDP. The third perspective concerns the degree of foreign trade diversification. Here South Korea and Mexico experienced different fates: the former positive due to a more balanced and risk-averse regional diversification, the latter negative owing to an over-dependence on one bilateral trade partner, the United States, whose economy was severely affected by the crisis.

The different answers from South Korea and Mexico to the crisis are not the exclusive outcome of technical decisions. They highlight the different development political economies of two key countries in East Asia and Latin America. The Mexican response to the Great Recession was essentially neoliberal and the implementation of fiscal policies was half-hearted; facing the dilemma between higher inflation (but by no means hyper-inflation) and plummeting growth and employment, Mexican policy-makers chose price stability, as they have done since 1982. By contrast, South Korea undertook a developmental statist response, despite the liberal orientation of President Lee Myung-bak and his main economic aides. This pragmatic reaction illustrates how, an orthodox discourse notwithstanding, the interventionist reflex is alive and well in East Asia. In the case of South Korea, this is not an altogether new attitude. Unlike Mexico and Latin America, South Korean economic liberalization since the 1980s was gradual, and some areas for state dirigisme have remained untouched after the demise of the EPB and other developmental institutions in the mid-1990s.

NOTES

* The author is grateful to the Centre for Korean Studies of the University of California Los Angeles, which funded a substantial part of this research with a grant from the Academy of Korean Studies.

1. *The Economist*, 17 February 2009; *Financial Times*, 3 February 2009.
2. *El Universal*, Finance Section, 8 February 2008.
3. These and subsequent figures for Mexico and Korea GDP growth in 2009 and 2010 are sourced from IMF (2010).
4. *La Crónica de Hoy*, 3rd October 2009.
5. *La Jornada*, 24 June 2010.
6. *El Universal*, 19 November 2009.
7. *CNN-Expansión.com*, 11 February 2009.
8. *Xinhua Press Agency*, 26 October 2008, http://www.spanish.xinhuanet.com/spanish/2008-10/26/content_748381.htm
9. *The Economist*, 28 October 2010.
10. *The Wall Street Journal*, 9 February 2011.
11. *Milenio Diario*, 4 June 2010; *The Economist*, 28 October 2010.

REFERENCES

Asociación Mexicana de la Industria Automotriz (AMIA) (2011), 'Estadísticas. Exportación por región', accessed at www.amia.com.mx/expr.html.

Banco de México (Banxico) (2009), *Política monetaria. Informe sobre el primer semestre de 2009*, September, Mexico City: Banco de México.

BBVA Research (2011), *México. Situación Regional Sectorial*, Mexico City: BBVA Bank.

Economic Commission for Latin America and the Caribbean (ECLAC) (2011), database of the Division of International Trade and Integration, accessed at www.cepal.org/comercio/SIGCI.

International Monetary Fund (IMF) (2011), *World Economic Outlook: Rebalancing Growth*, Washington, DC: International Monetary Fund.

Jones, R.S. and Yoo, B. (2010) 'Korea's green growth strategy: mitigating climate change and developing new growth engines', OECD Economics Department working paper series, no. 798, 28 July.

León-Manríquez, J.L. (2001), 'State capacity, state autonomy and economic performance: industrial policy in Mexico, 1950–2000', unpublished PhD dissertation, Columbia University Department of Political Science, New York.

Lowe-Lee, F. (2008), 'Korea feels Wall Street crisis . . . and reacts', *Korea Insight*, 4 November.

Moon, T.H. (2010), 'Green growth policy in the Republic of Korea: its promises and pitfalls', *Korea Observer*, **41**(3), 379–414.

Organisation for Economic Co-operation and Development (OECD) (2010), *OECD Economic Surveys: Korea*, Paris: OECD.

Park, Y.C. (2009), 'Global economic recession and East Asia: how has Korea managed the crisis and what has it learned?', Bank of Korea Institute for Monetary and Economic Research working paper series, no. 409, Seoul.

Villagómez, A. and L. Navarro (2010), 'Política Fiscal Contracíclica en México Durante la Crisis Reciente: Un Análisis Preliminar', Documentos de Trabajo del Centro de Investigación y Docencia Económicas (CIDE) no. 475, Mexico City.

World Bank (2011), *World Development Indicators Database 2011*, Washington, DC: World Bank.

4. On globalisation and region-building: the case of North America

Arturo Santa-Cruz

1. INTRODUCTION

It is commonplace nowadays to say that we live in 'a global order of strong regions' or, more succinctly, in a 'world of regions' (Buzan and Wæver 2003, 20; Katzenstein 2005) Regionalisation processes have certainly spread throughout the world, including the northernmost part of the western hemisphere, that is, Canada, the United States and Mexico – what is now usually referred to as 'North America'. By some standards, economic integration between the three countries is not far from the European Union's (Pastor 2010).

But what about the process of regionalism, that is, the building of institutions to solve collective problems, in North America (Breslin et al. 2002; Capling and Nossal 2009)? Here the story is different. Certainly since 1994 Canada, Mexico and the United States are bound together by the North American Free Trade Agreement (NAFTA), which from the start formally spun off to border development, environmental and labour matters, and in 2005 the three countries signed the Security and Prosperity Partnership. However, the question persists: Does North America – as a meaningful region – exist? That is, do Canada, Mexico and the United States share perceptions regarding interests, threats and values? More broadly, what is it that makes it possible now to talk about a world populated by regions? How has the globalisation process contributed to or hindered the emergence of a regionalised world? What can we learn from the regionalisation experience in the Pacific Rim when thinking of North America?

In order to address these questions, I first discuss the twin concepts and processes of globalisation and regionalisation. I argue that while both are complementary, the latter remains a second-best. I then consider the Asia Pacific experience, particularly the Asia Pacific Economic Cooperation (APEC) mechanism. My purpose here is to gain some insight by looking at an attempt at region building in some ways similar to the North American one. Thus, in section 4 I engage in a genealogical exercise, one that inquires into the emergence of North America as a regional referent. In the final section, I elaborate on the current status and aspirational nature of North America.

2. GLOBALISATION AND REGIONALISATION

The term globalisation conveys a sense of both ubiquitousness and spacelessness, of familiarity and extraneousness.[1] The global is usually opposed to the local, and since the latter is by definition circumscribed, the former appears as a borderless whole, a whole in which place ceases to be important. But since the local is also the space people know and identify with, the idea of the global can appear unknown and foreign. As an article in *The Nation* put it, 'The myth of globalization is that we no longer need to be connected to a place on the earth' (in Robbins 1998: 3) The difference in scale, thus, is the key factor that determines the imaginary border between local and global, known and unknown, self and other.

What really matters in the current upsurge of globalisation (some authors date it to the late nineteenth or early twentieth century) is the significance it has acquired (Robertson 1990: 26; Gilpin 2000: 294–5). The global is not simply the local writ large. It is an animal of an altogether different species. The actually existing global economy became a social (and economic) fact only in the last quarter of the twentieth century. It is since that time that technological changes and economic liberalisation brought the idea of a global economy home – wherever home happens to be. That is why the discourse on economic globalisation became widespread only recently.[2]

But economic globalisation somehow seems to have vanished into thin air – into the air we all breathe and therefore do not notice anymore. That is, just when globalisation had become a fact on the ground, regionalisation became the talk of the (global) town. Regional integration might then be the *differentia specifica* of the recent globalisation process. As national economies around the world became consolidated in the nineteenth and twentieth centuries, regionalisation came to play the role the national market had played in early economic thought, as in Friedrich List's pioneering idea of Germany as an *economic* unit (cf. Szporluk 1991). In the context of the 'American Imperium' porous regions emerged mainly in Asia and Europe (Katzenstein 2005). Thus, a century and a half after the German economist's writings on the 'national system' and the consolidation of the nation-state, regional integration became the touchstone of the global market (Väyrynen 2003).

The idea of regional integration, though, was born with an original sin: it was unable to command the passion and awe its predecessor, the nation-state – and its corresponding 'economy' – had. For economists, regional integration was at most a second-best. If their promised land has always been the materialisation of the ever-elusive welfare gains that only global integration can bestow upon consumers, regional arrangements could be no more than a means to that end. What matters to economists is the road to economic efficiency, be it a customs union or an optimal currency area; the political and institutional dimensions of regional integration are not their main concern.

For political scientists, on the other hand, the puzzle lies in explaining both the obstacles to and the underpinnings of regionalisation. Always ready to point to the primacy of politics over economics, political scientists are fundamentally concerned with the coalitions and institutions that allow or hinder processes of regionalisation and regionalism.[3] But for them, too, the regional level remains subordinated to the modern fountainhead of legitimacy and coercion, enmity and friendship, and ultimately, life and death: the state, the essence of the political (Schmitt 1976).

Thus, the traditional standing of regionalisation in the eyes of both economists and political scientists seems to correspond to the wider, popular mood toward regional integration projects. It is true, as Amitav Acharya notes, that 'regions, like nation-states, are to some extent imagined communities' (Acharya 2007: 651). As he explains, practices and socialisation processes are the fundamental tools for region building. However, be it the Association of East Asian Nations (ASEAN), NAFTA, APEC, or even the European Union, no regional integration project has come to have the *élan vital* of the imagined communities that came to possess a state – and an economy – of their own (Anderson 1998).

However, as 'global economy' became a household item in the late twentieth century, globalisation's stepchild came to be deemed legitimate. Economic regionalisation is now recognised as part and parcel of the globalisation process. Since the late 1980s, 'new regionalism' is in (Mansfield and Milner 1999). This is in part no doubt due to the change in trade policy that took place in those years in the (American) imperium as well as the dynamics in the European integration process at the time. The US adopted a more bilateral and even unilateral – as opposed to multilateral – approach, than had been the case since the late 1940s (Aho 1993: 19; Fry 2000: 119). Furthermore, as Dani Rodrik has noted, the fact that most WTO members are now also members of at least one regional arrangement 'suggests . . . that governments clearly regard regional and multilateral approaches as complementary. So we should stop thinking of these as mutually exclusive choices' (Rodrik 1998: 89). After all, like economic globalisation, regionalisation projects are also supposed to be about welfare gains to be realised through market relations between goods and factors of production – although in this case in a circumscribed, contiguous area.

3. INVENTING THE PACIFIC RIM

Considering the historical process by means of which the Pacific Rim was 'invented' surely will throw some light on both its current state and prospects. For it should be plain that no region of the world exists out there, waiting to be 'discovered' – they are all products of human conceptualisation – even if not all of them come to gain the same status (O'Gorman 2003). Furthermore, the commonsensical notion of economic regionalisation in a contiguous area highlights not only the aspirational nature of Asia Pacific as a region but also the symbiotic relationship between regionalisation and globalisation. Not that mere geographical contiguity makes for successful economic integration, but it certainly takes some effort to conjure up images of two shores of the Pacific Rim mostly separated by thousands of kilometres as a region.[4] For as Tom Manguson put it, the Pacific basin is 'akin to Pascal's horrible sphere, with periphery indeterminable and a centre that may be anywhere' (in Dirlik 1992: 55). That is why it seems that when talking about the Pacific Rim as a region, 'the strain of the public idea of geography [is] too severe', as President Franklin D. Roosevelt once remarked about a State Department proposal to consider Iceland part of the Western Hemisphere (Whitaker 1954: 160).

The APEC forum best illustrates this predicament. It was established in 1989 as a ministerial conference after an initiative from Australian Prime Minister Bob Hawke. Interestingly, though, the idea that eventually came to fruition was over 20 years in the making, and during this process it was not a forgone conclusion that it would include the Eastern shore of the Pacific. But at the end of the day it did, and at the 1989 inaugural conference in Canberra, there were 12 founding 'economies' (as its members are called) from both sides of the Pacific. They were Australia, Brunei, Canada, Indonesia, Japan, Malaysia, New Zealand, the Philippines, Singapore, South Korea, Thailand and the United States. Two years later Hong Kong, the People's Republic of China and Taiwan were admitted. In 1993 Mexico and Papua New Guinea joined the organisation; Chile followed suit in 1994. Peru, Russia and Vietnam have been members since 1998. Thus, APEC now has 21 members.

As the previous inventory makes evident, the section of the globe encompassing the economies bordering or in the Pacific constitutes a veritable collage. Upon a close look, it becomes apparent that there are two well-defined clusters: one in North East Asia and one in North

America, but there is not a trans-Pacific one. As Manuel Castells has noted, 'A Pacific region does not exist as an integrated or distinct entity . . . The economies of the Pacific, each of them, are interdependent in the Pacific and are deeply intertwined with the economies of the whole world' (Castells 1999).

Pacific Rim-wide regionalisation is thus clearly more a project than a reality. Interestingly, the project itself has not always been clear. Originally, the idea was that the trans-Pacific organisation would coordinate policy in three areas: trade, investment and aid for the less-developed members (Ravenhill 2001: 52). The first of the nine principles for the organisation approved at the 1989 inaugural meeting, though, was vaguer. It read: 'The objective of enhanced Asia-Pacific cooperation is to sustain the growth and development of the region, and in this way, to contribute to the growth and development of the world economy.' Hence, at the 1990 Ministerial Meeting in Singapore, APEC issued a Declaration on the Uruguay Round, and years later the Clinton administration openly used the trans-Pacific forum as a tool to move the Round, launched in 1986, forward. Although the actual effect of APEC on the last of GATT's rounds is hard to gauge, some commentators credit it with giving impetus to its conclusion in 1994. Thus, the image of APEC as a sort of avant-garde in trade liberalisation, as the grouping that embodied its *élan vital*, emerged.

The organisation's insistence on 'open regionalism', which means that liberalisation should be a voluntary process of unilateral measures, applied equally to members and non-members of the organisation and was instrumental in the increased expectations toward trade liberalisation that APEC would generate. But as a former Mexican minister, tongue-in-cheek, remarked: 'If you want to have a very destructive [APEC] meeting, you [ask]: "What do you mean by free trade?"' (Mattli 1999: 173). Thus, by the mid-1990s not all member economies were convinced that trade was the organisation's *raison d'être*. As a senior official of Japan's Ministry of Finance harshly put it in 1995, 'The Americans are wrong to regard APEC as being primarily about trade' (cited in ibid: 100; Ravenhill 2001). Indeed, several commentators have noticed that Asia-Pacific regionalism has – perhaps primarily – served a political purpose: the assertion of Asian culture and state sovereignty – hence the pervasive discourse on Asian regionalism (Fry 2000: 122; Poon 2001: 252; Capling and Nossal 2009: 154). There is thus a strong identity-based component in the Asian component of APEC. Not surprisingly, there is no consensus, even among the member economies, on what kind of animal APEC is. Or it might be that, after all, as a former Australian Foreign Minister put it, 'APEC is just four adjectives in search of a substantive' (cited in Dieter 1997: 157).

4. INVENTING NORTH AMERICA

In the opinion of many observers, Canada, Mexico and the United States are inexorably linked by geography – an approach that definitively seems more commonsensical than the one arguing for a trans-Pacific region (Pastor 2001; Hristoulas 2011).[5] However, I would argue that rather than emphasising merely physical factors, it is more useful to again take a historical stand in order to both understand the current state of affairs in the economic, political and social realms of this geographic region, and to look into its likely prospects. After all, as Tom Farer has noted, 'geography is a perception, not a fact' (Farer 1993: 339).

Obvious as it might sound, we might as well start from identifying, in political terms, the countries that conform to the region in question – and the answer is not straightforward. Thus, even though it is common in Mexico – and in Latin America in general – to use the term 'North Americans' (and even 'Americans'!) to refer to the nationals of the United States of America, it is clear that when people speak of North American they are not referring only to the citizens of that country.

Another common referent widens the scope of the region: the country of the 'gringos from the far North', Canada, is frequently taken to be – along with the United States – the other half of North America. Since both countries are 'sons of the same mother', it is not absurd to think that only the two of them make up the northernmost region of the western hemisphere. The myriad of features (among them cultural, economic, historic and linguistic ones) these countries share certainly contributes to this common understanding – in addition, needless to say, to the sole geographic factor. As Seymour Lipset has noted, Canada and the United States 'resemble each other more than either resembles any other nation' (Lipset 1990: 212).

It is worth remembering, however, that at least in the beginning of their relationship, Canada and the United States were far from constituting anything close to a community – as the fact that from the revolution of the 13 colonies not one but two nations were to be born ('twins separated at birth') (ibid.). Even after Canada became a confederation (1867), thus becoming relatively more independent from London, Washington still perceived Ottawa as an imperial outpost. Hence the Canada–United States border – the same one that decades later would be touted as the 'longest unarmed border in the word' – was in its beginning shot through and through by conflict. Thus, as J.L. Granatstein and Norman Hillmer point out, 'North America's peaceful character, its penchant for arbitration over warfare, was largely a myth' (in Haglund 2004: 23).

It would not be until the interwar period that the two countries set the foundations not only of what would eventually become a 'security community' but also a broader entity, one that would include economic and social aspects (Deutsch et al. 1966; Shore 1998). Thus, when Canada opened its first diplomatic post in 1926 – even though it was not to become a sovereign country until 1931 – it did so in Washington. From then on, the interests, and to some extent the identity, of the two countries would start to converge. Shortly before the outbreak of the Second World War, prime minister Mackenzie King pointed out: 'relations [with the USA] are so intimate and continuous that some people in Canada seem to imagine that they are not foreign relations at all' (Shore 1998: 352). Ten years after King left office, and revealing of the extent to which both countries conceived of their shared space as a commons, Ottawa and Washington subscribed a security agreement; it was appropriately called *North American* Air Defense Command (NORAD; my italics).

Getting to the point of thinking of North America as the geographic realm composed of the two most septentrional countries of the 'new world' was not easy – it took almost two centuries (Nossal 2004). The identity and the interests of both Canada and the United States were of course partially redefined during this long process. The two nations stopped seeing each other as an existential threat and came to consider the other as an ally in a joint endeavour – hence the oft-employed 'special relationship' term, used to describe the post-war relationship between the two countries.

It would take at least another two decades, however, before the concept of North America would come to encompass, in the collective imaginary, also the country that lies north of the Central American isthmus: Mexico.[6] The obstacles for this broadening of the common understanding had a lot more to do with cultural and historical cleavages than with geographic ones. From its inception, the border between the United States and Mexico had represented the hemisphere's 'great divide' – two sharply different strands of Western civilisation (O'Gorman 2003). Mexico's traumatic loss to its northern neighbour of over half of its territory during the nineteenth century, and the inauspicious beginning of the twentieth century certainly did not contribute to making the inclusion of Mexico into an imagined North American community easy.

Ottawa's relationship with Mexico, on the other hand, did not precisely act as a pulling factor. Due to its links to the British Empire, Canada did not originally – and for over a century after Confederation – consider itself as an American (that is, of the Americas, the Western Hemisphere) nation. In the context of the Second World War, with its new allegiance to the United States, Ottawa certainly widened its sense of belonging, but it stopped at the Rio Bravo. Canada and Mexico only established diplomatic relations in 1944. Afterwards, the relationship would be defined by its cordiality – a cordiality explained in large part by its exiguous character.

In any case, from the beginning both countries defined their relationship in terms of the one they had with their common, overbearing neighbour. This was still, broadly speaking, the state of affairs of the relationship between the three countries up until the late 1970s.

Then came a call made in 1979 by the then still presidential candidate Ronald Reagan, that his country subscribe with its two neighbours a 'North American Accord' (*New York Times*, 14 November 1979; Granatstein and Bothwell 1990: 314). Significantly, both Prime Minister Pierre Elliot Trudeau and President José López Portillo acted in concert to address the proposal: both dismissed it for going against the national interest of their respective countries.[7]

The tension in the fluid moment – as far as the definition of North America was concerned – would make itself evident a few years later. In 1985 Trudeau's successor, Brian Mulroney, suggested to President Reagan that they start negotiations leading to a Canada–United States Free Trade Agreement (CUSFTA). The Canadian initiative did certainly constitute a 180 degree turn in the foreign economic policy of that country, but the most interesting fact, for the purposes of this chapter, is that Mexico's inclusion was not part either of Ottawa's proposal or Washington's reply. Both countries considered it appropriate to start a new era in their relationship, in the region that was usually taken to comprise North America, in a bilateral fashion.

It would not be until a couple of years after CUSFTA's signing (1988) when, in another about face, Mexican President Carlos Salinas suggested to President Bush that their administrations start negotiations of what would become the North American Free Trade Agreement (NAFTA). Once again, regardless of whether or not the leaders of the two countries were thinking in terms of North America, or only of their bilateral relationship, it is telling that neither the Mexican initiative nor the US response to it considered it appropriate to include Canada in the eventual free trade area. As Gordon Ritchie – one of the principal Canadian negotiators of the CUSFTA – put it: 'Neither Mexico nor the U.S. originally expressed interest in making this a tripartite negotiation' (Ritchie 1991: 18). In a rather reactive fashion, since it was not particularly interested in deepening its relationship with Mexico, Ottawa would ask for admission into the negotiating process in February 1991. As Ritchie would add the following year: 'Even a free-trade agreement will not increase trade with Mexico to the point where it matters very much to most Canadians' (*The Gazette*, 7 April 1992). It is, therefore, not until the trilateral negotiations start, but more fundamentally until NAFTA comes into effect in January 1994, that a three-country North America enters the political economy lexicon – and the academic literature on regionalisation and regionalism.

Mexico, for its part, in economic terms certainly deepened its relationship with its two Northern neighbours in the following years; thus, during the Zedillo administration (1994–2000) trade with Canada increased by 107 percent, and with the United States by 160 percent. In relative terms, however, with or without NAFTA, Mexico's total trade with the United States has for decades hovered around 80 percent, whereas that with Canada has done so at around 3 percent.[8] Furthermore, there were no major initiatives intended to institutionalise the relationship in the nascent region.[9] Furthermore, both in Canada and the United States, but particularly in the former, the project to advance regional integration lost steam – and it even faced open opposition, particularly from some right-wing groups (Bow and Santa-Cruz 2009). In this respect, the trilateral relationship stayed on automatic pilot.

The situation would change radically, at least in Mexico, with the arrival of Vicente Fox to the presidency – the first executive to come from a party different from the Institutionalized Revolutionary one (PRI) in over seven decades. Thus, from automatic pilot the North American project was put on turbo mode, at least as far as Mexico's aspirations were concerned. The same day that he was elected to the presidency, Vicente Fox called for the creation of a strategic society with Canada and the United States (*Globe and Mail*, 16 January 2009). Still as president-elect, Fox visited Ottawa and Washington in order to propose a 'NAFTA-Plus', a new phase of the integration process which would include issues that had been left out of the negotiating agenda the preceding decade; to wit: labour mobility and the transfer of resources to the least developed parts of the region (fundamentally Mexico's southern states). Even though both Prime Minister Chrétien and President Bush (Jr) disregarded the ambitious Mexican initiative, due to the Fox administration's insistence on the matter some progress was made at least on the migratory side of the relationship with the United States. Somehow, at least the discourse on regional integration in North America seemed to take a breath of fresh air.

However, and regardless of what might have happened to the negotiations between Mexico and the United States on migratory affairs, the 9/11 terrorist attacks had a devastating effect not only on the bilateral relationship, but also on the trilateral realm. From then on, security became the undisputed priority of the Bush administration, and the reactions of its two North American neighbours evinced the differences that the two countries maintained in their relationship with their common neighbour. Thus, Ottawa suggested the creation of a 'Security Perimeter' in North America – one that, tellingly, did not include Mexico. Beyond the annoyance the Canadian proposal caused in Mexico's Ministry of Foreign Affairs, the fact was that three months after the fatal event, Ottawa and Washington signed an Intelligent Borders agreement, whereas the analogous version of it that Mexico signed with its northern neighbour, one that would also be leaner than the former, would not materialise until March 2002.

Albeit in a modest form, the regional project seemed to recuperate three years after the terrorist attacks. In March 2005, President Bush welcomed his North American counterparts at Waco, Texas, where the three of them launched the Security and Prosperity Partnership (SPP). Although SPP emphasised the security component over the prosperity one, it was certainly intended to make up for the deficiencies perceived in the integration process triggered by NAFTA. Thus, within the prosperity agenda, issues such as electronic commerce, energy, the environment, financial services, health and transport were included.[10]

However, the measures taken within the SPP framework were rather limited. According to Roberta Jacobson, director for Canada and Mexico at the State Department, at Waco the three leaders agreed that the regional integration process would move in an 'incremental' manner, that is, 'one step at a time'. Regarding the implementation of the agreement, Robertson points out that it was done cautiously, 'within the margins of what was politically feasible in the three countries'; in the Mexican case this meant respecting the limits imposed 'mainly with issues of sovereignty'. According to the foreign officer, 'people have found fault (with SPP) for not having a great vision', although she recognises that it 'doesn't have one, and did not have one from the beginning'.[11]

Similarly, the former director for North America at Mexico's Foreign Ministry, Alejandro Estivill, notes that SPP 'corresponds to a vision aimed at achieving what is possible, and not what is ideal'.[12] Given these rather modest objectives, the signature of an agreement to guarantee the compatibility of manufacturing standards in aeronautical products in September 2007 and, more importantly, the trilateral cooperation that took place during the human influenza pandemic in Mexico in 2009, look like real achievements (Anderson and Sands 2007).[13]

Due in large part to its association with the previous administration, the SPP ceased to exist under the Obama administration. As John Feely, deputy chief of mission at the US embassy in Mexico City notes, 'SPP was a good idea, but it is better to have a great idea';[14] however, that 'great idea' is still missing in North America. This is not to suggest that SPP was a waste of time; in addition to some very specific achievements – such as the ones mentioned above – such a mechanism left what, at least until 2009, seemed to be an important legacy in terms of regional institutionalisation: the North American Leaders Summit (NALS). Conceived to be held annually to deal with pressing issues in the regional economic and security agendas, five of them have already taken place (in Cancun,

Montebello, New Orleans, Guadalajara and Washington). For some observers, NALS represents the only real sign of governance in North America (Clarkson 2008: 439).

Thus, at least as far as Mexico is concerned, after close to two decades since NAFTA came into effect, the sense of belonging to North America has hardly shown any progress. According to a CIDE/Comexi poll, both in 2006 and 2008 only 7 percent of Mexicans define themselves as North Americans (while, on average, 58.5 percent regard themselves as Latin Americans) (González et al. 2008). As Alejandro Moreno has noted, 'the majority of Mexicans don't feel part of North America, either in cultural or geographic terms' (Moreno 2007: 81). Geography, as noted before, is after all also a perception.

What in fact has been taking place is that the two denser bilateral relationships of the region (between Canada and the United States, and between the latter and Mexico) have deepened in a parallel fashion. Thus, Ottawa has attempted to reconfigure its 'special relationship' with its immediate neighbour, attempting to distance itself from trilateral cooperation and negotiation mechanisms in order to avoid the 'Mexicanisation' of its relationship with its most important partner. A Security Perimeter – excluding Mexico – was indeed signed by Prime Minister Stephen Harper and President Barack Obama in February 2011.[15]

Mexico, on its part, has substantially increased the level of cooperation with its northern neighbour, particularly in the context of the 'war on drugs' pursued by the Calderón administration, as made clear by the 2007 Merida Initiative (and its 'Merida 2.0' or 'Beyond Merida' extension under the Obama administration). Indeed, as Feely from the US embassy points out, some of the activities that used to be undertaken under SPP have now been moved to the Merida Initiative.[16] Canadian involvement in the security issue, which has largely defined the current Mexican administration – and its relationship with Washington – has been rather symbolic (such as the training provided by the Royal Canadian Mounted Police to Mexican law enforcers). Thus, as a Mexican diplomat recently pointed out, 'Canada and Mexico still take the United States as the starting point for their bilateral relationship'.[17]

5. OF CONCENTRIC CIRCLES AND ASPIRATIONAL REGIONS

Even if all regions are invented, not all regions are born equal. Accordingly, as the APEC experience shows, regions do not always jell. Both Asia Pacific and North America, like the processes of globalisation and regionalisation of which they are part and parcel, are at a crossroads. They cannot move forward without endowing themselves with more meaningful institutions – that is, they would need to embark in a regionalising process. In their current state, they both remain more an aspiration than a reality.

As far as North America – the main focus of this chapter – is concerned, it seems clear that two decades after the trilateral negotiations leading to NAFTA started, more than as a region it is useful to think of it in terms of a set of four concentric circles. This schema clearly illustrates, for instance, that for Canada, North America is (for all practical purposes) synonymous with its territorial space plus that of the United States. Mexico, at least as far as Ottawa is concerned, is not part of this circle. On the other hand, the also very tight relationship between Mexico and the United States by and large leaves Canada out of the picture. The third circle, corresponding to the Canada–Mexico relationship, is much looser, illustrating both its exiguous character and its fundamentally monothematic (that is, economic) nature (lacking in strong political or social links). The last circle, encompassing the three countries, is the most tenuous one. The intensity of the political, social or strategic relationship does not add up to much. Despite the (disjointed) efforts to tighten the trilateral ties that have taken place in the last three lustrums, it would be wrong to assert that the three countries in question conform a meaningful region or that, as a Mexican diplomat put it, 'a genuine North American identity' exists (Katzenstein 2005; Clarkson 2008).[18] If not only an adjective in search of a substantive, North America remains more an adjective than substance.

NOTES

1. In this and the next section I draw on Santa-Cruz (2003).
2. For instance, whereas the *Social Sciences Citation Index* identified only 13 books or papers dealing with 'globalisation' during the five-year period 1980–84, in the equivalent 1992–96 period it listed 581 (Kelly and Olds 1999: 1)
3. As Richard Ashley (1983: 479) has put it, '*the logic of economy remains forever provisional, forever dependent upon the logic of politics*' (italics in original).
4. Although 'Asia-Pacific' and the 'Pacific Rim' are not identical, following common practice I will treat them here as synonymous.
5. Or as a Mexican intelligence officer recently put it: 'Mexico is by nature part of (North America's) Security Perimeter.' The official spoke at a seminar held under Chatham House rules; Mexico City, April 2011.
6. Interestingly, Mexico's first legal name, as it appears in the 1813 Declaration of Independence, is 'Northern America' (*América Septentrional*).
7. Although it should be noted that the Mexican president had entertained the idea of strengthening the links between the three North American countries. A memorandum to President Carter's National Security Adviser notes: 'He [López Portillo] has also vaguely discussed the idea of "North American interdependence", which would permit

Mexico, Canada, and the United States to deal with problems on a coordinated basis. The Canadians believe that the problems between Canada and the U.S. are different from those between Mexico and the U.S., and prefer to deal with the two of us on a bilateral rather than joint basis.' The referred Canadian position is by and large consistent with what we have observed in the two decades since. Memorandum for Mr Zbigniew Brzezinski, the White House; Visit of Mexican President Lopez Portillo, 13–17, February 1977, Carter Centre Archives.

8. Calculation based on data from the Ministry of Economy, Mexico.
9. Author's calculations based on data from Mexico's Treasury Ministry.
10. In August 2007, for instance, the North American Plan against Pandemic Influenza was launched. This plan became especially valuable two years later, in the context of the influenza outbreak in Mexico.
11. Author interview, Washington, DC, 15 July 2008.
12. Author interview, Mexico City, 3 July 2008.
13. See also Security and Prosperity Partnership of North America, 'Key Accomplishments since August 2007'. Available at: http://www.spp-psp.gc.ca/eic/site/spp-psp.nsf/eng/00086.html
14. Author interview, Mexico City, 3 July 2008.
15. 'Beyond the Border: A Shared Vision for Perimeter Security and Economic Competitiveness', A Declaration by the President of the United States of America and the Prime Minister of Canada, 4 February 2011. Available at: http://pm.gc.ca/eng/media.asp?id=3938.
16. Author interview, Mexico City, 19 April 2010.
17. The Mexican diplomat spoke at a seminar held under Chatham House rules; Mexico City, February 2010.
18. The Mexican diplomat spoke at the February 2010 seminar mentioned above.

REFERENCES

Acharya, A. (2007), 'The emerging regional architecture of world politics', *World Politics*, **59**, 629–52.

Aho, C.M. (1993), 'America and the Pacific century: trade conflict or cooperation', *International Affairs*, **69**, 19–37.

Anderson, B. (1998), *The Spectre of Comparisons: Nationalism, Southeast Asia and the World*, London: Verso.

Anderson, G. and C. Sands (2007), 'Negotiating North America: the security and prosperity partnership', Hudson Institute white paper.

Ashley, R. (1983), 'Three modes of economism', *International Studies Quarterly*, **27**(4), 463–96.

Bow, B. and A. Santa-Cruz (2009), 'From interests to identity? Opposition to North American integration in the United States', presentation to the *2009 Annual Meeting of the American Political Science Association*, Toronto, ON.

Breslin, S., R. Higgott and B. Rosamond (2002), 'Regions in comparative perspective', in S. Breslin, C. Hughes, N. Phillips and B. Rosamond (eds), *New Regionalisms in the Global Political Economy: Theories and Cases*, London: Routledge.

Buzan, B. and O. Wæver (2003), *The Structure of International Security*, Cambridge: Cambridge University Press.

Capling, A. and K.R. Nossal (2009), 'The contradictions of regionalism in North America', *Review of International Studies*, **35**(1), 147–67.

Castells, M. (1999), *La era de la información: Fin de milenio, Vol. 3*, Mexico City: Siglo XXI.
Clarkson, S. (2008), *Does North America Exist? Governing the Continent after NAFTA and 9/11*, Toronto, ON: University of Toronto Press.
Deutsch, K. et al. (ed.) (1966), *International Political Communities*, Garden City, NY: Anchor Books.
Dieter, H. (1997), 'El regionalismo en la región de Asia-Pacífico', in R. Bouzas (ed.), *Regionalización e integración económica. Instituciones y procesos comparados*, Buenos Aires: Grupo Editorial Latinoamericano.
Dirlik, A. (1992), 'The Asia-Pacific idea: reality and representation in the invention of a regional structure', *Journal of World History*, **3**(1), 55–79.
Farer, T.J. (1993), 'A paradigm of legitimate intervention', in L.F. Damrosch (ed.), *Enforcing Restraint: Collective Intervention in Internal Conflicts*, New York: Council on Foreign Relations.
Fry, G. (2000), 'A coming age of regionalism?' in G. Fry and J. O'Hagan (eds), *Contending Images of World Politics*, New York: St. Martin's Press.
Gilpin, R. (2000), *The Challenge or Global Capitalism: The World Economy in the 21st Century*, Princeton, NJ: Princeton University Press.
González, G., M.C.F. Guadalupe and J.A. Schiavon (eds) (2008), *México, las Américas y el Mundo. Política Exterior: opinión pública y líderes 2008*, Mexico City: CIDE.
Granatstein, J.L. and R. Bothwell (1990), *Pirouette. Pierre Trudeau and Canadian Foreign Policy*, Toronto, ON: University of Toronto Press.
Haglund, D.G. (2004), 'The comparative "continentalization" of security and defence policy in North America and Europe: Canadian multilateralism in a unipolar world?', *Journal of Canadian Studies*, **38**(2), 9–28.
Hristoulas, A. (ed.) (2011), *Reconsiderado la seguridad en América del Norte*, Mexico City: Miguel Angel Porrúa.
Katzenstein, P.J. (2005), *A World of Regions: Asia and Europe in the American Imperium*, Ithaca, NY: Cornell University Press.
Kelly, P. and K. Olds (1999), 'Questions in a crisis: the contested meanings of globalisation in Asia-Pacific', in K. Olds et al. (eds), *Globalisation in the Asia-Pacific: Contested Territories*, London: Routledge.
Lipset, S.M. (1990), *Continental Divide. The Values and Institutions of the United States and Canada*, New York: Canadian–American Committee.
Mansfield, E.D. and H.V. Milner (1999), 'The new wave of regionalism', *International Organization*, **53**(3), 589–627.
Mattli, W. (1999), *The Logic of Regional Integration: Europe and Beyond*, Cambridge: Cambridge University Press.
Moreno, A. (2007), 'Trust in North America: why do Mexicans distrust their continental neighbours?' *Norteamérica*, **2**(2), 63–84.
Nossal, K.R. (2004), 'Defending the "realm". Canadian strategic culture revisited', *International Journal*, **59**(3), 503–20.
O'Gorman, E. (2003), *La invención de América: Investigación acerca de la estructura histórica del nuevo mundo y del sentido de su devenir*, Mexico City: Fondo de Cultura Económica.
Pastor, R. (2001), *Towards a North American Community: Lessons from the Old World to the New*, Washington, DC: Institute for International Economics.
Poon, J. (2001), 'Regionalism in the Asia Pacific: is geography destiny?', *Area*, **33**(3), 252–60.

Ravenhill, J. (2001), *APEC and the Construction of Pacific Rim Regionalism*, Cambridge: Cambridge University Press.
Ritchie, G. (1991), 'A Canada–Mexico–U.S. Free Trade Agreement: watch out!', *Business Quarterly*, **55**(3), 18–23.
Robbins, B. (1998), 'Introduction part I: actually existing cosmopolitanism', in P. Cheah and B. Robbins (eds), *Cosmopolitics. Thinking and Feeling beyond the Nation*, Minneapolis, MN: University of Minnesota Press.
Robertson, R. (1990), 'Mapping the global condition: globalization as the central concept', *Theory, Culture and Society*, **7**, 15–30.
Rodrik, D. (1998), 'Comment to John Whalley's "Why do countries seek regional trade agreements?"' in J. Frankel (ed.), *The Regionalization of the World Economy*, Chicago, IL: University of Chicago Press.
Santa-Cruz, A. (2003), 'Introduction', in A. Santa-Cruz (ed.), *What's in a Name? Globalization, Regionalization, and APEC*, Guadalajara, Mexico: Universidad de Guadalajara.
Schmitt, C. (1976), *The Concept of the Political*, New Brunswick, NJ: Rutgers University Press.
Shore, S.M. (1998), 'No fences make good neighbours: the development of the Canadian–US security community 1871–1940', in E. Adler and M. Barnett (eds), *Security Communities*, Cambridge: Cambridge University Press.
Szporluk, R. (1991), *Communism and Nationalism: Karl Marx Versus Friedrich List*, New York: Oxford University Press.
Väyrynen, R. (2003), 'Regionalism: Old and New', *International Studies Review*, **5**, 25–51.
Whitaker, A. (1954), *The Western Hemisphere Idea: Its Rise and Decline*, Ithaca, NY: Cornell University Press.

PART III

Regional and global multilateralism

5. The numbers game in Asia-Pacific cooperation

John Ravenhill

1. INTRODUCTION

Multilateralism has not fared well in the first decade of the 21st century.[1] The Doha Round of WTO negotiations were on the verge of collapse when this chapter was completed in mid-2011. The 2009 UN Climate Change Conference (COP-15 in Copenhagen) ended in acrimony with little more than an agreement to keep talking. Early high (undoubtedly exaggerated) hopes that the G-20, given the role it accords rising and middle powers, would provide an effective boost to multilateral problem-solving at the global level were dashed by the ineffectiveness the grouping displayed at the 2010 Toronto and Seoul summits. Meanwhile, inter-state cooperation at the regional level in the Asia-Pacific has scarcely fared better. The Asia-Pacific Economic Cooperation grouping has stagnated since 1998, when proposals for an accelerated programme of trade liberalization badly divided its membership. The ASEAN Regional Forum, the principal vehicle for examining security issues in the Asia-Pacific, has increasingly come under attack for being little more than a 'talking shop' that has failed to move beyond confidence-building measures to address substantive issues (Emmers and Seng 2011). The global financial crisis once again exposed the ineffectiveness and fragility of ASEAN itself and the ASEAN-led regional institutions: the East Asia Summit in Pattaya, Thailand, scheduled for April 2009, was postponed because of civil unrest caused by former Thai Premier Thaksin's red-shirted supporters.

Dissatisfaction with the lack of progress in global and regional multilateral institutions played a significant role in two sets of developments within the Asia-Pacific region. The first was the articulation of proposals aimed at strengthening the regional institutional architecture. While some pre-dated the financial upheaval, they gained momentum in the midst of the crisis because it accelerated shifts in the global power distribution and generated expectations that Asian countries should take on greater responsibilities in global governance. The most notable of these proposals were those by former Japanese Prime Minister Yukio Hatoyama for the creation of an East Asian Community, and by former Australian Prime Minister Kevin Rudd for the establishment of an Asia Pacific Community. The second set of developments was an explosion in the number of bilateral agreements. Preferential trade agreements (PTAs) have attracted by far the most attention; relatively overlooked, but numerically – and some would argue substantively – more significant are the bilateral investment treaties (BITs) that many countries have entered into.

This chapter examines the relationship between the effectiveness of inter-state cooperation in the Asia-Pacific region and the number of participating states. It begins with a consideration of the theoretical literature on this subject. I then examine the actual experience of multilateral cooperation at the global and regional levels before considering the fate of the recent proposals for new forms of regional cooperation in the Asia-Pacific and the implications for the future regional architecture. I conclude by looking at the growth of bilateralism, and the potential to 'multilateralize' bilateral agreements.

2. THE NUMBERS GAME

Students of international relations, writing from various theoretical perspectives, have long believed that an increase in the number of participating states will have a detrimental impact on the effectiveness of multilateral cooperation. Theorists in the realist tradition see numbers as a distraction: they simply complicate the management of the global system, which inevitably, and properly from their perspective, is a matter for the great powers. Meanwhile, some students in the institutionalist tradition, following the arguments of Mancur Ólson (1965), see an increasing number of participants as reducing the prospects for successful cooperation because of the greater difficulties in organizing a winning coalition (flowing both from the problem that any individual state will receive a smaller share of the overall benefits and therefore be less inclined to invest scarce resources in working towards their realization, and from the increased transactions costs of coalition-building and maintenance that accompany a growth in the number of participants).

Pitted against this conventional wisdom are a variety of arguments that draw both on the experience of multilateralism and on theoretical approaches to cooperation that offer an alternative to what Miles Kahler (1992: 683) termed the 'misplaced pessimism' on numbers. Various institutionalist approaches, notably those that emerged from the neo-functionalist tradition, asserted that the disadvantages of managing greater numbers of participants can be offset by their facilitating the negotiation of larger 'package deals' that increase the benefits to all (Milner 1992) – although some cautioned of an unwelcome trade-off developing: the larger the numbers, the greater the potential gains . . . but the smaller the likelihood of their realization (Oye 1985). Snidal (1985), meanwhile, demonstrated that in theory it was possible for a winning coalition to be constructed even in the absence of a hegemonic power that some saw as essential to successful collaboration if Olson's logic of collective action applied.

From an entirely different perspective, other commentators pointed to the important role that middle powers can play – as entrepreneurs of ideas, as engineers in coalition-building, and as honest brokers among the major powers. Some of this literature in turn overlapped with constructivist arguments about 'epistemic communities' and 'norm entrepreneurs', which harked back to neo-functionalist propositions about the creative role that international secretariats could play in promoting multilateral cooperation at the regional and global levels. Having more states (or at least more of the right sort of state) involved in a negotiation might, therefore, other things being equal, increase the possibility that creative diplomatic solutions to difficult problems might be crafted. And, considerations of legitimacy also enter the equation: governance by a concert of powers is unlikely to be viewed favourably by those excluded from having a voice at the table, even when those with decision-making power act in a relatively benign manner. The consequence may be a situation where the excluded engage in free-riding or work destructively to undermine the status quo.

Concerns about the adverse impact of numbers on the effectiveness of multilateral cooperation also often seemed to betray a lack of understanding about how many international institutions actually operate. Some, of course (and here the International Monetary Fund and World Bank stand out), employ weighted voting formulas that favour the relatively powerful (or at least, those countries that had this status at the time of the institutions' establishment). Others, even though nominally operating within a framework of equal voting rights, are in practice governed through a process of minilateralism. The GATT/WTO is an excellent example. The adoption of the principal supplier rule in the GATT negotiations up until the Uruguay Round ensured that key decisions were the outcome of bargains between the United States, the European Union and Japan, and were subsequently 'multilateralized' to all GATT contracting parties through the application of the most-favoured-nation principle. Kahler (1992) records how several other global institutions also have been effectively governed through similar minilateral procedures.

How, then, to explain the recent (largely unsuccessful) experience of multilateralism – and what conclusions should be drawn for the Asia-Pacific region? The failure of the Doha Round and the UN Copenhagen Climate Change conference owe less to the numbers problem than to a change in the composition/interests of the key players, a consequence of the rise of China, Brazil and India. It was not the presence of countries such as the Kyrgyz Republic, Oman, Panama, Papua New Guinea and Mongolia (all new members of the WTO since the conclusion of the Uruguay Round) in the Doha Round negotiations that sank them. Rather, it was the inability of key players to reach agreement among themselves. These problems included conflicts among the EU, Japan and the United States, as well as between them and Brazil, China and India. It could be argued, of course, that these conflicts reflected a numbers issue – that the number of key players in the key minilateral decision-making group had increased – but this is a rather different statement of the problem and less persuasive an explanation than one that focuses on an increasing diversity of interests among the members of this core group. The failure of Doha reflected as much a failure of minilateralism as a negotiating process that fell victim to the numbers game.

What conclusions can be drawn from recent examples of successful multilateral cooperation? In this context, I would identify two important instances: the response of the G-20 in the immediate aftermath of the financial crisis; and action taken by the G7 to push down the exchange rate of the yen following the 2011 Tōhoku earthquake and tsunami. The G7 action was of particular note in that some considered the institution to be obsolete following the declaration by the leaders of the G-20 members at their third summit in Pittsburgh in 2009 that this new grouping would be the 'premier forum for international economic cooperation'. The G-7, a classic example of minilateralism, had, to the extent that any institution played the role, been the *de facto* governor of the global financial regime over the previous quarter of a century. Its interventions, notably the 1985 Plaza Accord, had sometimes dramatically shaped currency realignments. Its action in March 2011 to attempt to stem the appreciation of the yen was the first coordinated intervention that its central banks had agreed for 11 years. Besides concern for the ailing Japanese economy in the wake of the earthquake and tsunami, G-7 ministers were clearly concerned that the appreciation of the yen would be a significant element of a currency misalignment that threatened to stall the fragile global recovery. Shared interests among a small group of players that had the capacity to take effective action, and shared perceptions of the magnitude of the potential problem carried the day – albeit only temporarily pushing down the yen–dollar exchange rate.

The concerted response of the G-20 to the global financial crisis through coordinating their programmes of fiscal stimulus and by refraining from significant resort to protectionism was another instance of key countries sharing interests in avoiding a calamitous collapse of the global economy. It may have been, in the words of Wade and Vestergaard (2010), an example of the 'fellowship of the lifeboat', but the consequence was an effective coordination of national action, albeit one that did not address the underlying problems of the global economy whose resolution would have moved the structure of bargaining away from a positive sum towards more of a zero-sum game.

3. THE CASE FOR MINILATERALISM AT THE REGIONAL LEVEL

The two proposals launched in the last years of the first decade of the 21st century for new institutional configurations in the Asia-Pacific both reflected increasing unhappiness with the progress in multilateral cooperation in the ASEAN-dominated regional institutions. Both represented a push for minilateral leadership: in the case of the Hatoyama proposal, through a concert of the three major Northeast Asian powers; in the Rudd proposal, through an institution whose membership would be confined to regionally-significant countries.[2]

Rudd initially introduced his idea in a speech to the Asia Society Australia in June 2008. He declared that a 'regional institution which spans the entire Asia-Pacific region – including the United States, Japan, China, India, Indonesia and the other states of the region' was needed, and 'which is able to engage in the full spectrum of dialogue, cooperation and action on economic and political matters and future challenges related to security'. He added that 'none of our existing regional mechanisms as currently configured are capable of achieving these purposes' (Rudd 2008). While acknowledging that there was no appetite for additional institutions and meetings in the region, Rudd asserted that existing frameworks failed to provide a single forum for discussing the full spectrum of challenges facing the Asia Pacific, in particular, the management of major power relations. The Asia Pacific Community (APC) idea was influenced by the shift in the global power distribution, a trend accelerated by the global financial crisis. Beyond its wider geopolitical considerations, the APC was driven by the long-standing Australian fear of being excluded from East Asian regionalism (in the guise, for instance, of the ASEAN Plus Three grouping), and by its desire to ensure that the US continues to play a central role in the region.

Beyond the concern with the institution's membership (that it should not be exclusively East Asian) and scope (that it should include security as well as economic issues), the Rudd initiative also reflected a perception that the effectiveness of Asia-Pacific multilateralism was being undermined because it rested on the ASEAN 'convoy' principle – that is, a lowest common denominator approach in which all countries enjoyed veto power. This dimension was evident in the earliest statements of the Rudd proposal but was less prominent when the opposition of most ASEAN states to the proposal became obvious. In its early incarnation, what Rudd evidently had in mind was that the APC would be a minilateral institution: a meeting of 'regionally-significant' states just as the G-20 was to represent 'systemically-significant' states. His envoy, Richard Woolcott, is reported to have proposed that the APC take the form of an Asian 8, comprising the US, China, Japan, Russia, India, Indonesia, South Korea and Australia (Kelly 2008). It was to be a concert of powers, as the Australian co-Chair of a '1.5 track' conference on the proposal, held in Sydney in December 2009, inadvertently confessed (remarks of Michael Wesley quoted in Woolcott et al. 2009).

The Rudd initiative, handicapped by the lack of preparation and prior consultations of potential member states, ultimately foundered because of the opposition from ASEAN countries that resented the potential marginalization of their institution. Representatives from Singapore were particularly outspoken, with the Singapore government, already smarting at the inclusion of Indonesia but not the island state in the G-20, seething that it would be left out of a concert of regional powers.

The Rudd proposal effectively died when he was forced by his party to stand down as prime minister in June 2010. In the end, Rudd was able to save face when the member states of the East Asia Summit (EAS) agreed to admit Russia and the US as future members: victory was proclaimed on the grounds that the ambition to ensure US participation in an East Asian regional institution had been realized. But the EAS, arguably the weakest of the Asia-Pacific regional institutions, will have to evolve dramatically both in the scope of its discussions and in its organization, to realize the vision of a minilateral concert of powers that Rudd had originally put forward. Meanwhile, in claiming credit for bringing into being an expanded EAS, an ASEAN Plus Eight grouping, the Singapore government underlined the centrality of ASEAN to the regional architecture.

The East Asian Community idea, put forward by then Japanese Prime Minister, Yukio Hatoyama, was another attempt to shift the centre of gravity in Asia-Pacific regionalism away from ASEAN. The context was an improvement in relations between the three Northeast Asian powers, which permitted the inauguration of a Trilateral Summit in December 2008. The EAC can be interpreted as an attempt by the DPJ to rebalance its relationship with Washington and to establish for Tokyo a claim for economic leadership in East Asian regionalism (Mulgan 2009). Central to the creation of an East Asia Community would be successful management of the complex Sino–Japanese relationship and the achievement of a deeper Japanese economic engagement with the rest of Asia.

The goal of establishing an East Asian Community is certainly not new in Japan's foreign policy, dating back in its conceptualization to the 1970s. The central idea is based upon the successful experience of reconciliation in Europe through economic and financial integration. Through this cooperative approach, the regional states were expected to 'develop a multi-layered network of functional communities' (Hatoyama 2009). He also advocated the ambitious goal of a common currency for the EAC countries. Hatoyama suggested that the European Coal and Steel Community could be a model for closer economic integration in Northeast Asia. In particular, the joint development of gas fields in the East China Sea could provide a foundation for the EAC (Parameswaran 2009).

The EAC was supported by China and Korea at the second Trilateral summit in Beijing in October 2009. Nonetheless, it too soon foundered on issues relating to its membership and how it would fit with existing regional institutions. Responding to his critics, Hatoyama (2009) said that he was focusing first on the content of the EAC rather than on its ultimate structure and framework. Hence, instead of finalizing the EAC membership, he listed possible fields of cooperation. But his list of proposed activities suggested nothing that was not already being pursued within the ASEAN Plus Three and EAS groupings. And the membership issue would not go away. Foreign Minister Katsuya Okada stated in 2009 that Japan was not in favour of including the US but added that Tokyo could act as a 'connector' between Washington and the new grouping (Junbo 2009). Kurt Campbell, US Assistant Secretary of State for East Asian and Pacific Affairs, quickly responded that the US did not wish to be excluded from East Asian regionalism and that it would 'want an invitation' to the party as well (quoted in Junbo 2009). As with the Rudd proposal, the removal of the EAC's principal proponent from office (Hatoyama stepped down in June 2010) marked the end of the initiative.

Both the Hatoyama and Rudd initiatives reflected their conceptions of how national interests might best be pursued in the context of radical shifts in the distribution of economic and military power. They both also reflected perceptions that existing regional institutions, dominated by ASEAN, were not well-equipped to cope with the rapidly-changing context. Both sought to create a new core minilateral group to manage the increasingly complex regional agenda. Ironically, the failure of both initiatives served only to underline the importance of ASEAN to regional cooperation not just in East Asia but also the broader Asia-Pacific region.

Giving ASEAN pride of place in regional cooperation does confer a legitimacy that would be lacking in a concert of powers approach. And despite ASEAN's claim to be 'in the driving seat' of East Asian integration, it is difficult to think of significant initiatives for which ASEAN itself can claim credit. The major developments in regional cooperation in the last decade – whether in trade or finance (the Chiang Mai Initiative) – although launched under 'ASEAN Plus' auspices were actually not ASEAN initiatives but those of its partner states. ASEAN's requirement for cooperation to rest on consensus does not necessarily lead to the smallest states holding veto player status – they are often pressured to abstain rather than to block agreement, their compliance frequently being bought by arrangements that permit them opt-outs, longer adjustment periods, and so on. Clear boundaries exist to this *modus operandi*, however, with any intrusion on national sovereignty being off-limits. The inevitable result is that ASEAN-led institutions remain weak, of a 'soft law' variety, with consequent limitations on the scope and depth of cooperation. The region also suffers a leadership deficit because of the absence of effective minilateralism. Within East Asia, ASEAN Plus Three operates primarily as a series of ASEAN Plus One projects: the Chiang Mai Initiative is significant as the only genuinely *regional* institution, albeit one that was driven predominantly by Japan. Here the problem again is not necessarily one of institutional design but of the inability of the big players – China, Japan and Korea – to agree on the foundations for an effective minilateralism.

4. THE RUSH TO BILATERALISM

The first decade of the 21st century ushered in an era of bilateralism in East Asia. In contrast to the perceived failure of global and regional variants of multilateralism, cooperation at the bilateral level appears to have been successful, at least if measured by the number of treaties that countries have signed. The proliferation of PTAs has received the most attention. The involvement of regional states in bilateral investment treaties (BITs), in contrast, has gone largely unremarked. This section of the chapter examines the significance of this new bilateral cooperation and considers whether it lays a new foundation on which multilateral cooperation might be built.

Many East Asian countries have been active participants in BITs (Table 5.1), which continue to substantially outnumber the number of PTAs they have signed. More surprising, perhaps, is the distribution of bilateral investment treaties across countries, with China the most active

Table 5.1 Bilateral investment treaties concluded by East Asian states, May 2010

Brunei Darussalam	6
Cambodia	21
China	125
Hong Kong	15
Indonesia	62
Japan	15
Korea	90
Laos	23
Malaysia	6
Myanmar	6
Philippines	35
Singapore	39
Taiwan	22
Thailand	39

Source: UNCTAD (2010: Appendix 3).

player and Japan among the least active (being overshadowed by both Cambodia and Laos). In that most contemporary preferential trade agreements include an investment chapter, and the promotion of investment has become of increasing significance for some countries in negotiating these agreements (Manger 2009), PTAs, however, may be considered to some extent to be a substitute for BITs.

The explosion of interest in bilateral arrangements on investment reflects the failure of multilateral action on the matter – both the OECD's Multilateral Agreement on Investment and the attempt by industrialized countries to pursue investment issues through the WTO as one of the 'Singapore issues' foundered. It is also a reflection of the change in attitude of host countries, especially developing economies, towards foreign direct investment – the move away from the policies of economic nationalism popular in the 1970s, when the emphasis was on constraining investors and on expropriation, to a situation where states are keen to increase their attractiveness to potential investors to secure a place in global production networks (Moran 1998). Competition for investment has been found to be the factor most strongly associated with states' negotiation of BITs (Elkins et al. 2006). And support has been found for the argument that the presence of a BIT encourages investment into the developing economy partner (Neumayer and Spess 2005; Salacuse and Sullivan 2005), although there is no evidence that BITs are associated with enhanced rates of economic growth or that they are necessarily welfare-optimizing (Guzman 1998).

BITs represent a significant extension of legalization in international economic relations:

> Although BIT texts are often drafted in an open and imprecise manner – usually encompassing no more than ten pages – they can be described as hard law as they delegate the authority of interpretation and implementation to transnational arbitration bodies. (Berger 2008: 2–3)

In particular, by providing for investor–state dispute resolution, they directly grant foreign investors legal personality. Foreign investors often can take their claims against a host government directly to an international tribunal: they are not obliged to use domestic courts. Contemporary BITS are comprehensive in their coverage, providing not just for third party settlement of disputes but also a broad definition of investment, provisions for compensation in the event of expropriation, and constraints on governments' capacity to limit the inflow or outflow of funds.[3]

The relative neglect of BITs by students of international economic relations is surprising in that these treaties have resulted in greater incursions on national sovereignty than most commercial treaties. By substantially constraining the freedom of action of host states, they have provided much greater certainty for investors, and have helped overcome one source of insecurity – the change in the balance of bargaining power that occurs once investors have committed substantial resources to specific uses in host countries. Indeed, BITs have had so significant an impact on the bargaining relationship between investors and host countries that a backlash is under way: UNCTAD notes in its most recent *World Investment Report* that a number of developing economies have either denounced or are seeking to renegotiate some of their current BITs (UNCTAD 2010: 85–6). The investor–state dimensions of BITs have also attracted criticism in industrialized economies because of perceptions that they privilege foreign investors over their domestic counterparts: some members of the US Congress objected to Canadian companies' use of NAFTA's investor–state provisions; the Australian government's Productivity Commission has recently advised the government not to include investor-state provisions in the investment chapters of any PTAs it negotiates (Productivity Commission 2010).

What prospect is there for multilateralizing these investment treaties? Despite the similarity in content across many treaties (typically, they are less differentiated than PTAs), the answer seems to be relatively little. Indeed, the very absence of substantial differentiation may reduce pressures for multilateralization because the presence of individual treaties does not seem to complicate the operations of corporations across various countries. Moreover, in addition to the overall political sensitivity in elevating investment issues beyond bilateral negotiations, as seen in the inability of the OECD or WTO to forge agreement on multilateral treaties, the treaties are very much 'positional goods' intended to provide advantage to their signatories over their competitors for what is frequently perceived (inaccurately) as a fixed pie of foreign direct investment.

In the trade sphere, East Asian countries have been enthusiastic participants in the global push towards PTAs since the turn of the century. Currently more than 40 agreements are being implemented and a similar number are under negotiation. I will not rehearse the more general arguments that have accompanied the growth of bilateralism in international trade, notably whether these agreements in general represent a stumbling block or a stepping stone towards more liberal trade at the global level, but will concentrate on concerns about the barriers that these agreements raise to the management of supply chains across the region, and whether in themselves they will generate a self-sustaining momentum towards the multilateralization of agreements.

PTAs involving East Asian economies differ widely in design, scope and purpose. Some PTAs are narrow, focusing primarily on trade in goods, and aim for only minimal liberalization. Others are far more comprehensive with provisions that promote deep liberalization and regulatory cooperation or harmonization. Some are driven by economic motives while many others are driven primarily by political or diplomatic objectives. The net effect of this explosion of PTA activity together with wide variation in the agreements themselves is the creation of a dense and complex web of conflicting rules for the conduct of trade relations, which has the potential to increase the costs that businesses incur in managing their supply chains and those that governments face in administering customs procedures. One might reasonably expect, therefore, that a dynamic towards 'multilateralization' would be set in train as business and governments alike seek to reduce transactions costs.

Much of the recent academic focus on multilateralizing regionalism builds on the work of Richard Baldwin. In a seminal article, he argues that the exponential proliferation of PTAs and the higher trade costs associated with them are driving business and government to demand a more rational and global basis for international trade (Baldwin 2006). Baldwin suggests that trade liberalization (whether unilateral, preferential or multilateral) has been realigning the political economy landscape in favour of more trade opening, creating a self-perpetuating dynamic (the 'juggernaut effect'). The ascendancy of pro-liberalization forces generates pressure on governments to participate in more open trade arrangements, especially in a context where competitors are benefiting from discriminatory agreements that their governments have signed (the 'domino effect')

(Baldwin 1993). However, these market-opening arrangements in recent years have been dominated by PTAs, which, perversely, can increase trade costs and have potentially distorting side effects. The proliferation of PTAs therefore creates a third political economy effect – an interest in 'taming the tangle' of PTAs, in other words, in 'multilateralizing regionalism'.

The logical conclusion of Baldwin's argument is that the global proliferation of PTAs in tandem with the ongoing unbundling of production will generate political economy forces that favour the creation of larger and more coherent trade arrangements, a dynamic that will culminate eventually in full multilateralization (Baldwin 2006: 1507–8). This logic should make an observer optimistic that the tangle of PTAs in the Asia-Pacific region will be 'tamed'. Moreover, it is supported by evidence that broader PTAs would deliver larger welfare gains than are being achieved through the existing bilateral agreements (Kawai and Wignaraja 2008).

However, the political economy logic that Baldwin identified as driving the multilateralization of the 'spaghetti bowl' of preferential trade agreements rests on business playing a leading role in lobbying governments when disadvantaged: first, by competitors benefiting from discriminatory agreements and second, by a consequent proliferation of agreements with incompatible rules that complicates the management of their supply chains. While this logic seems persuasive in the European context, for example Augier et al. (2009), a number of the assumptions on which it rests may not be relevant to or may be far weaker in the Asia-Pacific region.

Three components of this political economy logic are particularly important. First, that business is the primary actor in driving trade agreements in the region. Second, that business is sufficiently adversely affected when competitors are benefiting from discriminatory trading agreements, and by the complications that a proliferation of agreements has for its supply chain management, that it will invest resources into lobbying governments to undertake trade policies that will resolve its problems. Third, that pro-liberalization forces have been sufficiently strengthened by the processes of globalization that they will prevail in conflict with residual protectionist interests. All three of these premises are questionable in the Asia-Pacific context. This is not to suggest that they are entirely irrelevant. Rather, it is that they may be so much weaker that outcomes in this region may be entirely different from those experienced in Europe (Ravenhill 2010).

The first set of assumptions relates to the role of business in trade policy-making. The literature in political economy on trade policy-making focuses almost exclusively on advanced industrialized economies, especially the United States – countries characterized by pluralist political systems. The political process in many countries in the Asia-Pacific region, especially in East Asia, is very different. The channels through which business influences the state are often informal and opaque. Again, this is not to suggest that business completely lacks influence, or to deny the likelihood that the state will wish to enhance national welfare through its external economic policies. Rather, it is to suggest that the capacity of specific businesses to influence policy-making may be uncertain, and that interests of individual businesses may not be the dominant factor in trade policy-making in many countries of the Asia-Pacific (for example see Chandra and Hanim 2010; Pongsudhiriak 2010).

Second, it is not evident that existing trade regimes have placed significant obstacles in the path of business management of their supply chains across the region. Several factors are important in this context. Governments in the region over the last three decades have put into place policies that have led to East Asia becoming the world's most integrated region for trans-border shipment of components despite the absence, until recently, of inter-state trade agreements. Governments introduced various measures, for example, duty drawback schemes and export-processing zones, which enabled components to be imported duty-free if the final product was exported. Through the work of APEC since its establishment in 1989, they have moved to reduce the transactions costs incurred by businesses operating across the region through, for instance, promoting greater transparency and efficiency in customs procedures, and through harmonizing regulations on product safety. Equally significantly, they have facilitated trade by lowering tariffs. This reduction has come about through three principal sets of policies: (1) through unilateral liberalization, which was most notable in Southeast Asia, and Australia and New Zealand in the 1980s; (2) through the regular rounds of GATT/WTO negotiations; and (3) through negotiating sectoral agreements. By far the most important of the latter is the WTO's 1996 Information Technology Agreement, which freed a substantial portion of trade in the single most important category of East Asia's exports.

The upshot is that tariff barriers around the region are relatively low. Even in the traditionally heavily-protected economies in Southeast Asia, the average MFN tariff rate on manufactures is currently less than 10 percent. But most trade takes place in product lines where MFN tariffs are already zero: the WTO (2011) has calculated, for instance, that close to three-quarters of the trade among the four largest ASEAN economies occurs in products with zero MFN tariffs. And where tariffs are still important, these sectors are usually protected for domestic political economy reasons and consequently often excluded from liberalization under the less-than-comprehensive coverage that has characterized the region's PTAs. To cite WTO data again, fully 22 percent of the value of trade between Japan and Mexico is subject to MFN tariffs despite the existence of a preferential trade agreement between the two parties (WTO 2011).

These two factors – relatively low tariffs, and the exclusion of sensitive sectors from agreements – coupled with the frequent unwillingness of countries in the region to sign agreements with their most important trading partners, have significant consequences for the political economy effects of the agreements: they seldom create major advantages or disadvantages for businesses that either benefit from them or are excluded from them. An important indicator to support this conclusion is the low utilization of the preferences within the agreements, especially in contrast to the utilization of the preferential schemes of the EU and the US. Businesses often do not consider that the benefits from the agreements justify the costs incurred in complying with their provisions, most notably the paperwork required to meet rules of origin provisions. And, again, to emphasize the difference with the logic driving multilateralization in Europe, business in the Asia-Pacific seems relatively unconcerned about the costs of proliferating PTAs and the 'noodle bowl' effect. Kawai and Wignaraja (2009) report that only 20 per cent of respondents to a survey of 841 firms in six East Asian economies indicated that multiple schedules of rules of origin added significantly to their business costs.

Flowing from this second set of considerations is the possibility that businesses will not invest significant resources into lobbying in favour of PTAs, in marked contrast to protectionist forces within economies across the region. In some countries in the region, such as Australia, Chile, New Zealand and Singapore, protectionist forces have lost most of whatever political clout that they once enjoyed. Elsewhere, however, the experience of negotiating PTAs over the decade has demonstrated the ongoing political strength of protectionist interests and, in some cases, their capacity either to entirely block an agreement that governments have wished to negotiate, or to emasculate it through the carve-out of substantial sectors.

Where, then, does this leave the logic of multilateralization? Proponents of multilateralization can draw little comfort from the analysis above. It casts doubt on the strength of any automatic multilateralizing effect that the proliferation of PTAs might have been expected to have set in train because of the disadvantages they are suggested to have posed for business groups. And, the relatively small costs that the noodle bowl imposes on business suggest that government-led efforts at multilateralization are likely to face difficulties when they encounter mobilized protectionist interests.

These arguments are pertinent to the prospects for the most prominent attempt to 'multilateralize' the noodle bowl in the Asia-Pacific region, the Trans-Pacific Partnership (TPP). The origins of the TPP lie in the Trans-Pacific Strategic Economic Partnership agreement – colloquially known as the P4 agreement – between Brunei, Chile, New Zealand and Singapore, which entered into force in 2006. In economic terms, the impact of the P4 was expected to be negligible as the economies of the signatories were already very open and the trade flows between them were small. Of greater importance was the deliberate attempt to design a high quality, ambitious 'model', which, unlike most Asia-Pacific preferential arrangements, included an accession clause for other parties to join in the future. In September 2008 the Bush Administration signalled its intention to join an expanded agreement, now renamed the Trans-Pacific Partnership, and Australia, Peru and Vietnam quickly followed suit (Malaysia also entered the negotiations after they began in March 2010).

The parties to the TPP negotiations aspire to create a similar high-quality agreement that goes beyond the P4 to address '21st century' trade issues, especially the domestic regulatory constraints that affect the ability of firms to enter, operate in, and exit foreign markets. In practical terms, this means that in addition to dealing with traditional issues (for example market access for goods and services and related disciplines), the TPP will also cover issues such as investment, government procurement, intellectual property and trade facilitation. The agreement will include an accession clause, providing for a future expansion of membership.

Given the small size of the economies of the Asian and Oceanic parties to the TPP, the overall welfare gains from the agreement are again likely to be small (especially as viewed from Washington). Although it includes a number of countries that have been very active (and effective over the years) in trade diplomacy – including Australia, Chile, New Zealand and Singapore – they lack the economic weight to form a powerful minilateral core for regional liberalization. The key to the TPP's potential for multilateralizing regionalism rests therefore on its capacity to attract some of the region's larger economies. Japan, increasingly concerned at Korea's success in negotiating bilateral agreements with the EU and the United States, has debated whether to seek membership, but a combination of ongoing political instability, pre-occupation with re-building after the Tōhoku earthquake and resistance from protectionist interests has caused it to postpone its decision. Without interest from the region's larger economies (whose participation in any event might only reinforce protectionist pressures in Washington), pro-liberalization interests in the US are unlikely to lobby enthusiastically for an agreement that has generated considerable concern among domestic interests that fear the impact of improved access for Vietnamese textiles or dairy (and other agricultural) products from Australia and New Zealand. The negotiators have indicated that a TPP agreement will not supersede existing bilateral treaties, possibly further complicating the management task of business which, in some relationships, for example those between Australia and New Zealand on the one hand, and Singapore on the other, will have to decide which of three preferential agreements to use. And the United States through the first seven rounds of negotiations has indicated its preference for having individual tariff schedules with each of its TPP partners rather than planning for a single multilateralized agreement (for further discussion see Capling and Ravenhill (forthcoming 2012), on which this section draws).

5. CONCLUSION

Effective regional cooperation in East Asia – and in the Asia-Pacific region more broadly – has been weakened by two problems: the overall number of states involved, and the absence of a minilateral core of states that have both the desire and the capability to provide leadership. Miles Kahler's (2000) judgment from the turn of the century continues to be valid today: Asian institutions remain highly informal; for the most part legalization has been explicitly rejected. ASEAN's dogged determination to cling to its central position in East Asian regionalism while seemingly incapable either of getting its own house in order or of providing effective leadership to broader East Asian or Asia-Pacific groupings has ensured both that cooperation remains shallow and that no substantial extension of cooperation (beyond the Japanese government-driven Chiang Mai Initiative) has occurred.

ASEAN's enlargement, now substantially more than a decade old, diluted its own cohesion through the addition of states that have proved to be reluctant to accept international obligations that limit their autonomy. But it is not just diversity in Southeast Asia that has inhibited regional institution-building: conflicting interests (complicated by an unwillingness to move beyond historical animosities) among the Northeast Asian Big Three of China, Japan and Korea – a natural 'minilateral' core – for East Asia, has left ASEAN 'in the driving seat' by default. The Hatoyama and Rudd efforts to build stronger regional institutions on the basis of a minilateral core both foundered on issues related to membership (and hence legitimacy).

In the meantime, states have increasingly pursued their interests through bilateral economic arrangements on trade and investment. That many of these remain shallow suggests that they often have been driven as much by political as by economic considerations. In itself, the primacy of the political does not bode well for the potential multilateralization of these agreements. Many appear to have been crafted to achieve either political and/or economic advantage that could be lost through their multilateralization.

NOTES

1. I understand multilateralism, following Ruggie (1992: 571), as having both a quantitative and a qualitative dimension: 'an institutional form which coordinates relations among three or more states on the basis of "generalized" principles of conduct'.
2. This section draws on Emmers and Ravenhill (2011).
3. For many years, however, China limited international arbitration to disputes involving compensation for nationalization and expropriation. Disputes pertaining to other aspects of investment had to be resolved in local courts or arbitrated through the China International Economic and Trade Arbitration Commission or other local fora, or settled through diplomatic means.

REFERENCES

Augier, P., M. Gasiorek and C. Laitong (2009), 'Multilateralizing regionalism: lessons from the EU experience in relaxing rules of origin', in Patrick Low and Richard E. Baldwin (eds), *Multilateralizing Regionalism*, Cambridge: Cambridge University Press.

Baldwin, R. (1993), 'A domino theory of regionalism', National Bureau of Economic Research working paper 4465, September, Cambridge, MA.

Baldwin, R.E. (2006), 'Multilateralising regionalism: spaghetti bowls as building blocs on the path to global free trade', *World Economy* **29**(11), 1451–518.

Berger, A. (2008), 'China's new bilateral investment treaty programme: substance, rational [sic] and implications for international investment law making', presentation to the American Society of International Law: International Economic Law Interest Group biennial conference, 14–15 November, Washington, DC.

Capling, A. and J. Ravenhill (forthcoming), 'Multilateralising regionalism: what role for the TPP?', *The Pacific Review*.

Chandra, A.C. and L. Hanim (2010), 'Indonesia', in Ann Capling and Patrick Low (eds), *Governments, Non-State Actors and Trade Policy-Making: Negotiating Preferentially or Multilaterally?*, Cambridge: Cambridge University Press, pp. 125–60.

Elkins, Z., A.T. Guzman and B. Simmons (2006), 'Competing for capital: the diffusion of bilateral investment treaties, 1960–2000', *International Organization* **60**(4), 811–46.

Emmers, R. and J. Ravenhill (2011), 'The Asian and global financial crises: consequences for East Asian regionalism', *Contemporary Politics* **17**(2), 133–49.

Emmers, R. and T.S. Seng (2011), 'The ASEAN regional forum and preventive diplomacy: built to fail?', presentation to the International Studies Association Annual Conference, 16 March, Montreal.

Guzman, A.T. (1998), 'Why LDCs sign treaties that hurt them: explaining the popularity of bilateral investment treaties', *Virginia Journal of International Law* **38**, 638–88.

Hatoyama, Y. (2009), address by H.E. Yukio Hatoyama, Prime Minister of Japan, 'Japan's new commitment to Asia – towards the realization of an East Asian Community', accessed 6 May 2011 at www.kantei.go.jp/foreign/hatoyama/statement/200911/15singapore_e.html.

Junbo, J. (2009), 'Why an East Asian Community matters', *Asia Times Online*, 22 October accessed at www.atimes/China/KJ22Ad03.html/.

Kahler, M. (1992), 'Multilateralism with small and large numbers', *International Organization* **46**(3), 681–708.

Kahler, M. (2000), 'Legalization as strategy: the Asia-Pacific case', *International Organization* **54**(3), 549–71.

Kawai, M. and G. Wignaraja (2008), 'Regionalism as an engine of multilateralism: a case for a single East Asian FTA', Asian Development Bank working paper series on regional economic integration no. 14, Mandaluyong City, Philippines.

Kawai, M. and G. Wignaraja (2009), 'The Asian "noodle bowl": is it serious for business?' Asian Development Bank Institute working paper series no. 136, April, Tokyo, accessed at www.adbi.org/working-paper/2009/04/14/2940.asian.noodle.bowl.serious.business/.

Kelly, P. (2008), 'Shape of the future', *The Australian*, 20 December, accessed at www.theaustralian.com.au/news/opinion/shape-of-the-future/story-e6frg74x-1111118369389.

Manger, M.S. (2009), *Investing in Protection: The Politics of Preferential Trade Agreements between North and South*, Cambridge: Cambridge University Press.

Milner, H. (1992), 'International theories of cooperation among nations', *World Politics* **44**(3), 466–96.

Moran, T.H. (1998), *Foreign Direct Investment and Development: The New Policy Agenda for Developing Countries and Economies in Transition*, Washington, DC: Institute for International Economics.

Mulgan, A.G. (2009), 'Hatoyama's East Asia Community and regional leadership rivalries', *East Asia Forum*, 13 October, accessed 4 April 2010 at www.eastasiaforum.org/2009/10/13/Hatoyama's_East_Asia_Community/.

Neumayer, E. and L. Spess (2005), 'Do bilateral investment treaties increase foreign direct investment to developing countries?', *World Development* **33**(10), 1567–85.

Olson, M. (1965), *The Logic of Collective Action*, Cambridge: Harvard University Press.

Oye, K. (1985), 'Explaining cooperation under anarchy: hypotheses and strategies', *World Politics* **38**(1), 1–24.

Parameswaran, P. (2009), 'Hatoyama's East Asia Community', *Asia Eye*, 16 October, accessed 4 April 2010 at http://blog.project2049.net/2009/hatoyamas-east-asia/.

Pongsudhiriak, T. (2010), 'Thailand', in Ann Capling and Patrick Low (eds), *Governments, Non-State Actors and Trade Policy-Making: Negotiating Preferentially or Multilaterally?*, Cambridge: Cambridge University Press, 161–85.

Productivity Commission, C.o.A. (2010), 'Bilateral and regional trade agreements: Productivity Commission research report', Canberra, accessed at www.pc.gov.au/__data/assets/pdf_file/0010/104203/trade-agreements-report.pdf.

Ravenhill, J. (2010), 'The "New East Asian Regionalism": a political domino effect', *Review of International Political Economy* **17**(2), 178–208.

Rudd, Kevin (2008), 'It's time to build an Asia-Pacific Community? address to the Asia Society, Australasia Centre, Sydney, 4 June, accessed at www.pm.gov.au/media/Speech/2008/speech_0286.cfm.

Ruggie, J.G. (1992), 'Multilateralism: the anatomy of an institution', *International Organization* **46**(3), 561–98.

Salacuse, J.W. and N.P. Sullivan (2005), 'Do BITs really work? An evaluation of bilateral investment treaties and their grand bargain', *Harvard Law Journal* **46**(1), 67–130.

Snidal, D. (1985), 'The limits of hegemonic stability theory', *International Organization* **39**(4), 579–614.

United Nations Conference on Trade and Development (UNCTAD) (2010), *World Investment Report 2010: Investing in a Low Carbon Economy*, New York and Geneva: United Nations.

Wade, R., and J. Vestergaard (2010), 'Overhaul the G20 for the sake of the G172', *Financial Times*, 21 October accessed at www.ft.com/cms/s/a2ab4716-dd45-11df-9236-00144feabdc0,dwp_uuid=73adc504-2ffa-11da-ba9f-00000e2511c8,print=yes.html.

Woolcott, R., T.N.T. Ninh and M. Wesley (2009), 'The Asia-Pacific: a community for the 21st century: conference summary record', 3–5 December, Asia Society Australia Conference, accessed at www.apc2009conference.org/userfiles/Microsoft%20Word%20-%20091215%20CONFERENCE%20SUMMARY%20RECORD%20_final_.pdf.

World Trade Organization (WTO) (2011), *World Trade Report 2011: Preferential Trade Agreements and the WTO: From Co-Existence to Coherence*, Geneva: World Trade Organization.

6. The principle of 'subsidiarity' and Asian unification

Yao Chaocheng

1. INTRODUCTION

Since the Asian financial crisis of the late 1990s, East Asia has begun to integrate, forming the beginnings of a regional community to resolve security and economic disputes. Across East Asia, governments and leaders are developing their own institutions and intraregional trade patterns. They even held their first truly regional meeting, the annual East Asia Summit (EAS) in 2005 in Kuala Lumpur, Malaysia, with the participation of ten Association of Southeast Asian Nations (ASEAN) members, China, Japan, Korea, India, and even two non-Asian nations, Australia and New Zealand. In subtle ways people across East Asia, like Europeans after World War II, are beginning to think of themselves as citizens of Asia. Presently the regional economic cooperation in Asia is developing fast and well with ASEAN as an axis and with the proactive participation of major Asian nations such as China, Japan, Korea and India. This process may lead to an Asian economic community in the future.

While pointing to a bright prospect, the process, however, is destined to encounter significant obstacles and difficulties, as Asia is too large and too diverse in terms of culture, religion, political systems and economic strengths to allow for easy community-building. Samuel Huntingdon predicted that the 'cultural fault lines' among some Asian nations would be difficult to repair and overcome (Huntington 1999). Daniel Twining (2010) commented that economically Asian nations may go together, but socially and politically shall still be divided from each other.

Others have argued that the most immediate threats were not associated with 'cultural fault-lines' but related to the ignorance of policy-makers and all those concerned not working on the issue positively. To live in peace, Asian people have to adopt a new way of thinking to resolve their disputes. The principle of subsidiarity[1] as a bottom-up democratic approach adopted in the process of European unification could be the key solution for Asia to overcome the impending obstructions. The Asian economic integration process has been carefully studied in comparison to Europe, in order to find out the relations and revelations. It is assumed that the principle in a democratic nature will promote an Asian economic integration process that in turn should also impact on China's political reform. In the process, conflicts shall inevitably happen. However it is the tension between particular interests and common benefits for all Asian nations that will keep the integration process open-ended and never complete as a necessary condition for steady improvements towards the final unification. A unified Asia, as a pillar alongside the European Union (EU) and the US forming a truly multi-polar world, would enable Asian nations to exercise sustainable control of their regional social, economic, cultural and political environment in a balanced manner of globalisation and regionalisation.

2. ASIAN ECONOMIC INTEGRATION PROCESS

Asia has been slow in responding to regional economic integration compared to Europe and North America. The first regional trade agreement was signed in Bangkok in 1975 by just five countries: Bangladesh, India, Korea, Laos and Sri Lanka. China entered the agreement in 2000. However, the Bangkok Agreement was only a preferential tariff agreement and has had only a limited function in reducing tariff barriers among members. In South Asia, the South Asian Association for Regional Cooperation (SAARC) was set up in 1985, but its economic cooperation process has been slow and remains at a low level. There had been no substantial development in trade liberalisation in South Asia until the signing of the Agreement on SAARC Preferential Trading Arrangement (SAPTA) in 1995. In December 2003, members of the Experts Committee of SAARC held a meeting in New Delhi, India, to make a final assessment of and give approval to the proposed programme for setting up the South Asia Free Trade Zone. In West Asia, the Gulf Cooperation Council (GCC) was established in 1981; its members are six Middle East countries including Saudi Arabia. It is a comprehensive sub-regional organisation which, however, only recently adopted regional economic integration as one of its objectives. The concurrent regional cooperation in Asia has seen a new momentum, particularly since November 2002 when China and ASEAN signed an FTA agreement in Phnom Penh, Cambodia. By 2010, the agreement had become effective.

On 7 October 2003, China, Japan, Korea and the ASEAN made a joint declaration on promoting the 10+3 FTA with a set time-frame up to the year 2020. Both Japan and Korea are also engaged in negotiations with ASEAN on separate bilateral FTAs. India, the largest economy in South Asia, has made active efforts to join in the faster economic cooperation process in East Asia. The first summit (EAS) was held in Kuala Lumpur, Malaysia in 2005. Since then, four EAS have been held respectively in the Philippines, Singapore, Thailand and Vietnam. On 23 May 2011, the three East Asian nations – China, Japan and South Korea, which account for roughly one-fifth of the world's trade – agreed to complete joint studies on a trilateral pact, which would pave the way for free trade negotiations. Though time consuming, it can be anticipated that a pan-Asia cooperation scheme shall finally evolve including ten ASEAN member nations, China, Japan, Korea and India with the participation of Australia and New Zealand and maybe other nations under the principle of open regionalism (Kumar 2007).

According to a WTO report, between September 2007 and January 2011 43 new FTAs had been established worldwide of which 14 are in Asia, representing nearly one-third of the total. According to the Asian Development Bank's annual report 2011, in the year 2010, economic growth rate reached 9 percent in Asia – twice the world average growth rate. It is forecasted that by 2050 the total Asian gross domestic product (GDP) will account for 51 percent of the global total (Greenwood 2011). Theoretically, regional economic integration will entail political integration. Once the East Asian Economic Community scheme is established, it is likely to attract other Asian nations of south, west central and north Asia, as well as the Middle East, and finally to expand into a 'Pan-Asian Economic Community'. Going further, a unified Asia may take shape.

While promising bright prospects, the unification process is destined to encounter many obstacles and difficulties. Asia is vast with substantial differences in culture, religion, political systems and economic strengths. Some well-known historical problems or territorial disputes still exist between China and Japan, China and India, and Japan and Korea, the four major nations that are involved in the regional cooperation scheme. These problems and disputes, together with cultural differences, ideological disparity and nationalism, may all act as obstacles in the Asian unification process. In the long run the social obstacles could be far more troublesome than the economic ones, and they can be destructive too.

3. THE SOCIAL OBSTACLES EXISTING IN THE ASIAN UNIFICATION PROCESS

3.1 Internal Obstacles

A regional economic unification must overcome economic obstacles, such as how to remove trade and non-trade barriers and how to achieve monetary stability in the region. However, in the long run of higher level unification, the social obstacles will be more troublesome than the economic ones and can be dangerous. Intra-regional obstacles are evidenced by a series of long-standing disputes that have intensified recently, including a maritime territorial dispute in the Sulawesi Sea between Malaysia and Indonesia, a dispute between South Korea and Japan over the Tokdo/Takeshima islets, and growing tensions between China and Japan over Japan's republishing of a controversial textbook and over a potentially energy-rich territory in the East China Sea.

Between China and India, the two big Asian nations, disputes exist with regards to the joint border and the Tibetan issue. The former dispute triggered war in 1962, while the latter remains a sensitive topic. Tensions continue to mount on the Korean peninsula and could lead to dangerous military confrontation. India and Pakistan are confronted with unsettled bilateral historical problems and disputes. Although bilateral relations have been improved since 2004, the problems and disputes are not yet thoroughly resolved. Among the historical problems and disputes that may obstruct the Asian unification process, Sino–Japan relations is the most decisive, including the disputes over the interpretation of World War II history and the gas field of the East China Sea. The former has been lingering for many decades and the latter has recently intensified.

In general terms, the most dangerous social obstacle in Asia is nationalism. The seminal book 'Clash of Civilizations' (Huntington 1996) resounds throughout the world because Huntington convincingly referred to nationalities or nationalism as the main causes of these clashes. When reviewing the conflicts and disputes taking place in Asia, it must be admitted that all are rooted in nationalism. On the one hand a sense of strong national identity can unite a nation into one, but on the other hand the promotion of nationalism can result in regional splits or international collisions which may go out of control.

3.2 External Interferers

The Asian unification process also encounters external interferers. At present, more than 30 FTA agreements are being negotiated among the 21 Asia-Pacific Economic Co-operation (APEC) members; almost all involve China and only four involve the US. The 1980s witnessed the tremendous growth of intra-regional trade and investment links (including Japan, the 'four tigers' (South Korea, Taiwan, Hong Kong and Singapore), ASEAN and China), creating de facto economic integration without any institutional framework. An East Asian Economic Group was proposed by Mahathir Mohamad, the former Malaysian Prime Minister in 1990, and the US responded by supporting APEC with the aim of preventing the emergence of an Asian economic bloc. In 1997, Japan proposed the establishment of an Asian Monetary Fund (AMF), but the proposal never took off due to US opposition (Stephenson 2011).

The amazingly sustained economic success of East Asia, especially China, may reinforce interventionist elements and tendencies in the EU and the US. In both Europe and North America, businesses increasingly need to take into account the opportunities and threats which these changes have brought about. In reaction to these challenges, both European and North American businesses may support an increasing pressure to not only maintain existing forms of selective protection against imports from East Asia, but also to develop new trade barriers. If the East Asian dynamism is maintained, further interventionist pressures and new protectionist initiatives are to be expected.

It can be foreseen that Washington shall work with Japan to promote shared interests in the East Asian regional framework, where Japan can serve as a US proxy on specific issues critical to both nations. The US does not want to find itself outside the Asian cooperation framework, so it may be working with Japan to create one that is more inclusive. Furthermore, the US has reinforced its strategic and military interests in the region. For example, when tensions over territorial claims in the South China Sea increased recently, the US jointly conducted military exercises with Vietnam, the Philippines and South Korea.

Besides, China is regarded as a challenge to the traditional strategic position of the US in Asia. The trend has triggered worries within the US Congress and among security analysts as to whether the United States can maintain its decades-long military predominance in the economically crucial Asia-Pacific region. Needless to say, Washington feels that its position might be seriously threatened by China in the long run.

3.3 China Threat

China's active diplomatic approaches and fast economic growth have raised questions in the US and throughout Asia concerning the nature of China's rise and its implications. Advocates of a China threat scenario have long argued that China desires regional hegemony and that US–China relations in this regard are a zero sum game. It is regularly proposed that China's rise will necessarily be highly disruptive to US pre-eminence in the global system, stability in Asia, and the international system at large (Economy 2005). Others paint a picture of China returning to the glory days of the Middle Kingdom, using its economic might to establish an empire with tentacles reaching out throughout most of

Asia and transforming its neighbours into little more than vassal states (Frank 1998). Still other analysts argue forcefully that China's rise can be managed through integrating the country into international norms and regimes, thereby ensuring that China has a stake in preserving the status quo. In this scenario, as the Chinese themselves have insisted, China's rise will be peaceful, serving an ameliorative function in international affairs: enhancing global security, promoting peaceful trade and addressing transnational challenges.

The rise of such a big country as China has been unprecedented in human history, as its economy has grown by 9.5 percent annually for the last 25 years. Since 1978, China's GDP per capita has risen relative to that of the world leader, the United States, in almost exactly the same way that Japan's rose between 1950 and 1973 (Wanand 2008). In 2010, China overtook Japan to become the world's second-largest economy in dollar terms (*Financial Times*, 25 February 2011). A British bookmaker is offering punters odds of 6/4 on China's surpassing the US to become the world's biggest economy before 2020. It is not for the first time that the world is facing a rising nation. However, a rising China should be different. The US had a population of about 30–40 million and Japan of 100 million when they rose to power. China, on the other hand, has a population of 1.3 billion. It is indeed the first time for the world to see such a populous nation rising. A rising China inevitably makes her neighbours psychologically worried. Some Asian nations fear that China will rise to become an intimidating superpower and a challenging force to the international order. The huge population, the growing economic capacity, the typical Chinese nationalism and passion, especially the nature of the political system, do serve as the justification for the contention of 'China threat'.

4. THE SUBSIDIARITY PRINCIPLE AND ASIAN UNIFICATION

4.1 Context

The history of Europe is a history of wars between kingdoms, religious and ethnic communities, nations and political ideologies. The two World Wars originated in Europe. In 1945, when Europe lay in ruins, European nations started engaging in innovative ways and means to settle their future conflicts through regional cooperation. Ever since, steady progress has been made towards political and economic unification. The unification process proved to be a necessary condition for lasting peace and a shared prosperity in Europe.

In the European unification process, a so-called principle of subsidiarity has played an important role. Subsidiarity denotes that any central authority should not attempt to work on solutions which can be solved at a more local or more immediate level. It is the subsidiarity principle that holds the EU together. It has strengthened the member states in their capacity-building for the common European good. It is a principle of general value and is applicable to each individual as well. Within the regional structure, it fosters autonomy, independence and self-reliance. A regional unification needs economic activities and also social activities. Deepening economic integration can push forward social integration, and only social integration can enhance the Asian regional unification to a high level.

4.2 The Subsidiarity Principle and the China Threat

It seems that China's growing economic capacity serves as the justification for the contention of the 'China threat'. However, this is not exactly the case. China is facing many internal and external problems, especially the internal ones, such as the high cost of economic growth, the increasing disparity between poor and rich, the inefficiency of the state-owned enterprises, a large number of unemployed and laid-off workers, environmental problems, energy shortage, as well as delayed reforms of the political system. All of these put a limit on China's economic development.

In remarkable public comments in summer 2010, China's Prime Minister Wen Jiabao said that Chinese officials 'must continue to liberate their thinking and make bold explorations' in reform. Without a 'reform of the political system', Wen argued, 'it will be impossible for the goal of economic reform and modernization to be realized.' China must reverse 'the excessive concentration of unrestrained power' and 'create conditions for the people to criticize and supervise the government . . . People's democratic rights and legitimate rights must be guaranteed' for economic growth to continue (quoted in Twining 2011: 13). As a former senior official of China's central bank, Yu Yongding, recently wrote, 'China's rapid growth has been achieved at an extremely high cost. Only future generations will know the true price.' Yu called China's inability to innovate its 'Achilles heel', and urged political reform aimed at 'breaking this unholy alliance' between government officials and business elites. 'Meritocracy is a prerequisite for good governance. But meritocracy has been eroded by a political culture of sycophancy and cynicism,' he wrote. China risks a 'serious backlash' that will stall growth unless it moves beyond a 'capitalism of the rich and powerful' (quoted in Twining 2011: 15). The Chinese government understands these domestic challenges and has tried very hard to overcome them. Especially with regard to the political development challenge, the government has been trying to implement schemes that give political space to the lowest level (that is, villages) to elect representatives from among more than one candidate, and from among candidates who are not all from the Chinese Communist Party (Wanandi 2008: 25–6). The principle of subsidiarity can help China to become a democracy.

The Asian unification process as a democratic process will no doubt accelerate China's political reform and its move towards democracy. This will help China to grow into a strong and solid pier of world peace instead of becoming a challenging force to the international order. Even if the Chinese GDP overtakes that of the US in the mid 21st century, it would not qualify China as a world leader. Therefore, China's rise would have to not only rely on economic growth, but also on the support of the forces of modern civilization and culture complying with the common international values in order to win the respects of other Asian nations.

China has re-positioned herself as an equal partner in regional and international cooperation, substituting the erstwhile Cold War position as the leader of the 'third world'. Under the new policy, China is trying to act as a promoter in the regional unification process, and not a leader, accepting ASEAN as the centre of the regional cooperation structure. The Chinese government has realized that pursuing a policy of equal partnership is the best way for China to gain the respect of other Asian nations. China has long followed an approach that opposes hegemonies and favours a multi-polar world. To be able to play a leading role in the Asian economic unification process China still needs to achieve the following: to become a tangible force big enough to influence the regional economy; to increase the scale of its economy; to have an adequately open market, a freely convertible currency and a sufficient amount of capital reserve to be used for overseas investment. Without these achievements China's influence on Asia and the world is still limited. Therefore, the middle solution is that China sticks to its existing policy of concentrating on her domestic political and economic affairs and in the meantime promotes regional social and economic cooperation in Asia through collective leadership in accordance with existing international values and norms.

4.3 The Subsidiarity Principle and Regional Structure

The subsidiarity principle was introduced by the Treaty of Maastricht and was further elaborated in a Protocol on the application of the principle attached to the Treaty of Amsterdam. It is the subsidiarity that holds the EU together. Without it, the Union would collapse (Rolly 1996). Following such a logic, the principle of subsidiarity can help Asian nations to learn to build up a super-state structure that suits the region best, to reconcile the principle of equality among nation states and citizens and to resolve disputes based on democratic and peaceful approaches. India's prime minister said his country could be secure only in a region of democracies; Japan's leaders hope to build an 'East Asian Community' modelled on the liberal principles of the European Union; and Southeast Asian statesmen have declared that regional stability requires democracy at home and abroad (Twining 2011). These examples show that the Asian nations have begun to embrace common political norms. In studies taken by the East Asia Barometer, a project examining public opinion across the region, majorities in nine Asian nations said that they desired democracy rather than any other type of political system. Though the study does not include China, in which such polling would probably be impossible, it seems likely that a survey would show that peace and democracy are equally desired by most Chinese people. In the future, these common political traits might help Asian nations to form the basic values of a stronger regional organisation (Rusciano 2011).

China as the largest economic body in Asia is positively participating in the East Asian economic integration process. Japan is committed to the idea of regional cooperation and community building because it views it as a way to overcome the challenges posed by China. In the meantime, despite the challenges it faces, Japan is still the region's largest economy in terms of GDP and is very important to the region in terms of trade, investment, finance and technology. As long as it gets its policies right, it will remain one of the most important members of the region. India is now already involved in the East Asia Summit, and its greater engagement with the region could be useful. The East Asia Summit, as a body dealing with strategic issues, should indeed be the right forum for India which has left its footprint in the region historically and because more will be expected of its participation in East Asia in the future. Learning from Europe, China, Japan and India should have more tolerance and magnanimity in their relations. If these three nations could put the historical resentments behind them and unite like Germany and France did, the Asian economic unification process would achieve velocity and gravity.

Within the regional structure Asians should be able to discover and solidify their common identity and become united step by step. Under the subsidiarity principle, Asians shall be able to repair the existing 'cultural fault lines' and manage the internal disputes and conflicts. If subsidiarity is applied as a main principle of the unification process it can help to improve the relations among Asian nations and contribute to a removal of the social obstacles in the process. An open and democratic regional unification process might not bring a final solution to all existing disputes and conflicts that are occurring continuously amongst Asian nations.

However, this unification process may provide a dynamic platform for democratic exchanges and peaceful negotiations within the framework of international laws for the common good. It is generally agreed that national interests can find higher gratification and fulfilment in international coordination and cooperation and consequently the synergetic efficiency of all Asian nations can be increased. The tension between particular interests and regional or universal benefits will keep the unification process open-ended as a necessary condition for steady improvement. A regional unification even demands continuous incompleteness of any endeavour to keep development in a dialectical state for constructive opposition and consensus building.

5. CONCLUSION: THE PRINCIPLE OF SUBSIDIARITY, GLOBALIZATION AND REGIONALIZATION

It is clearly evidenced that at present the main driving force of Asian unification is governments and politicians in a top-down manner without any far-reaching participation of non-state actors. However, it may not be possible to achieve Asian unification without the participation of civil society. As a strategic approach the governments of the Asian nations should take effective measures to encourage and promote mass exchanges among civil society actors, including scholars, particularly among the younger generation, in order to improve the understanding and minimize the misunderstandings amongst Asian nations. It is encouraging to see that in the Trilateral Statement made by China, Japan and South Korea on 22 May 2011, one of the main contents is the promotion of people exchanges such as the Asian Campus Programme to facilitate student exchanges, the Future Forum for the exchange of young people and the Tourist Projects to increase the number of intra-regional tourists to 25 million visitors by 2025. Step by step Asia shall be unified, but with a decentralised system of local and regional actors to cope with issues and problems in self-reliant ways using subsidiarity as a guiding principle. A unified Asia may open up to new markets, opportunities and avenues of social and economic upward mobility, transcending the spaces of the region.

Asia is experiencing new pressures for transformation from three forces: globalization and regionalization as well as democratisation. Yet it is also burdened with unresolved issues left over from its past. The world's last two remaining divided nations (China and Korea) need to find peaceful ways to create mutual understanding and cooperation.

Since it was possible for Germany to reunify in the course of European unification, it is also possible for China and Korea to be unified peacefully one day in the Asian regional unification process. If East Asia continues to grow with China, Japan and India driving its development – with an axle function performed by the ASEAN – it will indeed become the most important region of the globe and the balance of power will certainly shift. It is suggested that East Asia eventually could become like the European Union, which has a common currency, market and institutions to facilitate trade and even security policies. A shift from 'Pax Americana' to 'Pax Asia-Pacifica' could well be the answer. In time, only a cooperative Asian security system can replace the present US security umbrella (Ramos 2004).

It can be concluded that the economic barriers in Asia could be removed one by one in the process of economic integration, whereas the social obstacles have to be removed by applying the principle of subsidiarity, that is, the bottom-up democratic approach which should go hand-in-hand with top-down political initiatives. Resolving existing disputes do not only require the intelligence and consciousness of politicians, but also wide and positive participation by the Asian civil societies. A regional unification needs economic activities but also social and political activities. However, only the social and political activities can take regional integration to a higher level. Asians shall be able to repair the 'cultural fault lines' and to manage the prevailing internal disputes and conflicts. The subsidiarity principle can help Asian nations to remove the social obstacles that stand in the way of a united Asia. A unified Asia, along with the EU and US, forming the main poles of a truly multi-polar global order, would enable Asian nations to exercise sustainable control of their regional social, economic, cultural and political environment in a balanced manner of globalisation and regionalisation.

NOTE

1. See Article 3b of the Maastricht treaty and Article 5 of the Amsterdam treaty.

REFERENCES

Economy, E. (2005) 'China's rise in Southeast Asia: implications for the United States', *Journal of Contemporary China*, **14**(14), 409–25.

Frank, A.G. (1998), *Reoriented: Economic Globalization in Asian Age*, San Francisco, CA: University of California Press.

Greenwood, C.L. (2011), 'Asian Development Bank Annual Report, 2011', *Star of the Securities*, **19**, 44–7.
Huntington, S.P. (1999), 'Cultures in the 21st century: conflicts and convergences', keynote address at the Colorado College 125th Anniversary Symposium, pp. 7–8.
Huntington, S.P. (1996), *The Clash of Civilizations and Remaking the World Order*, New York: Simon and Schuster.
Kumar, N. (2007), 'Relevance of broader regional economic integration in Asia and a roadmap', in N. Kumar, K. Kesavapany and C. Yao (eds), *Asia's New Regionalism and Global Role*, Singapore: ISEAS Publisher.
Ramos, F. (2004), 'The price of Asian conflict', *Asian Economy*, **56**(4), 34–6.
Rolly, H. (1996), 'On belonging together and being different', in M.K. Raha and H. Rolly (eds), *Dimensions of Human Society and Culture*, New Delhi: Sage.
Rusciano, F.L. (2011), 'Civilizations don't clash, but the exploiters do', *Timur Kocaoglu*, **87**(12), 89–101.
Stephenson, S. (2011), 'Evaluating the contributions of RTAs to governance of services trade', *The Washington Quarterly*, **34**(3), 12–14.
Twining, D. (2010), 'Democratic partnership in Asia', *Policy Review*, October–November, 5–7.
Twining, D. (2011), 'Political reform: China's next modernization?', *Harvard Business Review*, January–February, 13–15.
Wanand, J. (2008), 'East Asian regionalism and global governance', in J. Wanand and T. Yamamoto (eds), *East Asia at a Crossroads*, Tokyo: Japan Centre for International Exchange, pp. 19–37.

7. Asia shaping the Group of 20 or the Group of 20 shaping Asia?

Hugo Dobson

1. INTRODUCTION

Although in existence since 1999 at the finance ministerial level, the upgrading of the Group of 20 (G20) to the leaders' level in November 2008 captured popular, media and academic attention. More recently, however, the abatement of the initial excitement surrounding the G20's emergence as the self-appointed 'premier forum for international economic cooperation' (as announced at the 2009 Pittsburgh Summit) and its reversion in 2011 to an annual, rather than semi-annual, event means that now is an opportune time to take stock of its impact, role, development and effectiveness, in addition to the division of labour amongst the 'Gaggle of Gs' and 'messy multilateralism' that now constitutes the architecture of global governance. So far, six G20 summits at the leaders' level have taken place: Washington (November 2008), London (April 2009), Pittsburgh (September 2009), Toronto (June 2010), Seoul (November 2010) and Cannes (November 2011). While finance ministers continue to meet regularly throughout the year, the next G20 leaders' summit at the time of writing was scheduled for June 2012 in Los Cabos, Mexico.

Within the ever-expanding literature on the G20, one focus of attention has been the new participants in G-summitry that are seen to provide the long sought-after legitimacy that the Group of 7/8 (G7/8) struggled with.[1] In particular, Asia's expanded membership has attracted attention; alongside Japan, as an original member of the G7/G8, the new additions are Australia, China, Indonesia, India and South Korea, giving rise to another alphanumeric configuration of the Asian Six (A6).[2]

The precedent that exists for giving Asia a voice within G-summitry is Japan's self-appointed role as Asia's representative within the G7/G8 since 1975. However, in a number of ways, expanded Asian representation within the G20 has increasingly made Japan's role an anachronism. First of all, the leaders of Australia, China, India, Indonesia, Japan and

Korea have attended all six G20 summits so far (with the exception of Australia at the 2010 Toronto Summit due to Kevin Rudd's replacement with Julia Gillard). In addition, the chair of the Association of Southeast Asian Nations (ASEAN), for example Vietnam at the summits in 2010, and the Secretary-General of ASEAN have also been added to the G20's attendance list. Thus, in terms of the number of seats being occupied at the summit table, Asian and European representation is balanced, whereas in the G8 Europe dominates, and there is no more need for Japan to act as the regional representative.

One result of this is that the overall tone of much media and academic coverage has focused upon the catalytic effect that membership of the G20 might have upon Asian regionalism as the A6 are forced into coordination and cooperation in responding to the G20's agenda and commitments with the goal of giving Asia a greater voice at the summit. To this end, at the 15th ASEAN Summit in October 2009, the decision was made to create a G20 contact group, including ASEAN Secretary-General, Chair and Indonesia. In particular, in the lead-up to the Seoul Summit of November 2010 as the first G20 summit to be held in Asia, voices calling for a coordinated Asian response reached a crescendo.

For example, some have suggested that in light of Asian regionalist projects, we can be optimistic about the emergence of a regional sub-grouping in the G20 that will encourage 'regional integration to the next level' (Siregar and Irman 2010: 12). In a similar vein, others have argued that Asia is in a position of strength in the G20 and it is crucial that Asian countries must caucus to effectively promote a range of initiatives relevant to both regional and global governance (Carin and Heap 2010: 13–14). In addition, Rana (2010) has advocated formalising ASEAN membership within the G20 but without explaining how this will concretely be achieved and ignoring the inevitable tension between representation, legitimacy and effectiveness that results from making a crowded table even more crowded. Instead, Rana suggests that ASEAN+3 could meet before the G20 to coordinate positions but this ignores Australia and India, suggesting that ASEAN+6 would be a more appropriate forum. Finally Rana has suggested that Asian countries should work with the informal Singaporean-led Global Governence Group (3G), which seeks to represent smaller countries and ensure the UN is not eclipsed by the G20. This kind of outreach could be effective in strengthening the G20's legitimacy but will not necessarily make Asia's voice any louder or clearer. Other advocates place themselves somewhere between the two poles of advocating a full-blown Asian caucus and calling for minimal coordination in the G20 (Parello-Plesner 2009; Young 2009).

In contrast, Ito Takatoshi has struck a note of caution by arguing that 'Asia has not coordinated to maximize its effectiveness. But, one may wonder, is there a common agenda for Asia? Asian leaders should examine whether Asia collectively has anything to contribute to the global agenda, or an Asian agenda to press' (Ito 2010: 8–10). The chapter concurs with Ito's initial point and comes to pessimistic conclusions in answering his subsequent questions.

This conclusion stands in contrast to much of the literature on Asia's role in the G20 for the reason that the majority of it is normative and bears little relation to the actual development of the G20 and the nature of Asian countries' participation so far. Certainly Asia's numeric representation in the G20 has increased and China, Japan and South Korea did meet informally on the periphery of the G20 Washington Summit of November 2008 to increase their levels of bilateral currency swap agreements. However, evidence of actual coordination or cooperation similar to that of BRICS (Brazil, Russia, India, China and – from April 2011 – South Africa) is thin on the ground, especially as the initial sense of crisis that led to the upgrading of the G20 dissipates (Mo and Kim 2009). For example, the G20 was mentioned three times in the Japan–China–South Korea Trilateral Summit's Declaration of May 2011 in terms of promising coordination and compliance that has ultimately failed to materialise. In understanding why, this chapter highlights the concrete behaviours and motivations of the individual A6 in the six G20 summits so far and suggests that few attempts have been made to coordinate an Asian approach in G-summitry. On the one hand, what emerges are divergent agendas amongst the A6 as regards the future of the G20, mostly starkly represented by Japan that seeks to secure the continuation of the G8 whilst others seek to ensure its eclipse by the G20 and capitalise on their seats at the top table. On the other hand, a high degree of convergence is clear, as each country in the A6 has sought to carve out and claim the same identities and roles in the G20 whether as an innovator in global governance or bridge between the developed and developing worlds. This divergence and convergence can be seen across a range of other behaviours including responding to the norm of internationalism in promoting global governance, hard-nosed realist defence of the status quo and national interest, in addition to regional leadership. Finally, the shadow that the US hegemon casts over the G20 summits should not be forgotten. Not only is this the key challenge for global governance mechanisms like the G20, but each country, Asian or not, regards the summit as a forum in which it can manage its core bilateral relationship with the US.

2. INTERNATIONALISM AND INNOVATION IN GLOBAL GOVERNANCE

The first behaviour shared by a number of the A6 has been to respond to the norm of internationalism by acting as a responsible member of international society and seek to innovate in terms of global governance mechanisms. Australia represents one of the most salient examples of this, and the rise of the G20 has been cited as a significant foreign policy victory for Australia generally and former Prime Minister Kevin Rudd individually. Ahead of the Washington Summit, reports circulated claiming that the upgrading of the G20 to the leaders' level was Rudd's initiative, communicated to, and originally resisted by, President George W. Bush in a telephone conversation.[3] A year later, another newspaper claimed that after the Pittsburgh Summit the rise of the G20 was both 'a major win for Australia and developing nations that have pushed hard for the broader body to reflect the shift in power to the developing world', and for Kevin Rudd 'the culmination of a nearly two-year campaign to convince larger nations to support the broader body, which includes China, India, Brazil, Indonesia and other developing nations'.[4]

The reasons for Australia's enthusiastic response to the G20 can be explained by Rudd's personal ambitions (and G-summitry is characterised by the emphasis it places on the input of individual leaders and the interpersonal relationships they construct). However, it can also be explained as a long-standing normative driver in Australian foreign policy as highlighted by Michael Fullilove, 'the one foreign policy theme that has united our otherwise diverse post-war prime ministers has been the desire to join (and, if necessary, erect and strengthen) institutions through which Australia can influence international decisions and touch the international flows of power' (Fullilove 2010). This strong proclivity is evident in Gillard's recalling of Australia's heads of G20 diplomatic missions in order to articulate her position: 'it's not the Australian way to stand on the sidelines when we've got something to contribute . . . We are internationalist by instinct. We believe in multilateral forums . . . through Australian eyes we see the G20 as a serious strategic opportunity, not just for us but for the global economy'.[5] This was also seen as part of Gillard's effort to secure the role of G20 host in 2014.[6] Thus, as part of a continuum from ANZUS (Australia–New Zealand–United States) to APEC and beyond, the G20 would appear to demonstrate that 'Australia is going global'.

Australia has backed this 'vision' up with performance. One concrete measure of internationalism is compliance with the pledges made at G20 summits. According to compliance studies conducted by the G20 Research Group at the University of Toronto, one increasingly salient outcome is the difference in compliance between G8 members of the G20 and new members, with the former scoring higher than the latter. However, Australia bucks this trend by ranking highly overall and the highest of newcomers to G-summitry (G20 Information Centre 2011).

Similarly, South Korea and Japan have demonstrated internationalist impulses and the desire to innovate. The Koreans were the first Asian and non-G8 hosts of a G20 summit and seized the opportunity to make clear their leadership qualifications. Sakong Il, Chair of the Presidential Committee for the G20, stated that '[t]he G20 members, especially the G7, know we'll be more than willing to lead. Leadership doesn't mean working alone. Leadership means getting harmony, getting cooperation and getting support'.[7] To this end, South Korea sought to ensure the G20 lived up to previous commitments on issues that were inherited from previous summits such as reform of the IMF, banking regulations and the ongoing Doha Development Agenda (DDA); progress was achieved on some (reform of IMF voting rights), although there was little or no momentum on others such as concluding the DDA. In addition, little progress was made on exchange rates but South Korea sought to shape the future agenda of the G20 by promoting development as an issue for discussion at the G20.

As regards innovation, South Korea was also conscious of the fact that after Seoul, the G20 would revert to an annual summit process and thus it was presented with a chance to shape the G20 before it metamorphosed from crisis to steering committee. Thus, it has promoted initiatives like the Business 20 meeting of global CEOs and engaged in a number of outreach activities with non-G20 countries and international and regional organisations. In terms of compliance, South Korea's performance has improved in direct response to the Seoul Summit to become one of the most compliant countries of the new additions to the G20 alongside Australia. As will be demonstrated below, hosting the Seoul Summit was a key event in motivating South Korea.

Japan has similarly sought to demonstrate its internationalist credentials. It did not follow the 17 countries and regions (including China and Indonesia) that introduced protective measures after the 2008 Washington Summit despite their leaders' promises. Prime Minister Aso Taro spearheaded the provision of assistance to the IMF with US$100 billion and the plan of doubling member countries' contributions to the IMF's general fund from US$320 billion. Japan's contribution in these terms has been described as 'unmatched . . . China followed while Japan led' (Kirton 2009: 7). This can be seen in Japan's tradition of innovation in G-summitry, for example by creating a time and space for the Group of 5 (G5) of Brazil, China, India, South Africa and Mexico to meet independently and with the G8 at the 2008 Hokkaido–Toyako Summit as G13, in addition to a G16 that included Australia, Indonesia and South Korea to work towards reductions in emissions. Finally, according to compliance studies, Japan ranks highly. However, as will be discussed below, Japan's internationalist and innovative tendencies within the G20 specifically have been tempered by more hard-nosed realist motivations.

India is no newcomer to G-summitry having attended G8 summits as a member of the G5 with qualified status until the G20 was promoted to the leaders' level in 2008. India clearly gets the recognition in the G20 that it has demanded and not received in the G8's outreach and dialogue processes, and Prime Minister Manmohan Singh has attended all six G20 summits, whilst operating from a position of strength as India's economy proved to be relatively resilient during the crisis. As a result, India can claim a degree of impact on the G20's final declarations. For example, a great deal of similarity was noted between the Pittsburgh Summit's declaration and Singh's policy prescriptions on a range of issues including supporting financial institutions and coordinating exit strategies.[8] In addition, India could even claim the position of innovator in global governance as it was the India–EU Summit of 30 September 2008 in Marseille that represented one catalyst for the upgrading of the G20 to the leaders' level at Washington.

However, beyond this India has little to claim in terms of providing leadership. Its levels of compliance are low and Simon Cox has demonstrated that India is 'mostly indifferent to the G20', quoting Vijay Kelkar, a former IMF Executive Director, who stresses that India can do little at the present time to shape the international system (Cox 2010: 4).

Also standing in contrast to the leading internationalists and innovators of Australia, South Korea and Japan, Indonesia's behaviour has been circumspect. President Susilo Bambang Yudhoyono has attended all six summits and Indonesia has supported efforts to reinforce the role of the IMF, strengthen financial supervisory regulations and the establishment of a donor agency by developed countries similar in role to the IMF. It has chaired working groups on reform of the World Bank and the IFIs, and anti-corruption measures. Yudhoyono also highlighted climate change in his speeches at Pittsburgh and promoted food security at the World Economic Forum in Davos as a particular issue.[9] Thus, in some ways Indonesia has responded positively to the status it has been accorded through the membership of the G20. However, its low levels of compliance with G20 commitments suggest that this tentative activity is motivated and limited by other factors discussed below.

Finally, China traditionally demonstrated open hostility towards G-summitry by ignoring or dismissing its communiqués and emphasizing the legitimacy of the United Nations Security Council (UNSC). Since 2003 China has joined G8 summits as part of an enlarged dialogue meeting or as a member of the G5. However, the G20 meeting of finance ministers and central bank governors was regarded positively as, in the words of one leading Chinese economist, a 'timely gift for a Chinese government, which wishes to have closer cooperation with the G7/8 but does not want to be part of it for the time being' (cited in Chin 2010: 118). Since then, the upgrading of the G20 to the leaders' level and its self-appointment at the Pittsburgh Summit as 'the premier forum for international economic cooperation' have also been positively welcomed by China and place it in a central position (G20 Information Centre 2009). However, beyond expressing support for further institutionalisation by creating, and even hosting, a permanent secretariat, China has done little to shape the work of the G20, has not always complied with commitments, and as will be seen below has been motivated by more realist concerns.

3. STATUS AND STATUS QUO

There is a strong tendency within the A6 towards protecting the new-found and hard-fought status within the G20, although this is expressed differently. In the case of Australia, a degree of status anxiety is evident. Australia's media reported a secret memo leaked from the UK's Foreign and Commonwealth Office ahead of the 2009 London Summit that designated Australia, along with Canada, Mexico and Russia, as 'second division' countries, whilst 'high-priority states' were the US, France, China, India and Saudi Arabia.[10] Similarly, one Australian diplomat described the G20 as: 'potentially the most significant new diplomatic initiative in the world since the founding of the United Nations', but stressed that 'Australia is lucky to be a part of it – if the forum is to last beyond the financial crisis of the past few years and Australia is to keep a spot at the top table, that place must be earned'.[11] Thus, degrees of not only internationalism but also developmentalism are evident in motivating Australia's participation within the G20. A similar status anxiety can be seen as one of the underlying motivations behind South Korea's efforts to reinforce its claim to a seat at the top table of summitry, especially when doubts had been expressed previous to the Seoul Summit as to its qualifications to lead (Japanese Prime Minister Kan Naoto and Finance Minister Noda Yoshihiko providing two vocal critics).

When drawing up the membership of the G20 finance ministers meeting in 1999, it was decided that Indonesia would be invited at the expense of Thailand. In short, 'Thailand was the nexus of the Asian banking crisis, but Indonesia was more influential in the region. Indonesia in; Thailand out'.[12] Although hardly equitable, this demonstrates that membership of the G20 can be arbitrary and suffers from the legitimacy problems that beset the G8. In any case, Indonesia's participation is based on this recognition by other powers that Indonesia is an important regional power, as well as a growing economy, and provides greater legitimacy for the G20 in terms of geographical, political, cultural and religious representation.

Participation in G-summitry is nothing new but in the G20 process, Yudhoyono has not lost any opportunity to emphasise Indonesia's newfound status and arrival on the world stage. Ahead of the Seoul Summit, he declared that with Indonesia's membership of the G20 it was now 'world class' and envisioned world power status in the near future.[13] To this end, Indonesia wants the G20 to be a permanent institution: 'an economic and civilizational powerhouse' in Yudhoyono's words, which ultimately promotes Indonesia's position in the world and its claims to stand alongside the BRIC countries to form BRICI, whilst allowing it to carve out a role for itself as a spokesperson for the developing world and a bridge between it and the developed world (roles that are also being claimed by other A6 countries, as discussed below) (Chin 2010: 112–14). However, Yudhoyono's ultimate goal is for Indonesia to grasp this opportunity and become 'a regional power with a global impact'.[14]

China has been probably the most high-profile member of the upgraded G20 summit and is the rising power that all other summiteers want to court. However, its participation appears to be concerned with status as its previous misgivings towards the G8 evaporate now that it is centre-stage in the G20. As regards its concrete role in the G20, rather modest assessments have characterised China's role stressing its position as a developing country lacking in capabilities and willingness (Tu 2009: 50). On specific issues, China has come forward with specific proposals. For example, ahead of the G20 London Summit, Zhou Xiaochuan, Governor of the People's Bank of China, received praise for his promotion of Special Drawing Rights (SDRs) as the new international reserve currency in place of the dollar. Zhou has also suggested reforms of the IFIs but only ones that tinker with the system and hardly express China's long-term normative vision. China's contributions to the G20 have not only been modest but also opaque and driven by national interest (for example, ensuring that Hong Kong and Macao were not classified as tax havens and breaking G20 pledges on anti-protectionist measures). Thus, China's newfound relationship with the G20 is hardly an epiphany and strong doubts linger. For example, the effectiveness of an expanded and *ad hoc* forum where 20 leaders meet around a crowded table and have only ten minutes each to have their say has been questioned by China, as has the legitimacy of the G20 with some voices dubbing it a 'transitional mechanism', instead placing continued emphasis on the role of the more formalised and legalised institutions such as the UN as the legitimate architecture of global governance, and even going so far as to suggest the creation of an Economic Security Council within the UN that would essentially be doing the work of the G20 but within the more legitimate framework of the UN (Chin 2010: 118–19). China's recent assertive reactions to bilateral issues with Japan and regional security have suggested a hard-nosed realism that leads analysts to wonder what kind of collective, collaborative behaviour can be expected from China in fora like the G20.

In contrast, although Japan is concerned with status, this is by maintaining the status quo as represented by the G8. As a latecomer denied a permanent seat on the United Nations Security Council (UNSC), the G8 holds a special position in Japan's international relations as it has been recognised as an original member since the inception of the summit process in 1975. In addition, it has instrumentalised the summit to demonstrate its role as a responsible member of international society and has adopted the role of representative of Asia within these chiefly European and North American gatherings. In terms of status, identity and acceptance, the G8 has mattered to Japan and this has been evident in mediating its actions within the G20. Whilst demonstrating its commitment to a concert approach to the global economic and financial crisis through the G20, as outlined above, Japan has also sought to avoid the institutionalisation of the G20, especially at the expense of the G8, and ensure that the latter is not consigned to the history books. This can be seen in various prime ministers' statements before and after the summit from Aso, who declared in 2009 that 'Japan believes that the importance of the G8 has increased', to Hatoyama Yukio, who declared later that year that 'the G8 should not be discarded [and making the G20 the premier forum] does not make the G8 irrelevant', through to Kan, who wrote that 'the importance of the G8, underpinned by a shared sense of fundamental values such as freedom and democracy, remains unchanged' (Kan 2010).[15]

3. BRIDGING DEVELOPED AND DEVELOPING COUNTRIES

A third role within the G20 over which members of the A6 converge in seeking to claim is that of a 'bridge' between the developed and developing countries. In the case of South Korea, this role was central to its preparation and hosting of the first Asian G20 Summit. President Lee Myun-Buk had been advocating development as an agenda item for the G20 for some time previous to Seoul and at Pittsburgh was already carving out a bridging role for South Korea (Lee 2009). Sakong Il stressed that the living memory of South Korea's developmental experience, from the Korean War through to membership of the OECD and financial crisis in the 1990s, qualified it to play this bridging role (Sakong 2009). Hosting the G20 allowed it play this role to an extent but never at the expense of securing other successful summit outcomes.

In the case of India and Indonesia, both countries have regarded themselves as in a position to play this role. On the one hand, Director-General of the Federation of Indian Chambers of Commerce and Industry, Rajiv Kumar, highlighted India's duty at the Seoul Summit was to 'bring sanity back' to the G20 summit process and make the world's leaders realise that 'we're in it together, and we sink or swim together', suggesting a bridging role in attempting to bring back the cohesion that was seen to characterise the initial crisis-triggered summits.[16] India's strength in this position is a result of its relatively strong performance through the crisis, thereby allowing it the opportunity to promote reform of the World Bank and IMF and even lead the developing countries.[17] Although India has claimed this identity, as mentioned above, it has failed to back this up with concrete action.

On the other hand, Yudhoyono was more successful in advocating a widely cast invitation at the initial Washington Summit and protecting the developing nations through a Global Expenditure Support Fund to ensure their continued growth. These efforts continued at the London Summit within discussions of the reform of the IFIs and the specific assistance that developing and poor countries required. Thus, motivated by a worsening situation at home in terms of its ability to meet debt repayments, Indonesia played a central role in the G20's decision at London to shift funds from the IMF and World Bank to regional development banks, particularly the Asian Development Bank (Chin 2010: 112–14).

4. REGIONAL LEADERSHIP

What is obvious by its absence has been Japan's traditional role of Asia's representative. Japan is now one of six Asian participants, with attention particularly focused on China but South Korea as well. Japan lost in its bids to host the first G20 Summit in Asia to South Korea and subsequently its response has been to question China and Korea's ability to provide leadership thereby creating tensions, rather than cooperation, amongst Asia's representatives.

In fact it is Australia who can probably boast the best record amongst the A6 for seeking to promote a regional response. Australia's Department of Foreign Affairs and Trade advocates outreach to non-G20 members, especially within its regional neighbours, and holds regular meetings to this end.[18] Again, this appears to have been driven initially by Rudd, particularly as part of the broader Asia-Pacific Community initiative that embraces the Asia Pacific countries 'to engage across the breadth of the security, economic and political challenges we will face in the future' and seeks to create 'an overarching and effective regional architecture, and engendering a stronger sense of the need for a region-wide will to work and plan cooperatively and in as coordinated a fashion as possible' (Frost 2009). Similarly, Australian Foreign Minister Stephen Smith has placed the emphasis much more on AP10 than the A6 in the G20 as 'a political driver of stronger global cooperation and governance, responding to the range of global challenges that will confront us in this the Asia-Pacific century'. The focus of this proposal is not East Asia, or Southeast Asia, but Asia-Pacific.[19] However, in her above-mentioned speech, Gillard only mentioned Asia Pacific once and stressed a role for the East Summit in implementing the G20's agenda in terms of regional financial stability. Thus, there is the question of which region Australia wants to promote in the G20.

Indonesia is similarly conflicted. Its traditional constituency is as a spokesperson for ASEAN (despite the recent participation of ASEAN in its own right) and a representative of developing countries and non-G20 countries. However, the question is whether it wants to continue to play the role of ASEAN's spokesperson or has it outgrown this role and now sees itself as an independent power, unconstrained by its membership of ASEAN and standing alongside the BRICs as emerging powers. Advocates of a post-ASEAN foreign policy welcome Indonesia's membership of the G20 as an opportunity to press ahead with an independent foreign policy and that 'Indonesia should free itself from an undeserving obligation to follow the wishes of any state or grouping of states, including ASEAN, if by doing so we sacrifice our own national interests' (cited in Desker 2010). However, in contrast, at the 15th ASEAN Summit in October 2009, Yudhoyono tried to assuage concerns that 'Indonesia has a new club, new home, namely G20 [and] will no longer make ASEAN its main home', by stressing the importance of ASEAN.[20] To this end, he did suggest at the Pittsburgh Summit that the rotating chair of ASEAN be invited. Thus, it is unclear which group Indonesia wishes to be identified with, and beyond the rhetoric its role has been concerned more with its own interests than regional coordination.[21]

In contrast, India has done little to promote an Asian position at the G20. Any discussion of groups and identities has been framed within possible divisions in the G20 between debtor and creditor countries, and India sought to paper over the cracks at Seoul in order to maintain harmony and we-ness within the group. In a similar vein, South Korea has responded to a range of domestic, bilateral and internationalist audiences in seeking to ensure the success of the G20. However, one outcome of this was Korea's avoidance of coordinating too closely with its Asian G20 partners for fear of creating a caucus that might stymie and fracture the work of the G20. In other words, it appears as if South Korea sacrificed any ambitions to regional leadership ambitions for global leadership in order to burnish its image at home and abroad as firmly positioned at the centre of global governance and international summitry.

5. HANDLING THE HEGEMON

Membership of the G20 process provides countries with the opportunity to manage their most important bilateral relationships, either with the traditional hegemonic US or with a rising China. On this most basic level, Indonesia has used the G20 summit as an opportunity for conducting meetings on the periphery of the summit to manage its relationships with both these countries. India and Japan have used the opportunity for their respective leaders to meet Obama for the first time as part of a 'getting to know you' exercise.

As host of the Seoul Summit, South Korea's actions in the G20 exhibited a stronger bilateral flavour. Lee attempted to instrumentalise the summit as part of a wider redefinition of the US–ROK relationship into a range of different areas that include economic, social, cultural, scientific and technological cooperation. In this context, the Seoul Summit was identified (although ultimately unsuccessfully) as the deadline for the conclusion of a Korean–US Free Trade Agreement (Snyder 2009).

For Australia, the bilateral aspect of multilateralism represents a balancing act that has resulted in mixed messages. On the one hand, Paul Dibb (2009), former Deputy Secretary of Defence, argued that 'the global financial crisis will hasten the relative decline of America and improve China's status. That simple statement in itself reflects the crucial geopolitical nature of this global financial crisis for Australia'. However, at the same time, Australia does not want to be seen to be too close to China as was evidenced in Rudd's sensitivity to accusations of his privileging the relationship with China at the expense of the US. This even manifested itself in Rudd avoiding being seated next to the Chinese ambassador to Britain, a long-standing friend, on a BBC news programme ahead of the London Summit.[22]

6. CONCLUSION

Reviewing the position of each country in the A6, Australia has been one of the most proactive countries in advocating revision of the architecture of global governance and coordinating an Asian response therein. However, there are questions as regards how far it will promote these changes, in what form and to what end? In the case of China, it probably means more to the G20 than the G20 means to China. What the G20 means to China can be understood in terms of recognition, rather than as an opportunity to provide global, let alone regional, leadership. India has shown little inclination to lead or contribute to the G20's work. Indonesia's concerns revolve around moving from the regional to global level but it continues to suffer from domestic problems that have the potential to undermine this ambition. For Japan, the emergence of the G20 has presented a challenge rather than an opportunity. It has worked towards the success of the G20 as the 'premier forum for international economic cooperation', even demonstrating a leadership role on occasions, whilst displaying a reactionary preference for the G8 and the status that goes with membership of this more select grouping. Finally, South Korea's participation in the G20 is an opportunity to demonstrate its ability to provide leadership in global governance, particularly in the face of a number of doubters before the Seoul Summit, and burnish President Lee's domestic legacy. Little room was left for a regional leadership role, which was notable by its absence from the Korean host's efforts.

Thus, the picture painted in this chapter is one of not only, but predominantly, national interest shaping the participation of the Asian members of the G20 so far. There is no common agenda and no caucus. Rather, fragmentation amongst the A6 can be seen both in participation, which has been largely unilateral, uncoordinated and driven by national interest/status anxiety, and on the issue of the evolving architecture of global governance, where there appears to be little agreement on the legitimacy, effectiveness and future of the G20. As regards identities and roles within the G20, it appears to be a case of too many cooks spoiling the broth as countries jockey for the position of innovator in global governance, representative of the developing world and bridge with the developed world.

One question that emerges is whether the existing institutional arrangements are sufficient for Asia, or any region, to have its voice heard at the G20. In thinking about these questions, we can refer to Huigens and Niemann's definition (2009) of actorness using the criteria of 'recognition', 'authority', 'autonomy' and 'cohesion', and it would appear from the above analysis that the A6 is weak in all of these criteria. In any case, the G20's record in supporting these elements of actorness is patchy. To encourage regionalism and inter-regionalism, the G20 would have to invite the leaders and the respective regional hubs. It seems to cover some bases – the EU, North and South America, East, South and Southeast Asia – but membership of an elite club – a top-down, exclusive, hierarchical rather than bottom-up form of multilateralism – is not conducive to developing regional identity. Also, some of the choices of regional representatives are contentious – why South Africa and not Nigeria as the only African representative, and why Saudi Arabia and not Egypt for the Middle East? Finally, the focus so far on the decisions surrounding the G20's membership has been placed on its role not as a bridge between regions but a bridge between developed and developing countries.

There is also the question of what role might be played by non-G20 Asian countries. For example, Singapore has played a proactive role in attempting to shape the G20 and enhance its legitimacy by giving voice to the non-G20 countries of the world through its 3G initiative. Its leadership within this pressure group has centred upon strengthening the position of the UN and other multilateral bodies, whilst promoting a 'variable geometry' in the way in which the G20 makes decisions across different sectors in which non-G20 countries have a stake (Chowdhury 2010). However, this represents a somewhat tautological position, as these traits are at the heart of the G20 process, as outlined in Paul Martin's original proposal (Martin 2005). So, what is motivating Singapore to take a position that is self-evident and already embedded in G-summitry? It appears to be seeking to carve out a similar middle-man, bridging role as some of the other Asian countries that have secured a seat at the top table.

Looking ahead to future summitry, the six pillars of the French G20 presidency: reducing imbalances and fostering economic coordination, reforming the international monetary system, tackling commodity price volatility, improving financial regulation, contributing to development and fighting against corruption are likely to reappear at future summits as 'legacy issues', in addition to which new issues will be added as part of the Mexican G20 presidency in 2012. In this context, there is much that an A6 can contribute. However, it is also becoming increasingly clear that the G20 lacks the ideological glue that binds a smaller group like the G8 together, and this is equally true of the A6. In the absence of a sense of 'group-ness' or 'together-ness', the more likely outcome is a 'variable geometry' or constantly shifting coalition of countries on specific issues.

NOTES

1. The G8 consists of Canada, the EU, France, Germany, Italy, Japan, Russia, the UK and the US (66 per cent of global economic output but only 14 per cent of population);

the G20 includes the G8 plus Argentina, Australia, Brazil, China, India, Indonesia, Mexico, Saudi Arabia, South Africa, South Korea and Turkey (accounting for 90 per cent of global output and 67 per cent of population).

2. If one were to include the four other G20 members from the Asia-Pacific region (Canada, Mexico, Russia and the US), this would constitute an AP10. Although the Asia Pacific Economic Cooperation (APEC) forum has supported the G20's role and recommendations in securing growth, comparatively little attention has been placed on such a configuration within the G20. However, this chapter will refer to it where relevant.
3. *The Australian*, 30 October 2008.
4. *The Age*, 26 September 2009.
5. Speech to the G20 Heads of Mission Dinner, 20 March 2011. Available online at: http://www.pm.gov.au/press-office/speech-g20-heads-mission-dinner (visited on 7 July 2011).
6. *The Sydney Morning Herald*, 23 March 2011.
7. *Wall Street Journal*, 28 May 2009.
8. *The Times of India*, 27 September 2009.
9. *Agence France-Presse*, 28 January 2011.
10. *The Financial Times*, 13 March 2009.
11. *The Age*, 23 March 2011.
12. *The Globe and Mail*, 18 June 2010.
13. *Jakarta Globe*, 13 October 2010.
14. *The Economist*, 31 March 2010.
15. 'A Japan–Europe Partnership to Surmount Global Challenges', 5 May 2009. Available online at: http://www.kantei.go.jp/foreign/asospeech/2009/05/05speech_e.html (visited on 30 June 2011); 'Press Conference by Prime Minister Yukio Hatoyama following his attendance at meetings at the United Nations and the Pittsburgh G20 Summit', 25 September 2009. Available online at: http://www.kantei.go.jp/foreign/hatoyama/statement/200909/25naigai_e.html (visited on 30 June 2011).
16. *The Wall Street Journal*, 10 October 2010.
17. *The Wall Street Journal*, 25 June 2010.
18. Australian Government Department of Foreign Affairs and Trade (2011) 'The G20'. Available online at: http://www.dfat.gov.au/trade/g20/index.html (visited on 30 June 2011).
19. 'Asia Pacific: Toward a 21st Century Community', 3 December 2009. Available online at: http://www.foreignminister.gov.au/speeches/2009/091203_asia-pac.html (visited on 7 July 2011).
20. *The Star*, 26 October 2009.
21. *The Jakarta Post*, 3 April 2009.
22. *The Age*, 31 March 2009.

REFERENCES

Carin, B. and P. Heap (2010), 'Asians can think: a time for Asian leadership', *East Asia Forum Quarterly*, **2**(4), 13–14.

Chin, G. (2010), 'The emerging countries and China in the G20: reshaping global economic governance', *Studia Diplomatica*, **63**(2), 105–23.

Chowdhury, I.A. (2010), 'The Global Governance Group (3G) and Singaporean leadership: can small be significant?', ISAS working paper no. 108, 19 May.

Cox, S. (2010), 'India in the G20: enjoy the silence', in Anon (ed.), *India in the G20: Macroeconomic Policy Coordination, Regulation and Global Governance*, London and Delhi: Centre for Economic Policy Research and National Council of Applied Economic Research.

Desker, B. (2010), 'Is Indonesia outgrowing ASEAN?', *RSIS Commentaries*, 29 September.
Dibb, P. (2009), 'Geopolitical implications of the global financial crisis', *East Asian Forum*, 30 March, accessed 7 July 2011 at www.tinyurl.com/67lzolg.
Frost, F. (2009), 'Australia's proposal for an "Asia Pacific Community": issues and prospects', Parliament of Australia Parliamentary Library research paper no. 13 2009–10.
Fullilove, M. (2010), 'With friends in high places: Australia's G20 membership', Brookings Institute, 13 March, accessed 6 July at www.brookings.edu/opinions/2010/0313_australia_fullilove.aspx.
G20 Information Centre (2009), 'G20 leaders' statement', University of Toronto, accessed 16 August 2011 at www.g20.utoronto.ca/2009/2009communique0925.html.
G20 Information Centre (2011), 'G20 analysis', University of Toronto, accessed 16 August at www.g20.utoronto.ca/analysis/index.html.
Huigens, J. and A. Niemann (2009), 'The EU within the G8: A Case of Ambiguous and Contested Actorness', May, College of Europe Department of EU International Relations and Diplomacy Studies EU diplomacy papers.
Ito, T. (2010), 'Towards a new world financial architecture', *East Asia Forum Quarterly*, **2**(4), 8–10.
Kan, N. (2010), 'Japan's responsibilities: the G8, the G20 and APEC', in M. Koch and J. Kirton (eds), *G20: The Pittsburgh Summit*, London: Newsdesk.
Kirton, J. (2009), 'A committed contributor: Japan in G8 and G20 governance', April/May, accessed 28 January 2011 at www.g7.utoronto.ca/scholar/kirton-japan-sheffield.pdf.
Lee, M. (2009), 'Pittsburgh: bridging the Washington–London G20 summits and beyond', in M. Koch and J. Kirton (eds), *G20: The Pittsburgh Summit*, London: Newsdesk.
Martin, P. (2005), 'A global answer to global problems: the case of a new leaders' forum', *Foreign Affairs*, **84**(3), 2–6.
Mo, J. and C. Kim (2009), 'Power and responsibility: can east Asian leadership rise to the challenge?', September, HGCY working paper series.
Parello-Plesner, J. (2009), 'KIA – Asia's middle powers on the rise?', *East Asia Forum*, 10 August, accessed 21 April 2011 at http://tinyurl.com/3ptexw3.
Rana, Praduma B. (2010), 'How can Asia raise its pitch at G20', *China Daily*, 6 July.
Sakong, I. (2009), 'Korea and the G20 summit next November', *East Asia Forum*, 22 November, accessed 30 June 2011 at www.tinyurl.com64zxp5n.
Siregar, M. and T.W. Irman (2010), 'The global agenda: a bigger role for Asia', *East Asia Forum Quarterly*, **2**(4), 11–12.
Snyder, S. (2009), 'Korean leadership in the G20 and the US–ROK alliance', *East Asia Forum*, 30 September, accessed 7 July, 2011 at www.tinyurl.com/5uxfyka.
Tu, X. (2009), 'China: a revisionist rather than a revolutionist', in M. Koch and J. Kirton (eds), *G20: The Pittsburgh Summit*, London: Newsdesk.
Young, S. (2009), 'The case for an East Asian caucus on global governance', *East Asia Forum*, 24 April, accessed 21 April 2011 at http://tinyurl.com/dm8hhm.

8. From G8 to G20: a shift of the dynamics of global economic governance?

Hong Yousheng and Fang Qing

1. INTRODUCTION

If the Group of 7/8(G7/G8) has been a major mechanism of the global economic governance (GEG) since it was formed in 1975 by the Western advanced countries, then the Group of 20(G20), with membership of both them and the emerging economies, has now become the premier forum of global economic co-operation rather than merely a temporary arrangement as it was first conceived in the aftermath of the 2008/09 global financial crisis. This evolution from G7/8 to G20 has brought about important shifts in GEG dynamics, not just to accommodate the rising influence of emerging powers like China but also geographically, from the Atlantic region to the Asia-Pacific (Elek 2010). What both the incumbent G7/8 members and new members of the G20 configuration have in mind for the evolving purpose and influence of this new global governance structure is of great importance. For example, will the United States continue its support of the G20 as 'a new and less hierarchical approach to global governance', or alternatively return to G8 for maintaining 'its hegemonic leadership role' (Alexandroff 2010: 45)? On the other hand, are the emerging economy members willing and able to co-ordinate their own standpoints in the G20 arena? The new Asia-Pacific G20 members of Indonesia, South Korea and Australia may play a key role here, as is discussed in this chapter.

2. THE UNITED STATES, EUROPE AND THE G20

The most salient characteristic of G20 is the emerging economies' participation in this core new GEG institution. However, is this vertical shift of the GEG dynamics represented by G20 a substantial change or just a temporary and superficial phenomenon? This depends not only on continuously increasing the power and governance capability of the emerging countries but also on whether this shift can be recognised, accepted and supported by the established developed countries, especially the US and the EU member states. The evolution from G8 to G8+O5 (Outreach Five Countries[1]), then to G20 was promoted by the US and Europe, which shows that both acknowledged that, in an ever globalising world, the influence of the emerging economies and the rising 'Global South' of developing nations generally can no longer be ignored. This was especially apparent in the 2008/09 global financial crisis, and applies to other pressing global challenges facing humanity in the early 21st century.

To both Europe and the US, the emergence of the G20 and its associated geopolitical structural shifts threaten to weaken Western power and influence. In French President Nicolas Sarkozy's 'relative power age' view, the major nation-state is no longer able to dominate the world as was the case in the past. Former British Prime Minister, Gordon Brown, argued that Europe should develop stronger collective capacities to influence the global governance agenda, arguing that only when Europe is open to the world can it shape wider multilateral co-operation on global issues. German Chancellor Angela Merkel's idea of creating an 'economic NATO' was seen by many as an attempt to consolidate Western geoeconomic power in the face of the declining developed country influence (Yuan 2009). However, such ideas of maintaining Western global hegemony are countered by European dissatisfaction with the US-dominated global financial system. Indeed, many European countries have recently shown their wish to co-operate more closely with the emerging economies to reshape world economic order within the existing framework of G20. For example, hosting nation France expects to include the reform of international monetary system in the agenda of the 2011 G20 Summit.[2]

While the US remains the world's most powerful country, its hegemonic position is under threat on various fronts (Beeson and Bell 2009). Two highly controversial wars in the 2000s (Afghanistan and Iraq), being the trigger for a major global financial crisis in 2008, and seeing a relative decline of its influence in various international arenas over the last decade has caused much self-reflection amongst US policy-makers and other decision-making elites. Global geopolitical shifts of power, the re-ascendance of China, and ensuing changes in the global agenda and accepted norms of international behaviour have all provided those in Washington with much food for thought. Despite its relative decline, the US still maintains strong capabilities for influencing global governance structures, both established and emerging. Moreover, the accommodation of new Asia-Pacific powers in the G20 presents the US with certain opportunities given it is still the pre-eminent great power in the region. It is also not possible for the G20 to advance substantially in any real direction without American support.

The G20 also provides a common opportunity for both the US and Europe to share their responsibility for providing global public goods to a broader international community where rising powers such as China, India and Brazil take on greater global responsibilities and duties (Wang and Cheng 2010). However, the scope for Western countries to use the G20 to serve their own specific national interests is likely to be limited. For example, the US ultimately failed to persuade other G20 members to impose the collective pressure on China to amend its 'managed' exchange rate system. Furthermore, Mahbubani (2010) has argued that Europe and the US should get used to the idea that the norms and ideas embodied in Western civilisation present only one of many options on which to found global governance in the 21st century. This is perhaps easier for Europe to accept than the United States, not least because the European Union does not have so many hegemonic positions to defend as the US, but also because to date Europe has shown itself relatively more open to G20-led reform of global governance systems and structures.

3. ASIAN MEMBERS OF THE G20: A 'FRAGMENTED' ASIA?

The G20 accommodates many new Asia-Pacific nations, and reflects the shift in global economic gravity further towards the region (Arrighi 2007). The six Asian G20 members – China, Japan, India, South Korea, Indonesia and Australia[3] – have the potential to make a significant impact within the group, however there is much disagreement amongst scholars concerning the matter. Ito (2010) argues that Asia is too fragmented and that: 'After so many years of under-representation in the International Monetary Fund, Asia has not co-ordinated to maximise its effectiveness. But, one may wonder, is there a common agenda for Asia?' (p. 10). Meanwhile, Carin and Heap (2010) contend that, with political gridlock in the US and feebleness in Europe, Asia and its natural allies in the G20 need to 'move into the policy vacuum and use G20 to institutionalize broader and more inclusive approaches to global decision-making' (p. 14). Yet their argument seems unrealistic because there is no 'revolutionary' amongst the G20 Asian members yet that is ready to subvert the existing international order. Moreover, as Hugo Dobson argues in his chapter, thus far Asian G20 members seem mostly preoccupied with using the Group as a platform on which to project their own national interests at this early stage. In terms of their motivations and policies towards G20, the six Asian members can be divided into three categories, each represented by China, Japan and South Korea (Tiberghien 2011).

The first category comprises China, India and Indonesia, what we may call the 'revisionists' in the current international order. As the rising regional powers, they wish to participate in the core GEG mechanisms and play important roles. Their contributions to the G20, however, are greatly restrained by some crucial factors such as their comprehensive strength, complex domestic situation, and relative lack of international governance experience. With specific regard to China, through carrying out a strategy of domestic market reform and 'opening-door' policies for more than 30 years, its economic transformation and growth trajectory has been staggering, and it is now standing as the world's second largest national economy. China is increasingly firmly regarded as a regional power, and we could argue that it has strong interests to take on global governance roles to consolidate its position as a global power. At the same time, the Chinese government has long insisted that China identity is still that of a developing country, with all the capacity constraints that infers when taking on global governance responsibilities. Beijing instead has chosen to afford top priority to the imperatives of domestic development and lifting more of China's citizens out of poverty. The G20 provides China with an opportunity to participate in GEG relatively equally with developed countries and other developing countries. At the same time, as the world's second largest economy and with more than US$3 trillion of foreign exchange reserves, China is expected to be a pivotal G20 player in the longer-term (Tiberghien 2011). China has already made important contributions here, for instance in the co-ordination of the members' policies to deal with the 2008/09 global financial crisis, and proposed new reform measures for the international monetary and financial systems. Still, China has attracted much criticism from Western scholars in particular, such as Alexandroff (2010) who labelled the nation a 'part-time' global leader that is, 'principally focused on its domestic development, and it remained reluctant to assume enhanced global responsibilities' (p. 45). In fact, there has been no real fundamental change of the Chinese government's position of keeping a low profile for the nation and declining a leadership in global governance (Liu 2010).

Japan represents the second category on its own. As a big economic power already well embedded within the GEG centre, Japan is a defender of the status quo and is resistant to the possibility of the G20 replacing the G8. However, Japan has been an active G20 player. As Kirton (2009) observed, 'In G20 as well as G8 governance, Japan thus remains a committed contributor and indeed a leader', and, 'Japan has proved to be a

G20 leader far more than China has' (pp. 6–8). Yet there is a bottom line to Japan's G20 interests according to Rathus (2011) who argues that, 'Japan is attempting to keep G20 as the *de facto* junior partner to G8'. Although then Japanese Prime Minister Yukio Hatoyama stated at the 2009 Pittsburgh G20 Summit that the Group had become a premier forum of global economic co-operation, he further stated that the G8 mechanism should not be abandoned. This position has been maintained by successive Japanese governments for four reasons: (i) it is easier to achieve results in G8 meetings rather than in the larger, diverse and hence more cumbersome G20; (ii) for a similar reason, the G8 is underpinned by a stronger shared sense of values, such as political liberty and democracy; (iii) the G8+O5 mechanism already allowed for dialogue between developed countries and developing countries; (iv) whilst major economic issues are discussed in G20 in principle, G8 has established precedents for additionally discussing political and security issues. From a regional perspective, Japan is further worried that a developed G20 at the G8's expense could possibly undermine its position as a world leader and Asia's principle representative in global governance forums. The G8 remains the most exclusive global club to which Japan belongs, unlike China not being a permanent member of the United Nations Security Council. Tokyo also tried to prevent the G20 from further institutionalising by opposing the proposal to establish a G20 secretariat supported by China. In this sense, Japan shares similar anxieties to Europe and the United States concerning a future strong G20 and the geopolitical implications that come with this.

South Korea and Australia comprise the third category within Asian G20 members. As developed economies, their attitudes and positions towards the Group lie between the above two categories. Whilst like China, India and Indonesia they are also 'revisionists' regarding the current international order, and desire to play an important role in G20 with strong aspirations to perform leadership roles, they have been reluctant to propose new ideas that may subvert the Western-dominated international system. Their middle-power status also makes them natural intermediary players. In the case of South Korea, its economic success has brought with it geopolitical influence, becoming a member of the Organisation for Economic Co-operation and Development (OECD) in 1996 in recognition of its development achievements since the early 1960s. Nevertheless, its international influence remains limited and in its regional context is rather overshadowed by the great power neighbours of China, Japan and Russia. However, the enhancing of the G20 status to summit level after the 2008/09 global financial crisis provided South Korea with new opportunities to raise its global profile, hosting the 2010 G20 Summit in Seoul. Il Sa-kong, Chairman of the 2010 Summit Co-ordination

Committee, remarked that 'Korea, as chair of G20 is supposed to lead the informal global economic steering committee for establishing the new global economic order and new global standards. For the first time, Korea is tasked to show its global leadership' (SQ Interview 2010: 88). South Korea's President Lee Myung-bak followed this up by stating that, 'It is now incumbent on the global community to translate the momentum that has been generated toward establishing a forum that can take a genuine global leadership role for longer-term issues. The Seoul Summit will play a decisive part in ensuring shared growth beyond crisis.'[4]

However, many Korean scholars are clearly conscious that there is not much room for South Korea to take the lead, considering its level of economic power and international status. As Kim (2010: 56–7) argued, as the host of the Seoul Summit, South Korea can 'play the role of mediator for the two most fundamentally confrontational groupings within G20', that is between the US-led developed country sub-set and the emerging economies sub-set, and simultaneously take advantage of its own geopolitical superiority to play a role of communicable bridge between the US and China. It is interesting that, compared with Japan who wants to continue its world leader and Asian leader roles, South Koreans do not show much desire to be an Asian leader but are eager to act as a world leader. This may explain too South Korea's reluctance to promote exclusive Asian co-ordination and co-operation within the G20.

In summary, each Asian G20 member has shown its own preference for doing things in its own way and they lack a co-ordination amongst them as well as a strong alignment of mutual interests. The G20's 'Asian moment' is therefore not expected by many analysts and the developed country elites still dominate this emerging GEG institution. As Tiberghien (2011) comments, this may be generally explained by 'weak regional institutionalization among the three Northeast Asian neighbours, and to the dominance of foreign policy considerations in the short-term (and foreign ministries) over economic considerations (and economic ministries)' (p. 4).

4. ASIA'S REGIONAL COOPERATION AND GEG

Asian members have hitherto pursued their own respective national interests in the G20 process, this being consistent with neo-realist expectations concerning state behaviour in global governance diplomacy. Yet globalising and other transnationalising forces, creating stronger interdependent linkages between states, have compelled them to pursue increasingly common goals through an expanding range and levels of international institutions. 'National interests' may thus be pursued through mutual co-operation and co-ordination amongst states. Therefore, the G20 may help advance GEG through its members putting forward proposals based on national interests. For example, all G20 members have a common interest in creating strong, sustainable and balanced growth in the world economy.

With this same principle in mind, it is possible for Asian G20 members to further their regional co-operation with the Group based on their respective national interests, and to play an increasingly important role in GEG as well as the reconstruction of world order in the future. Asia is characterised by its diversity and pluralism, and this obviously poses a challenge when speaking with one voice in G20 diplomacy. Such diversity is, of course, an issue at the world level with respect to find sufficient commonality to advance global governance. It is one of the G20's essential functions, moreover, to reflect different interests and desires, and co-ordinate diversified national interests and policies. At the same time, the formation of 'regional bloc' positions may actually work against the co-ordination of global economic policies, and could hinder the progress of GEG objectives. Thus, the GEG should not be based on regional blocs, and regional integration is not a necessary prerequisite for advancing global governance *per se*. Hence, Asian G20 members should try to effectively promote GEG processes through their own unique wisdom and approaches, based on seeking common ground amongst all other members, whether Asian or non-Asian.

We contend there are three main ways in which Asia could make its successful contributions to GEG, added to what they could do in the G20. The first is on the national level. Asian emerging countries, by increasing their own economic strength, have bought about improved development and prosperity throughout the region, which lays a solid economic basis for GEG. While the 'Washington Consensus' has been universally questioned in the international community in recent years, more and more attention has been given to the development model employed by some Asian emerging economies based on their own national conditions (Ramo 2004). The World Bank report, *The East Asian Miracle*, also explores this model and points out its differences from the ones constantly abided by in traditional Western economic theory, such as the positive role played by governments in seeking markets and providing funds for companies (Yang 2007). The success of the alternative model issues a confident voice in the Western-led world, diversifying the ways to national industrialisation. The good economic performance of the emerging Asian economies and their participation in GEG will provide more options to restructure the Western-dominated system, which could promote the G20's creditability to act as a steering committee for the world economy specifically.

Secondly, since the regional and global governance are closely interconnected, Asian regional co-operation could provide rich experiences for GEG. Through bilateral and multilateral co-operation with formal or informal integration, institutions, conferences, forums and other means of communication, the Asian countries are achieving a more effective management of their regional economic affairs. As Mahbubani and Chesterman (2009), remarked: 'These open and inclusive regional processes provide a framework to manage competition and alleviate inherent tensions among regional states. The inclusiveness of such consensus-based processes reassures small and medium-sized states that their views would not only be heard but would also be taken into account' (p. 5). The successful co-operation on the regional level provides the prerequisite for the higher level of global co-operation as illustrated by East Asia's regional co-operation (Zhang 2010: 249), and is relevant to GEG mechanism designs. For example, the pattern of Asian regional co-operation could be used for reference to the G20's institutional innovation, such as to explore some new co-ordination networks for balancing elite leadership with other various economies in order to improve its legitimacy.

Thirdly, on the global level, most Asian countries actively participate in various forms of GEG. The major powers in Asia hold permanent or non-permanent memberships of the UN Security Council. In this well-established global governance structure, Asia's developed economy powers and emerging economy countries have made their own contributions to important matters in the Council's affairs, including additionally reform of the UN itself. Asia's emerging economies are playing an increasingly important role in other global institutions, including the IMF, World Bank and World Trade Organisation (WTO), by which they are involved more deeply in their management and reconstruction. With their rising power and influence, they also have contributed to a great extent in the transformation of the underlying GEG structure itself, from G8 to G8+O5 and then to G20.

Asian emerging countries are also involved in other global-spanning coalitional alignments. For example, China and India are the members of the high-profile BRIC group along with Russia and Brazil, which regularly holds meetings to discuss each other's ideas and policies relating to global governance and other international affairs. Australia and Indonesia are also members of the 17-country Cairns Group that champions the interests of competitive agricultural exporters. Thus, there is the question of whether Asian G20 members may seek closer alignments with non-Asian members of the Group rather than form a regional coalition. The former may prove to be a more likely outcome than the latter as the G20 evolves over time.

5. CONCLUSIONS

The rise of emerging developing countries like China and India has brought about significant reconfigurations in global structures of power, with implications for global economic governance. As one would expect, these emerging countries seek an increase in their influence in international institutions, as well as their restructuring to reflect global structural changes. Perhaps nowhere is this more evident than in the G20. This chapter has discussed the positions and approaches of its Asian members. We have seen how these have differed in many ways, although some categorisation of common positions and interests are also evident. It has also been made clear that if G20 is destined to foster a more effective co-governance structure or compromise between the incumbent advanced G7/8 countries and the emerging countries, this undermines Japan's position somewhat by diluting its Asian representative influence. This mainly explains why Japan has resisted any move for the G20 to supersede the G7/8. Other Asian nations – new to the G-process – have on the whole viewed the G20 in a more positive light, seeing the governance structure as an opportunity to champion their interests and ideas with greater emphasis on the international stage. At the same time, the United States and major European powers are likely to exert considerable influence over the G20 and other GEG institutions for some time yet. They still have sufficient power to moderate the G20's progress, with implications for all other member nations.

NOTES

1. Brazil, China, India, Mexico and South Africa.
2. 'Welcome from the French G20 presidency', available at: http://www.g20.org/index.aspx (accessed: 18 August 2011)
3. Australia is also considered part of the Oceania region.
4. Lee M.B., 'The road to Seoul: shared growth beyond crisis', available at: http://www.g8.utoronto.ca/newsdesk/seoul/seoul-lee-mb-en.html (accessed: 16 June 2011).

REFERENCES

Alexandroff, A.S. (2010), 'Stuck in transition: conflicting ambitions for the G20's future', *Global Asia*, **5**(3), 42–6.

Arrighi, G. (2007), *Adam Smith in Beijing: Lineages of the Twenty-First Century*, London: Verso Books.

Beeson, M. and S. Bell (2009), 'The G-20 and international economic governance: hegemony, collectivism, or both', *Global Governance*, **15**(1), 67–86.

Carin, B. and P. Heap (2010), 'Asians can think: a time for Asian leadership', *East Asia Forum Quarterly*, **2**(4), 13–14.

Elek, A. (2010), 'A testing time for the G20', *East Asia Forum Quarterly*, **2**(4), 18–19.

Ito, T. (2010), 'Towards a new world financial architecture', *East Asia Forum Quarterly*, **2**(4), 8–10.

Kim, Y.K. (2010), 'The rise of G20 and Korea's response', *SERI Quarterly*, **3**(4), 49–57.

Kirton, J. (2009), 'A committed contributor: Japan in G8 and G20 governance', presented at the National Institute of Japanese Studies International Workshop on Japan (still) Matters: What Role in the World?, 30 April–1 May, University of Sheffield.

Liu, Z. (2010), 'A summary on the symposium of G20 institutionalization and China's participation in global economic governance', *International Perspectives*, **5**(2), 98–103.

Mahbubani, K. (2010), *New Asian Hemisphere: Inevitable Shifting of Global Power to the East*, Beijing: Contemporary China Publishing House.

Mahbubani, K. and S. Chesterman (2009), 'Asia's role in global governance', special report presented at the Global Redesign Initiative: Singapore Hearing on Asia's Contribution to the Redesign of Global Governance, 1–2 December, Singapore.

Ramo, J.C. (2004), *The Beijing Consensus: Notes on the New Physics of Chinese Power*, London: The Foreign Policy Centre.

Rathus, J. (2011), 'Japan and the G20: Ambivalence and the China Factor', *East Asia Forum*, available at: http://www.eastasiaforum.org/2011/02/12/japan-and-the-g20-ambivalence-and-the-china-factor (accessed: 15 June 2011).

SQ Interview (2010), 'Seoul's G20 host comes full circle', *SERI Quarterly*, **3**(4), 86–91.

Tiberghien, Y. (2011), 'East Asian politics and the great G20 game: convergence and divergence in Chinese, Korean, and Japanese approaches', East Asia Institute Fellows Program working paper no. 29.

Wang, G. and J. Cheng (2010), 'G20 mechanization and global governance reform', *International Outlook*, **105**(3), 8–18.

Yang, J. (ed.) (2007), *The International System Transformation and Multilateral Organizations: China's Response and Choice*, Beijing: Shi Shi Publishing House.

Yuan, P. (2009), 'The transformation of international systems and China's strategic choice', *Contemporary International Relations*, **241**(11), 39–44.

Zhang, Y. (2010), *The Logics of the Weak in International Politics: ASEAN's External Relations with Major Powers in the Asia-Pacific Region*, Beijing: Sciences Academic Press.

9. Regional answers to the global crisis? Asia-Pacific multilateral organisations and the economic downturn

Jörn Dosch

1. INTRODUCTION

In April 2010, the Association of Southeast Asian Nations (ASEAN) leaders adopted a declaration on sustainable recovery and development which reiterates the organisation's determination to overcome the negative impacts of the global economic crisis to maintain regional growth (ASEAN Secretariat 2009). In March 2009, the Parliament of Mercosur stressed that the bloc 'must unify and coordinate its position to face the crisis in the G20, WTO, the IMF and the World Bank' (Xinhua General News Service 2009). In November 2009, in the response to the crisis leaders of 21 Asia Pacific Economic Cooperation forum (APEC) economies demanded 'a new growth paradigm and an expanded trade and investment agenda that will strengthen regional economic integration (REI) in the Asia-Pacific region' (APEC 2009). In January 2010, the foreign Ministers of the Forum for East Asia–Latin America Cooperation (FEALAC) expressed their 'determination to continue working together to accelerate economic recovery by sharing our own experiences, wisdom and best practices that both regions obtained as they got over the past crises' (FEALAC 2010).

However, the more interesting and challenging question addresses the extent to which the rhetoric has been followed by targeted policy action. This chapter compares the four organisations from two different angles: first, which of the two regional organisations, ASEAN or Mercosur, has been more efficient and effective in responding to the crisis and why? Second, which of the two multilateral cooperation structures, regionalism or inter-regionalism has made the more significant contributions to countering the crisis?

The next section briefly outlines the state of the theoretical and practical discourses on regional integration and inter-regionalism with special emphasis on the four empirical cases ASEAN, Mercosur, APEC and FEALAC. This will be followed by a discussion of the four organisations' respective contributions to crisis management. It is argued that the academic literature almost completely neglects the role and influence of extra-regional actors, including foreign donors, in regional cooperation processes in both Asia and Latin America. However, as the chapter tries to demonstrate, regional and inter-regional responses to the crisis have been most successful when policy efforts were promoted, (financially) supported or even driven by extra-regional actors, such as the European Union and the US.

2. REGIONALISM AND INTER-REGIONALISM IN ASIA AND LATIN AMERICA

There can be little doubt about the fact that ASEAN has been one of the most popular research objects in the study of regionalism, second only to the European Union. Fashions in the study of regionalism have come and gone: functionalism, federalism, transactionism, neorealism, liberal institutionalism, regime theoretical approaches, and most recently social constructivism – but no matter from which theoretical angle scholars have looked at ASEAN, the main findings have been strikingly similar for some four decades. In essence, all major studies have arrived at similar conclusions, which were already outlined by the pioneers in the analysis of Southeast Asian regionalism. For example, Pushpathavi Thambipillai (1980) concluded that within Southeast Asia the desire not to unite politically but to preserve autonomy would prevail. And in an early article published in 1971, Xuto stated: '[The] newly independent countries of Southeast Asia are naturally sensitive about their newly-acquired independence and sovereignty, which tend to be jealously guarded against any real or imaginary infringement. Effective regionalism is likely to lead to weakening individual sovereignty and independence and Southeast Asian countries may be reluctant to commit themselves fully to it' (reprinted in Xuto 1982: 49).

Although the studies mentioned here were published decades ago, most of their findings remain resilient. Today and in spite of the 2007 ASEAN Charter that codifies the norms, rules and procedures in regional cooperation, more than four decades of regional co-operation have not generated any kind of supra-nationality. National sovereignty rules (see Dosch 2008). The ASEAN Secretariat in Jakarta, which was established in 1976, contributes to the management of the organisation's day-to-day business and, to a degree, works as the organisation's internal think-tank but does not have autonomous decision-making power. At the same time few would dispute ASEAN's achievements in political and economic regionalism based on a coordinated, inter-governmental approach to regional governance. Nicola Phillips identifies four central elements of regional governance that allow for a comparison of regionalisms in different geographical settings, most importantly East Asia and Latin America:

1. Stable set of international economic strategies;
2. Distinctive set of governance structures which enables regional economic governance;
3. Set of normative or ideational constructs that not only makes possible a given set of regional governance structures but also makes possible the very definition of the region;
4. Convergence of domestic coalitions and political economy structures across the region, which would facilitate the coherent construction of regional political projects. (Phillips 2003: 218).

While these four categories offer indeed a very suitable framework for comparison, there is one feature that, by and large, has always distinguished East Asian from Latin American regionalism. As Manfred Mols (1988) proposed in a pioneer study on comparative regionalism that is still relevant and valid today, while East Asian states have followed a non-legalistic approach to inter-governmental cooperation based on soft institutions, non-binding decision-making and consensus-building, Latin Americans have adopted a model closer to the Europan integration characterised by legally binding commitment. It is generally acknowledged that East Asia's (particularly ASEAN's) non-legalistic or 'soft institutionalised' cooperation has generated more benefits for its member states and the region in general than Latin America's legalistic or 'hard institutionalised' regionalism. The former has allowed for more flexibility in dealing with specific policy challenges of regional governance than the latter.

In quantitative terms, however, until about half a decade ago, Latin America had created more regional organisations and cooperation fora than East Asia. In 1960, Guatemala, Honduras, El Salvador and Nicaragua founded the Central American Common Market (CACM). Costa Rica acceded in 1962. In 1969, Bolivia, Chile, Colombia, Ecuador and Peru signed the Cartagena Agreement which established the Andean Community. Chile left the organisation in 1976. Venezuela joined in 1973 but withdrew in 2006. In 1980, the Treaty of Montevideo established the Latin American Integration Association (ALADI) as a successor to the Latin American Free Trade Association (LAFTA).

Current members are Argentina, Bolivia, Brazil, Chile, Colombia, Cuba, Ecuador, Mexico, Paraguay, Peru, Uruguay and Venezuela.

The 1991-established Mercosur, the Southern Common Market grouping of Argentina, Brazil, Paraguay and Uruguay (Venezuela signed an accession agreement in 2006 but has not yet been formally admitted), has achieved the highest level of consolidation on the long list of integrative experiments carried out within the region. The fast progress made in its first implementation phase (until 1994) boosted it into the realm of an elected interlocutor for conducting commercial negotiations with the various actors in the global arena. Based on the decision to aim at creating a customs union, all member countries in 1994 made a commitment under the Ouro Preto Protocol (OPP) to implement a common external trade policy. However, the impasse that encircled Mercosur as from 1998 triggered broad academic discussions and brought about repeated 'relaunching' attempts at a political action level (Stuhldreher 2010).

As in the case of the Asian variant of regionalism, the phenomenon of inter-regionalism – the process through which patterns of relations between geographical regions are institutionalised (Sanchez Bajo 1999: 927) – is often marked by certain common characteristics such as 'soft' institutional structures and processes, which in turn are characterised by informality, consensus orientation and pragmatism. A second common feature is the somewhat controlled shift of contentious issues from the official level (track one) to the non-governmental level (track two) in order to discuss these issues non-controversially and to avoid a political stalemate among the parties. Taking into consideration all existing inter-regional arrangements, which also exist between Asia and Latin America, Europe and Africa etc., it becomes obvious that they differ with regard to membership, the degree of institutionalisation, and the policy areas covered by the arrangement.

Inter-regionalism emerges as a response to specific configurations and the increasing complexity of the international system. Hence, in light of a perceived erosion process of nation-states' steering mechanisms in the era of globalisation, inter-regionalism just as regionalism appears to offer state actors new action corridors and a tool to explore and to regain (lost) political steering competencies. According to Hanns Maull, this allows states to pursue the following three objectives: (1) accumulation of wealth through intensified trade and investment relations as well as through deepened forms of transnational division of labour; (2) cooperative management of general problems of interdependence (rule-setting, regime creation, crisis prevention) and of specific conflicts of interdependence (tariff and nontariff barriers, dumping); and (3) strengthening of the major industrialised region's bargaining power with regard to the definition of the rules of the international economic system (Maull 2000: 149). Consequently, inter-regionalism serves as a political vehicle for the deepening of interdependence, the mutual increase of material and nonmaterial resources, and the resolution of conflicts through the use of accompanying measures and additional cooperation between governmental and nongovernmental actors. It performs certain balancing functions, and contributes to multilateral institution and identity building in international relations (Hänggi et al. 2006; Doidge 2007; Robles 2008; Rüland et al. 2008). The vast majority of studies in inter-regionalism have focused on relations between East Asia and Europe, particularly with regard to EU–ASEAN relations and the Asia–Europe Meeting (ASEM). However, inter-regionalisms have also emerged elsewhere with APEC being one of the pioneers.

APEC was formed in 1989 and currently comprises 21 economies from four regions (or subregions, depending on one's perspective): East Asia, Oceania/Australasia, North and South America. A key feature of APEC's agenda is 'open regionalism'. In stating this, APEC members commit themselves to non-discriminatory trade and investment policies in accordance with the WTO's most-favoured-nation (MFN) principle. As such, APEC differs considerably from preferential trading agreements such as NAFTA and the EU. Unlike many of the East Asian intra-regional dialogues, APEC has the rudiments of an institutional structure, with a secretariat based in Singapore and annual meetings. In this respect, it has developed consistency as an international forum. Keohane and Nye (2001: 2) describe APEC as 'multicontinental interdependence'. APEC peaked shortly after its founding: the Bogor Declaration of 1994 committed the member states to the elimination of trade barriers by 2010 for developed economies and 2020 for developing countries but no concrete efforts followed to achieve this goal. The APEC Bogor summit coincided with the enthusiastic approach of the first Clinton administration towards multilateralism. Washington supported APEC as a cornerstone of the Clinton administration's policy goal to sustain economic dynamism in the Asia Pacific. Back then, the Office of the US Trade Representative identified APEC as the regional centrepiece to US efforts to open markets and expand trade. This enthusiasm has long since disappeared. Under the administration of George W. Bush, the US largely employed the APEC Leaders' Meeting as a security forum, evidenced by the dominance of the 9/11 attacks in the 2001 Beijing summit agenda, and the condemnation of North Korea's nuclear weapons programme at the 2006 Hanoi summit. Nevertheless, APEC has also focused upon developing a unified response to WTO and climate change issues, which were central to the Hanoi and Sydney (2007) APEC leaders' summits. However, APEC has arguably failed to achieve its initial promise, and one has to be sceptical about its ability to deliver its much-vaunted model of open regionalism. In 2009, President Obama made his first visit to Asia, attending the Singapore APEC summit which – despite a lack of concrete achievement – could at least be interpreted as a new momentum for APEC (Davison 2011).

Compared to APEC, the Forum for East Asia–Latin America Cooperation (FEALAC) is less institutionalised. The forum has 18 Latin American and 16 Asian member states (including Australia and New Zealand). In addition to the different level of institutionalisation, the main difference between APEC and FEALAC is the absence of the United States in the latter. Besides, while the Asian membership in APEC and FEALAC is almost identical, the latter also comprises the smaller Latin American economies and Cuba. FEALAC provides a framework for increasing dialogue and cooperation on a wide array of economic, political and social issues without, however, trying to generate major inputs to international order building. FEALAC nevertheless provides an interesting example for a growing trend in international relations that is spearheaded by Asian and Latin American state actors: multilateral cooperation across continental borders outside the Europe–US–East Asia triad. In their Manila Action Plan of 2004 the members of FEALAC stated that, through the process of inter-regional cooperation, they expected to achieve a more equal distribution of the benefits resulting from globalisation as well as prevent the marginalisation of any sector of the human society. While FEALAC has often been criticised due to its poor outcome-oriented performance, its low profile, the inability to influence the policies of the governments which take part in its meetings and, ultimately, its reduced visibility, FEALAC nevertheless contributes to the strengthening of regional identities both in Latin America and in East Asia as much as it helps some of the participating states to reduce their peripheral position in the world order and strengthen their negotiation power vis-à-vis the US and the European Union (Abad 2010). In the next step the chapter will look at the way and extent to which these four organisations and fora have responded to the challenges of the global economic crisis of 2008–09.

3. ASEAN'S AND MERCOSUR'S RESPONSES TO THE GLOBAL ECONOMIC CRISIS

Trade statistics show that due to the impact of the global financial crisis on Southeast Asia, ASEAN's total merchandise trade backtracked from US$1,897.1 billion in 2008 to US$1,536.8 billion in 2009. However, this 19 per cent decline was less than the 22.6 per cent decline in worldwide trade. Besides, ASEAN's trade surplus with the rest of the world reached

US$61.2 billion in 2009, which more than doubled from the previous year (US State News 2010). Does this demonstrate the success and strength of ASEAN in dealing with the challenges of the crisis? It is not that long ago that ASEAN had been accused of not being able to react effectively to situations of crisis. ASEAN's handling of the regional financial crisis of 1997–98 was seen as ineffective inside and outside the region. On this point Bantarto Bandoro (1998: 98–9) wrote, 'ASEAN is not only at the crossroad, but it is also on the brink of depression and disintegration'. This worst case scenario, however, never materialised and both ASEAN as an institutional body and the process of regional integration are more robust today than in the late 1990s.

Among observers there is widespread agreement that the ASEAN countries had put their houses in order after the deep crisis of the late 1990s. Immediately before the 2008–09 global crisis the Southeast Asian economies were growing strongly, in the range of 5–8 per cent, as they have been for most of this decade. Budget deficits were generally modest. Where they were larger, as in Malaysia and Vietnam, they were funded by buoyant domestic savings or large foreign aid flows. Moreover, all but Vietnam – the Southeast Asian country that displayed the most crisis vulnerability symptoms – were running current account surpluses, resulting in rapidly accumulating foreign exchange reserves, especially in Singapore and Malaysia. There have been no cases of serious financial collapse or bank runs (Lopez 2009). ASEAN suffered too, as the decline in trade volumes demonstrates, but clearly to a lesser extent than other regions.

On the occasion of several official ASEAN meetings and summits since the outbreak of the crisis in late 2007, heads of state and ministers have emphasised their determination to spur economic integration and adopt bold measures, particularly on trade facilitation and elimination of non-tariff barriers, to stimulate intra-ASEAN trade as the best approach towards easing the impact of the crisis. In a nutshell, heads of state 'stressed the importance of deepening ASEAN integration to maintain its resilience while remaining open to global and regional trade'.[1]

On paper, this strategy has been successful. The ASEAN Free Trade Area (AFTA), which was realised on 1 January 2010, eliminated duties on 99.65 per cent of all tariff lines under the Common Effective Preferential Tariff Scheme for the ASEAN Free Trade Area (CEPT-AFTA). For Cambodia, Laos, Burma/Myanmar and Vietnam, tariffs on 98.96 per cent of total tariff lines have been adjusted to within the 0–5 per cent range. The ASEAN Trade in Goods Agreement (ATIGA), which consolidates all ASEAN's existing initiatives, obligations and commitments on intra-ASEAN trade-in-goods (including both tariff and non-tariff elements) into one single comprehensive document, also entered into force on 17

May 2010 (US State News 2010). The benefits seem clear cut. 'A larger single market such as ASEAN will provide a stronger economic base to ride out global shocks and thus the integration of ASEAN into ASEAN Economic Community will be crucial for the long term sustainable growth' (Mthangavelu 2008).

While ASEAN's achievements in economic integration should not be played down, they need to be put into perspective. The impact of a Southeast Asian Free Trade Area is limited because, unlike in the case of Europe for example, intraregional trade as a proportion of the countries' total trade is small: less than 20 per cent. The most important trading partners for the individual ASEAN members are the United States, Japan and the European Union but not the neighbouring economies. According to a World Bank study of AFTA, the slow pace of intraregional trade liberalisation is not a stumbling block though. The more important fact is that 'the ASEAN agreement has been a force for broader liberalization . . . AFTA members have been responding to lower internal tariffs by reducing also their trade barriers on imports from outsiders. In this sense, AFTA has been clearly beneficial for the promotion of freer world trade' (Calvo-Pardo et al. 2009: abstract; 23).

This finding is confirmed by ASEAN's attempts to liberalise trade with extra-regional economies. For example, in 2002 ASEAN and China agreed on the establishment of a China–ASEAN Free Trade Area (CAFTA). It is often referred to as the world's biggest Free Trade Area, comprising 1.7 million consumers with a combined gross domestic product of US$2 trillion and total trade of US$1.3 trillion. On 1 January 2010, trade between China and the six 'old ASEAN members' (Brunei, Indonesia, Malaysia, the Philippines, Thailand and Singapore) became duty-free for some 7,000 products. CAFTA will be joined by Vietnam, Laos, Cambodia and Myanmar in 2015.

Part of ASEAN's relative success in strengthening internal and external trade relations is due to the absence of a hegemonic trading partner. The Southeast Asian economies have been relatively unconstrained in their diversification of trade relations. By comparison, one of Mercosur's main challenges has been to reduce the member states' dependence on the US market, not only in terms of trade but also with regard to financial markets. The US fiscal crisis had been far more significance for Latin American economies than initially assumed. All Mercosur member states have experienced greater financial stability since 2003. Many analysts attribute this half-decade boom to high global commodity prices, since all the countries in the Mercosur are export economies (oil in the case of Venezuela, while the other countries are dependent on agricultural exports). Growing Chinese demand for commodities has played a strong part in the generation of this mini-boom. As the financial crisis began, Mercosur seemed to offer a protective, if symbolic, shell to weather the storm. However, subsequent developments in late 2008 proved the pundits wrong. The impact of the international crisis on the real economy of these countries became particularly evident after the last quarter of 2008. Until then the effects had been mainly financial, with no impact on growth rates, which, in spite of the deceleration taking place in the last part of that year, were significant on average (Stuhldreher 2010: 190). For example, in October 2008, the Argentine government announced that it would nationalise the country's private pension system, which, with close to US$30 billion in assets, was the largest investor in the country's capital markets. The change was intended to protect people's pensions from market fluctuations, but the immediate affect was the exact opposite. In the following days, the Buenos Aires stock exchange fell more than 20 per cent and many investors sold their Argentine bonds (Weisberg 2008).

Even though Mercosur was never designed to immunise its members from the fluctuations of global commodity prices, the crisis has revealed the extent of the region's dependency on external economic factors (ibid.). In March 2009 the Parliament of Mercosur decided to gather the economy ministers of the bloc in a special session to deal with the current economic downturn (Xinhua General News Service 2009a). A communiqué stated: 'The bloc's contraction tendency in the flow of commercial trade could affect the viability and the strategic meanings of the Mercosur . . . Mercosur must unify and coordinate its position to face the crisis in the Group-20 (G20), World Trade Organization (WTO), the International Monetary Fund (IMF) and the World Bank.' Several high-level meetings have taken place in response to the crisis. For example, in December 2008 social protection measures in the face of the world financial crisis were discussed at a Mercosur summit. Related initiatives included the planned creation of the Mercosur Fund of guarantees for micro, small and medium-sized companies and the Mercosur Fund of familiar agriculture (Xinhua General News Service 2008). There is no documented evidence available, however, showing that any of these talks or proposals resulted in concrete policy action or demonstrating that Mercosur as a collective actor has added any value to the crisis-related actions of the individual member states. Mercosur's general and persisting problem is disunity within the bloc itself. 'The trading group has been riddled by problems and myriad exceptions to the rules since its inception in 1991. Bilateral trade disputes between members, particularly Argentina and Brazil, have been common' (EIU Views Wire 2010).

The above notion about the 'myriad exceptions to the rules' is important as it illustrates the consequences and downside of Latin America's legalistic approach to regionalism. The respective national interests of Mercosur member states and different levels of economic development make it difficult for governments to adhere to the manifold rules they have agreed to in multilateral negotiations. However, while non-adherence might play to the interests of domestic constituencies, it renders the agreed cooperation framework useless and leads to frustration and setbacks in the regional integration process. ASEAN faces a situation of even greater diversity and disparity of national interests in relations among members. However, the non-legalistic approach to regionalism, the so-called ASEAN way, allows for more flexibility and a lesser degree of disappointment if integration turns out to be a bumpy road, as it usually does.

4. APEC'S AND FEALAC'S RESPONSES TO THE CRISIS

Overall, the Asia-Pacific region has been at the forefront of the recovery from the global economic crisis of 2008–09. Yet, this is more the result of massive stimulus packages in China, Japan, the United States and smaller economies such as Singapore (as well as massive financial bailouts in OECD countries that prevented further economic freefall) than targeted policy action by regional organisations. However, of all the four organisations and fora discussed in this chapter, APEC has demonstrated the strongest explicit commitment to crisis solving. The 2009 Singapore summit committed APEC to advancing 'APEC's inclusive growth agenda in 2010, and develop a multiyear programme to build capacity for structural reforms and SME development, employment creation, and the development of social safety nets' (APEC 2009).

As a result, the possibility of creating an Asia-Pacific Free Trade Area or more specially the revival of the Bogor goals of 17 years ago has resurfaced on APEC's agenda (*The Nation* 2010). Since 2008, APEC has initiated several programmes and projects to address, inter alia, the financial crisis through SME support, employment creation and social safety nets in APEC. The main task of APEC's several working groups, however, has been information and analysis gathering and, based on this intelligence, the coordination of member states' policies. While the 2009 Singapore meeting drew the usual misgivings and call for a 'fresh model of economic integration' (McClatchy-Tribune Business News 2009), describing APEC as a talking shop or a toothless tiger is not entirely justified. Summit meetings are first and foremost photo opportunities, but with its numerous working and sub-groups APEC has provided a useful mechanism for the discussion and coordination of policy responses to the crisis. More cannot be expected from an inter-governmental organisation that does not have a supra-national mandate to speak and decide on behalf of its members. FEALAC's situation is similar while being significantly less institutionalised than APEC.

FEALAC discussed the possibility of strengthening its role in contributing to member states' efforts to mitigate the negative impact of the global financial crisis on their respective real economies and thereby sustain economic development. However, it was decided to defer any practical decision on that issue until the 4th Foreign Ministers' Meeting which was held in Tokyo in January 2010. The Tokyo Declaration stressed the importance of the G20, IMF and World Bank in tackling the global financial and economic crisis and reinforced the member states' 'determination to continue working together to accelerate economic recovery by sharing our own experiences, wisdom and best practices that both regions obtained as they got over the past crises' (FEALAC 2010). These opportunities were not further specified. Yet, FEALAC can be described as a framework that allows members to garner support for initiatives among like-minded states and contribute to agenda setting in preparation for deeper institutionalised and/or global multilateral settings, such as G20. The same applies to APEC which has strongly supported the WTO's goal of successfully concluding the Doha Round free-trade talks in 2011. APEC and – to an even lesser extent – FEALAC might not produce many tangible outcomes (such as negotiated treaties and trade agreements) but every opportunity for communication and harmonisation of viewpoints is generally a good one. At the same time, the low level of institutionalisation makes it difficult to see how FEALAC could make a concrete contribution to the further strengthening of trade and investment relations between the two regions which have developed robustly over the past 15 years but are still – by quite a margin – less significant than both regions' respective economic relations with the US and Europe. Between 1995 and 2009 intra-regional trade in East Asia and Latin America has increased at about 55 per cent. FEALAC members as a whole contribute about one-fifth of global trade, and absorb about 20 per cent of FDI. However, intra-FEALAC trade is asymmetrical with East Asia accounting for 88 per cent (Tsardanidis 2010).

5. THE ROLE OF EXTERNAL ACTORS

In addition to a broad range of internal regional dynamics, 'processes of regional cooperation are almost always also influenced by the actors external to the system' (Gilson and Yeo 2004: 28). These external federators

> are actors or situations which provoke regionalist reactions and/or pursuits of cultural or situational identities via assistance, pressure, or simply by their mere existence. The Soviet Union and the United States contributed in a substantial way to the formation of an integrated Europe, and Washington was a principal external federator in nearly all efforts of Latin American integration. (Mols 2004: 61)

External stimuli do not have to be of a direct and explicit nature but can also include distant events and developments that at first glance do not seem to bear much importance for other regions. For example, at least until recently 'many [in Asia] believed that the euro as a symbol of EU's success story of integration would have a stimulating effect on their own regional cooperation' (Xu 2004: 119).

More often than not, the direct involvement of an external actor is crucial for the success or failure of regional cooperation schemes. This observation is not necessarily identical with the neo-realist claim that regional cooperation requires the involvement of a hegemonic stabiliser to be assured of real progress, that is, institutional evolution. However, it is hard to overlook or undermine the importance of the American factor in APEC, for example. While North America is part of the Asia-Pacific region according to APEC's own definition, the organisation came about as an East Asia–Australian initiative and the US can be described as a quasi external actor in relation to the concept of multilateral institution-building in East Asia which found its first cornerstone in APEC. The forum has been most successful and effective during periods when the organisation could be sure of pro-active US involvement and less visible when it depended on leadership from within East Asia. In the early 1990s APEC provided a 'win–win' opportunity (to borrow the Chinese catch-phrase) for both the US and medium powers in the Asia Pacific. The 'upgrade' of APEC in the wake of the global economic downturn was mainly due to renewed US interest in the organisation by the Obama administration – and the fact that the 2011 APEC summit took place in Honolulu.

The involvement of external actors is not always as obvious as it is in the case of the US role in APEC and does not have to be of a hegemonic nature. A central element in Southeast Asia's regionalism that is almost completely neglected in the academic discourse, and hardly ever features in the media either, is ASEAN's cooperation with foreign donors.[2] Few realise that foreign donors currently disburse funds of at least US$50 million annually on behalf of the integration of the ASEAN region. This might not look like an impressive amount but is more than the triple the size of ASEAN's official annual budget of US$14 million (each member state makes the same annual token contribution of US$1.4 million which is mainly absorbed by the Secretariat's operational budget). The general goals of this foreign support include capacity-building for officials of the ASEAN Secretariat and member states' governments and funding for the operation of regional centres for cooperation on a broad range of economic and security issues, and more specifically speeding the establishment of a customs unit, strengthening regional intellectual-property regimes, and empowering civil society to further ASEAN's plan to create a fully integrated regional community by 2015. The European Union – both the European Commission (EC) and individual member states – has been spearheading the support for Southeast Asian integration. Pledged EC support for ASEAN alone amounted to approximately US$55 million during 2008–10. Several senior government officials in Southeast Asia told this author that ASEAN would not be able to exist without the financial and technical assistance of external actors.[3]

Between 1996 and 2007 the EC disbursed nearly €100 million in overseas development aid (ODA) for several major projects to promote and foster ASEAN integration, ranging from capacity-building programmes at the ASEAN Secretariat to the standardisation of national Intellectually Property Rights (IPR) regimes in ASEAN member states and harmonisation of customs procedures throughout Southeast Asia in preparation for the envisioned ASEAN Customs Union. For the period 2008–10 the Commission has earmarked €37 million for the support of ASEAN Integration. In its *Regional Programming for Asia Strategy Document 2007–2013*, the European Commission identified 'support to regional integration (through ASEAN/SAARC and ASEM)' as the first of three priority areas (European Commission 2007). In addition to the Commission's contributions, individual EU member states (particularly Germany, France, the UK, Denmark and Sweden) have funded development projects broadly targeted at the support for regional integration either at the ASEAN Secretariat or in ASEAN member states. According to this author's rough estimates, the total of EU member states' current ODA for ASEAN at least equals the amount of the European Commission's ODA. This means that financial support for ASEAN from EU sources alone (at the current exchange rate) amounts to an annual average of currently approximately US$33 million or 2.4 times ASEAN's official annual budget.

Both the ASEAN–US Enhanced Partnership Plan of Action (2006) and several EU–ASEAN cooperation programmes such as the ASEAN Programme for Regional Integration Support (APRIS) provide technical assistance and capacity building to assist ASEAN in achieving its objective. At the core of the Customs Union is the initiative to create an ASEAN

Single Window (ASW) for customs clearance; for example the harmonisation of the ten national customs regimes. On ASW alone there are between 1,000 and 2,000 donor-funded activities across 50 sectors. According to an external evaluation report on the European Commission's support to ASEAN,

> no other aspect of economic integration has attracted more donor attention than customs harmonisation as it is in the natural interest of the [European Commission] and other donors to ease the access of exporters to the Southeast Asian markets and thereby strengthen trade relations. Slow and complicated customs procedures are seen as a main hurdle to trade facilitation. (European Commission 2009: 22)

In comparison, despite well-developed and institutionalised relations between the EU and Mercosur, the EU–Latin American axis has never achieved the importance of its EU–Southeast Asia counterpart. For example, free trade talks between the two blocs, originally announced in 1999 at the first Ibero–American summit, have been suspended since 2004 owing to discord over agricultural tariffs and subsidies paid to European farmers.

6. CONCLUSION

This chapter has discussed the responses of four regional and intra-regional organisations and fora – ASEAN, Mercosur, APEC and FEALAC – to the global economic downturn of 2008–09. The introduction raised two questions: first, which of the two regional organisations, ASEAN or Mercosur, has been more efficient and effective in responding to the crisis and why? Second, which of the two multilateral cooperation structures, regionalism or inter-regionalism has made the more significant contributions to countering the crisis?

The first question can easily be answered. When we revisit Nicola Phillips' four elements of regional governance, for example, (1) a stable set of international economic strategies; (2) a distinctive set of governance structures; (3) a set of normative or ideational constructs; and (4) a convergence of domestic coalitions and political economy structures across the region, which would facilitate the coherent construction of regional political projects, we find that Mercosur only scores higher on one, while ASEAN leads on three. Mercosur is stronger on governance structures as all member states are democracies, hence regional governance is not constrained by disagreement on broad political norms and values. ASEAN, however, has the more elaborate, stable and successful strategy in dealing with the international environment due to its ability to speak with one voice in international relations. While the 'ASEAN Way' has been criticised as being too weak and 'informal' to provide a suitable normative base for deep economic integration, it has nevertheless effectively worked as a trademark 'ideational construct' that served ASEAN well as a framework for inter-governmental cooperation. Last but not least ASEAN's ability to facilitate the construction of regional projects is also higher than Mercosur's despite the fact that Mercosur is more homogenous in terms of the political systems in its region than ASEAN. The difference is that there is broad agreement among the state elites in Southeast Asia on the direction of the integration process as expressed, for example, in the project of the ASEAN Community 2015. While neither ASEAN nor Mercosur might have been effective in addressing the impacts of the global crisis through direct, coordinated policy responses, ASEAN's superior institutional setting has put the organisation in a better position than Mercosur to weather the storm.

The second question, however, misses the point. ASEAN and APEC have been more effective in dealing with the global crisis than Mercosur and FEALAC. ASEAN falls into the category of regionalism, APEC is an inter-regional scheme. This result does not prove the superiority of one mechanism over the other. In relative terms, ASEAN and APEC have been more successful in playing their part in crisis management, albeit more through ongoing economic integration – especially in the case of ASEAN – than direct targeted policy action. In the case of APEC the US has revived its formerly low interest in Asia-Pacific multilateralism resulting in an upgrading of the organisation in the aftermath of the economic downturn. With regard to ASEAN, there is reason to assume that Southeast Asian regionalism would not have achieved the current level of inter-governmental cooperation and advances towards economic community-building without the substantial financial and capacity-building contributions of foreign donors, including but not limited to, the EU, the US, Australia and Japan.

NOTES

1. Chairman's Statement of the 14th ASEAN Summit, 'ASEAN Charter for ASEAN Peoples', Cha-am, 28 February–1 March 2009, http://www.aseansec.org/22328.htm.
2. The following findings are based on this author's primary research in Southeast Asia between 2008 and 2010, including dozens of interviews with ASEAN officials, national government officials, foreign donor organisations and other stakeholders.
3. According to author interviews in Jakarta, Kuala Lumpur and Hanoi which were conducted in 2009 and 2010.

REFERENCES

Abad, G. (2010), 'Non-triadic interregionalism: the case of FEALAC', in Jörn Dosch and Olaf Jacob (eds), *Asia and Latin America. Economic, Political and Multilateral Relations*, London and New York: Routledge.

APEC (2009), 'Sustaining growth, connecting the region', leaders' declaration to the 17th APEC Economic Leaders' Meeting, Singapore, 14–15 November.

ASEAN Secretariat (2009), ASEAN leaders' statement on sustained recovery and development, Ha Noi, 9 April, accessed at www.asean.org/24512.htm.

Bandoro, B. (1998), 'The implication of economic turbulence: ASEAN on the brink of depression and disintegration', *Indonesian Quarterly*, **26**, 298–300.

Calvo-Pardo, Hector, Caroline Freund and Emanuel Ornelas (2009), 'The ASEAN free trade agreement: impact on trade flows and external trade barriers', World Bank policy research working paper series 4960, New York.

Davison, R. (2011), 'Globalization and regionalism in the Asia-Pacific', in M. Connors, R. Davison and J. Dosch (eds), *The New Global Politics of the Asia Pacific*, 2nd edn, London and New York: Routledge.

Doidge, M. (2007), 'Joined at the hip: regionalism and interregionalism', *Journal of European Integration*, **29**(2), 229–48.

Dosch, Jörn (2008), 'Sovereignty rules: human security, civil society, and the limits of liberal reform', in Donald K. Emmerson (ed.), *Hard Choices. Security, Democracy, and Regionalism in Southeast Asia*, Stanford, CA: Walter H. Shorenstein Asia-Pacific Research Center Books.

EIU Views Wire (2010), 'Latin America/EU economy: re-invigorating trade ties', New York, 3 June.

European Commission (2007), *Regional Programming for Asia*, strategy document 2007–2013, accessed at http://eeas.europa.eu/asia/rsp/07_13_en.pdf.

European Commission (2009), *Evaluation of EC Co-operation with ASEAN*, ref. 1262, vol. 2, accessed at http://ec.europa.eu/europeaid/how/evaluation/evaluation_reports/reports/2009/1262_vol2_en.pdf.

FEALAC (2010), Fourth Foreign Ministers' meeting of the Forum for East Asia–Latin America Cooperation, Tokyo Declaration, 17 January 2010.

Gilson, J. and L.H. Yeo (2004), 'Collective identity-building through trans-regionalism: ASEM and East Asian regional identity', in W. Stokhof et al. (eds), *The Eurasian Space: Far More Than Two Continents*, Singapore: ISEAS.

Habib, H.A. (1995), 'Defining the "Asia Pacific region"', *Indonesian Quarterly*, **23**(4), 302–12.

Hänggi, H., R. Roloff and J. Rüland (2006), 'Interregionalism: a new phenomenon in international relations', in H. Hänggi, R. Roloff and J. Rüland (eds), *Interregionalism and International Relations*, London: Routledge.

Keohane, R. and J. Nye (2001), 'Introduction', in J. Nye and J.D. Donahue (eds), *Governance in a Globalizing World*, Washington, DC: Brookings Institution Press.

Lopez, G. (2009), 'ASEAN's response to the global crisis, policy net', 29 April, accessed at www.policy-net.org/blogs/%7Bc59d79c1-ab42-4170-8572-4d613ae05d61%7D/aseansresp.

Maull, H. (2000), 'Europa und Ostasien: Eine neue Dimension des Inter-Regionalismus?' [Europe and East Asia: a new dimension of inter-regionalism?] in K. Schubert and G. Müller-Brandeck-Bocquet (eds), *Die Europäische Union*

als Akteur der Weltpolitik [*The European Union as an Actor in World Politics*], Opladen, Germany: Westdeutscher Verlag.
McClatchy-Tribune Business News (2009), 'APEC goes through the motions', editorial, 18 November, Washington.
Mols, M. (1988), 'El Regionalismo en America Latina y el Sudeste Asiatico: aspectos comunes y diferencias', in L. Tomassini (ed.), *Nuevas formas de concertacion regional en America Latina*, Grupo Editor Latinoamericano, Anuario RIAL.
Mols, M. (2004), 'Is there an Asianisation of Asia? The new millennium in Asia and the identity debate', *Panorama: Insights into Southeast Asia and European Affairs*, **6**(1), 57–64.
Mthangavelu, S. (2008), 'Global financial crisis: impact on Singapore and ASEAN', Eaber working paper series paper no. 49, The Australian National University, Canberra.
Phillips, N. (2003), 'The rise and fall of open regionalism? Comparative reflections on regional governance in the Southern Cone of Latin America', *Third World Quarterly*, **24**(2), 217–34.
Pizarro, R. (1999), 'Comparative analysis of regionalism in Latin America and Asia-Pacific', CEPAL International Trade and Development Finance Division, December, Santiago.
Robles, A.C. (2008), *The Asia–Europe meeting (ASEM): The Theory and Practice of Interregionalism*, Abingdon and New York: Routledge.
Rüland, J., G. Schubert, G. Schucher and C. Storz (eds) (2008), *Asian European Relations. Building Blocks for Global Governance?*, London: Routledge.
Sanchez Bajo, C. (1999), 'The European Union and MERCOSUR: a case of interregionalism', *Third World Quarterly*, **20**(5), 927–41.
Stuhldreher, A. (2010), 'MERCOSUR's relations with East Asian countries: a critical assessment', in J. Dosch and O. Jacob (eds), *Asia and Latin America. Economic, Political and Multilateral Relations*, London and New York: Routledge.
Thambipillai, P. (1980), 'Regional cooperation and development: the case of ASEAN and its external relations', PhD dissertation, University of Hawaii, Honolulu.
The Nation, Thailand (2010), 'Growth, currency crisis top APEC ministers' agenda', 8 November.
Tsardanidis, C. (2010), 'Inter-regionalism: a comparative analysis of ASEM and FEALAC', in J. Dosch and O. Jacob (eds), *Asia and Latin America. Economic, Political and Multilateral Relations*, London and New York: Routledge.
US State News (2010), 'ASEAN's economy resilient, surpasses global performance amidst world economic crisis', 26 August.
Weisberg, J. (2008), 'The Economic crisis and mercosur', North American Congress on Latin America, November, accessed at https://nacla.org/node/5269.
Xinhua General News Service (2008), 'Mercosur to study social protection measures amid world financial crisis', 15 December.
Xinhua General News Service (2009), 'Mercosur to hold special meeting on global financial crisis', 18 March.
Xu Mingqi (2004), 'The Euro and East Asian monetary co-operation', in W. Stokhof et al. (eds), *The Eurasian Space: Far More Than Two Continents*, Singapore: ISEAS.
Xuto, S. (1982), *In Retrospect: Views and Comments from Selected Writings*, Bangkok: Social Science Association of Thailand.

10. Intra-regional geopolitical dynamics in Northeast Asia

Cheol Hee Park

1. EAST ASIA IN THE REGIONAL–GLOBAL NEXUS

East Asia, or the Asia-Pacific in general, places itself as the economic powerhouse of the world as well as global geopolitical dynamics in the 21st century. Regardless of a debate on the decline of American power, the global power shift to East Asia is steadily on the move (Mahbubani 2008). This does not necessarily mean that North America or Europe is on the downturn. Nor does it mean that East Asia is going to feature as a consolidated whole against the West. Still, undeniably, East Asia is drawing more attention than before, especially in the context of a rising China.

East Asia has long been a centre of global dynamism. The discourse on East Asian dynamism is not solely the story of the 21st century. In the latter half of the 20th century, the developmental model of Japan and the so-called East Asian tigers had drawn worldwide attention, especially after the two oil shocks in the 1970s (Evans 1995; Woo-Cumings 1999). In particular, Japan has been regarded as a country to learn from (Johnson 1982). Vogel labelled Japan as Number One as early as 1979 (Vogel 1979). Finding the secret of Japan's economic success and political stability has long occupied social scientists worldwide (Katzenstein 1978; Curtis 1988; Calder 1988). Scholars also spotlighted the 'flying geese model' in East Asia where Japan took the lead and 'four tigers' in East Asia – South Korea, Taiwan, Hong Kong and Singapore – followed. East Asian economies that accepted the Japanese model of development emerged as a new focus of academic research (Haggard 1990; Wade 1990; Woo 1991; Amsden 1992). However, since the bubble economy ended in Japan in the early 1990s, Japanese socioeconomic performance has muddled through. Scholars began highlighting problems related to Japanese political economy instead of its success story (Lincoln 1999; Carlie and Tilton 1998; Grimes 2001; Vogel 2006).

From the end of the 1990s, two phenomena have emerged as a new focus of academic debate, replacing the discussion on the rise of Japan.

One is, without doubt, the rise of China. Discussions over how the rise of China will affect regional and global order flourished. Power transition and its impacts on the global order have constituted a major point of debate (Goldstein 2005; Shambaugh 2005; Kang 2007; Ross and Feng 2008). The other topic that has emerged is a debate on East Asian regionalism. However, opinions are divided as to whether or not East Asian regionalism is smoothly on the move. The number of publications on the possibilities and challenges of East Asian regionalism or multilateralism has drastically increased (Lincoln 2004; Pempel 2005; Frost 2008; Green and Gill 2009). The geographical focus of regionalism has also shifted from the Asia-Pacific to East Asia.

These two new discourses, the rise of China and the emerging East Asian regionalism, have so far been addressed separately as if the two were mutually exclusive. Many scholars have devoted their attention mostly to the presumed global impacts of China's rise, focusing on the question as to whether or not China will be a revisionist power (Johnston 2003: 5–56; Goldstein 2005). However, only a few have linked the rise of China with its implication for emerging regionalism in East Asia. This does not necessarily imply that China is an engine of emerging regionalism. Nor does it suggest that East Asian regionalism can be achieved without the participation of China. Rather, how the rise of China is perceived among regional neighbours and how geopolitical dynamics in Northeast Asia is reshaped in the context of China's rise should be duly discussed in order to access the potential for upgraded regional integration.

Also, when regionalism is debated, the weight and role of the three Northeast Asian countries has to be taken into consideration. ASEAN countries have long been in the driver's seat of regional integration in East Asia (Acharya 2009: 172–92). However, China, Japan and South Korea constitute a critical mass in the region in almost all dimensions, including politics, diplomacy, economy and security. Cooperation among these three regional powers is critically important for the progress of regionalism in East Asia, but it can never be taken for granted. From the outside it looks as if regional integration in Northeast Asia was smoothly on the rise. Still, from the inside, as Rozman (2004) points out, Northeast Asian regionalism is stunted. Without upgrading cooperative ties among China, Japan and Korea, the steeplechase for regional cooperation is likely to face lots of expected and unexpected hurdles (Pempel 2006: 239–54).

This chapter analyses changing geopolitical dynamics in Northeast Asia with a focus on cooperation and conflict among South Korea, Japan and China. The following combines a microscopic analysis of evolving ties among intra-regional countries with a telescopic and macroscopic analysis of regional cooperation in Northeast Asia.

2. NORTHEAST ASIAN REGIONAL INTEGRATION FROM A TELESCOPIC VIEWPOINT

Aaron Friedberg once pointed out that East Asia will remain as a 'cockpit of great power conflict', because, unlike Europe, no conflict-mitigating elements had been developed in East Asia (Friedberg 1993/1994: 5–33). To him East Asia was ripe for conflict and rivalry. On the other hand, Pempel (2005) suggested that East Asia was ripe for cooperation. Whether East Asian regional cooperation is smoothly growing is highly contentious. Still, it is also true that market-driven, bottom-up, private-sector initiated regional cooperation, which is often called regionalisation, permeates East Asian countries.

Associative interactions among East Asian countries have grown significantly over the past decade. The share of intra-regional trade has increased from 34.2 per cent in 1980 to 49 per cent in 2007, surpassing intra-regional trade among NAFTA countries which stood at 42.0 per cent in 2007 (Park and Hong 2010: 9). Considering that intra-regional exports reached 68 per cent and intra-regional imports recorded 61.8 per cent of total trade in 2007 among the EU 27 countries, intra-regional trade among East Asian countries lags behind Europe. However, intra-regional imports among East Asian countries increased from 31.6 per cent in 1980 to 51.6 per cent in 2007. Also, intra-regional exports among East Asian countries have gone up from 36.8 per cent to 45.4 per cent in 2007 (Park and Hong 2010: 12). In terms of the flow of overseas direct investment, global-level flows decreased from US$2.5 trillion in 2007 to US$2.2 trillion in 2008. However, during the same period, intra-regional direct investment among East Asian countries increased from US$263 billion to US$269 billion (Park and Hong 2010: 7). According to the Japan Aviation Association, the number of intra-regional travellers using air transportation has steadily increased from 366 million in 2000 to 473 million in 2004 and to 590 million in 2007 (JAA 2008: 49). Changing economic transactions between Korea and the two neighbours show the same tendencies. The trade amount between South Korea and China was only US$6.4 billion in 1992, but reached US$188.4 billion in 2010. South Korea's trade with Japan stood at US$31.2 billion in 1990, but increased to US$92.5 billion in 2010 (MOFAT 2011: 155–61). By every standard, regional interdependence is steadily on the rise.

The institutional nexus among East Asian countries has also been thickened. Before the Asian economic crisis in 1997, the Asia-Pacific Economic Cooperation (APEC) worked as the main regional forum for advancing cooperative ties among Asian countries. However, the Asian economic crisis worked as a catalyst for enhanced institutional ties among

East Asian countries. First, East Asian countries, primary victims of the crisis, shared a loose identity and awareness that national borders mean less in the age of a globalising economy. Tides of foreign currency shortage hit not only Indonesia and Thailand but also South Korea. It is in this context that ASEAN invited three Northeast Asian countries, China, Japan and South Korea, to an ASEAN meeting in December 1997, which became the ASEAN Plus Three (APT) forum. Second, China shifted its foreign policy orientation in the wake of the Asian economic crisis. Until the mid 1990s, China showed either indifference to regional affairs, as was demonstrated by its attitude towards the North Korean nuclear development programme between 1992 and 1994, or an aggressive stance towards its regional neighbours, which was attested by the Taiwan Strait crisis in 1996. Accordingly, China was regarded as a potential threat to regional order (Burnstein and Munro 1998). After the Asian economic crisis, however, China began actively engaging in regional affairs (Shambaugh 2004/5: 64–99). China, together with Korea and Japan, participated in multilateral forums like ASEAN Plus Three. Also, China started to get actively involved on the issue of North Korea's nuclear programme as a participant in the Four Party Talks. China went further to toss the idea of concluding an FTA agreement with ASEAN countries. Alarmed by the active Chinese approach, Japan moved to expand the membership of ASEAN Plus Three to establish the East Asian Summit (EAS), which included Australia, New Zealand and India (Fukushima 2009: 103–27).[1]

Within the ASEAN Plus Three framework, the three heads of government of the three Northeast Asian members began meeting separately from 1999. This mechanism eventually developed into a Three-Way Summit among Northeast Asian leaders from 2008. This reflects the recognition that the big three in Northeast Asia have their independent role to play rather than being led by the weak in the world of the strong. In addition to ASEAN Plus Three and the Three-Way Summit, the Six Party Talks were established in 2003 as an institutional framework to handle the most thorny security issue in the region, which is the denuclearisation of North Korea.

Because of these tightening network of multilateral and mini-lateral talks, contacts among Northeast Asian leaders have regularly taken place. The South Korean president, Japanese prime minister and Chinese prime minister meet in a series of multilateral settings every year such as ASEAN Plus Three (APT), the Asia–Europe Meeting (ASEM), Asia-Pacific Economic Cooperation (APEC), Three Way Summit among Northeast Asian leaders and East Asian Summit (EAS). This shows a changing context of organisational linkages among three Northeast Asian countries. For example, in 2008, the South Korean president and the

Japanese prime minister met five times. In 2009, the South Korean president had summit meetings with the Japanese prime ministers six times. It can be concluded that, from a telescopic standpoint as well as from an aggregate level analysis, regional cooperation is making an upward movement in Northeast Asia.

3. INTRA-REGIONAL DYNAMICS AMONG NORTHEAST ASIAN COUNTRIES FROM A MICROSCOPIC VIEWPOINT

Though it looks as if regional cooperation is smoothly on the move from a telescopic angle, geopolitical dynamics among the three Northeast Asian countries reveal more complexity if seen from a microscopic angle. A cursory look at South Korean and Japanese attitudes towards China's rise illustrates this point. After 1992, when South Korea and China normalised diplomatic ties, South Korea showed a fever-like favouritism towards China. In 2004, China became the biggest trading partner for South Korea, surpassing the United States. In a single year, 2009, South Korea exported US$86.7 billion to China while importing US$54.3 billion from China.[2] As of 2009, 67,000 South Koreans are studying in China, second only to 103,889 South Korean students in the United States, and 63,000 Chinese are studying in South Korea (*Yonhap News* 2010).[3] Unlike John Mearsheimer's prediction that South Korea, like other countries in East Asia, would join a balancing approach against China (Mearsheimer 2005: 47–8), South Korea has hardly shown signs of balancing against China. Instead, what can be witnessed is hedging or accommodation (Kang 2009: 1–28; Han 2010). At least South Korea made the decision of not making a choice between an ally, the US, and a partner, China (Chung 2008). At the same time Japan felt unease about China's rise as a regional and global competitor, which urged it to adopt a balancing strategy towards China, at least as far as the decade between 1996 and 2006 was concerned. In order to cope with China Japan has strengthened its alliance partnership with the United States (Christensen 1999). Under the guardianship of the United States, which encouraged Japan to assume more of a regional security function, Japan turned more proactive and assertive with regard to defence issues (Arase 2007: 560–83). Instead of accommodating China, Japan has taken balancing action against China.

The three nations in Northeast Asia do not necessarily agree on the regional security and diplomatic architecture, though economic and human transactions link them more tightly than before. If we highlight geopolitical dynamics among three Northeast Asian countries, two different phases can be discerned in terms of conflict and cooperation among them. The period between 1998 and 2007 may be characterised as a phase when South Korea and China teamed up against Japan. However, the period between 2008 and 2011 may be categorised as a phase when South Korea and Japan worked together while both nations had uncomfortable ties with China.

4. PHASE ONE (1998–2007): STRATEGIC CONVERGENCE BETWEEN SOUTH KOREA AND CHINA AGAINST JAPAN

The year 1998 was a turning point in trilateral ties among South Korea, Japan and China in several ways. It was in 1998 that the three Northeast Asian countries began to show diverging attitudes towards North Korea. South Korean president Kim Daejung adopted the so-called 'sunshine policy' to engage North Korea in an attempt to denuclearise the Korean Peninsula. China also shared the perspective of embracing North Korea. However, the Daepodong missile launch and abductees issue that unfolded in 1998 served as a force for moulding negative images of North Korea. Also, in 1998, East Asian regionalism entered a new stage. After experiencing the Asian financial crisis in 1997, when the United States was viewed as an enforcer rather than a rescuer, China, with a new diplomatic principle, began actively engaging with its regional neighbours (Shambaugh 2004/5). South Korea also became energetic in weaving the regional network for peace and prosperity in East Asia. Japan did not step backward, but, in the eyes of the Japanese, the new regionalism drive was perceived as an aggressive counter to the former Japanese leadership in East Asian affairs, especially with regard to Southeast Asia which Japan regarded as its economic sphere of influence. Furthermore, in 1998, historical controversies showed different dynamics. In 1998, South Korean President Kim Daejung initiated forward-looking relations with Japan, which Japan welcomed, while Chinese President Jiang Zemin expressed increasing frustration over Japan's historical past. However, from around 2001 when the contentious issue of Japanese high school history textbooks and Koizumi's Yasukuni shrine visit emerged as controversies between Japan and its two neighbours, South Korea and China began taking a similar stance towards historical issues. Thus, three sets of issues – the North Korea problem, the historical controversy, and the regionalism drive – constituted focal points that affected the complex and dynamic relationship among the three Northeast Asian countries. In most of these issue areas, South Korea was perceived by the Japanese as tilting too much towards China at the expense of Japan, possibly including the United States.

Above all, what made Japan most fretful about South Korea's friendly move towards China was the North Korea question. During the Cold War period, few if any Japanese raised questions about the existing security ties between the United States and Japan and South Korea respectively. South Korea belonged to the liberal camp and contained North Korea. However, the progressive South Korean government led by Kim Daejung began engaging North Korea in the hope of opening up the country and eventually denuclearising the peninsula. Considering that China had long been a protector of North Korea, this policy shift signified a turn towards China at the expense of Japan and the United States. Japan could not actively follow suit to engage North Korea. First of all, after the Daepodong missile launch in 1998 that threatened Japan physically for the first time after the end of World War II, North Korea was perceived as a country that could destabilise Japan and the region. After the missile launch, Japan decided not only to participate in the Missile Defence programme led by the United States but also to launch military satellites (Park 2004). Second, convinced that North Korea was abducting innocent Japanese citizens in the late 1970s and early 1980s, conservative Japanese sounded the alarm bell against North Korea and refused to improve the relationship with the latter until the issue was satisfactorily resolved. On 17 September 2002, Prime Minister Koizumi showed his willingness to catch up with the South Korean engagement policy by visiting North Korea and signing the Pyongyang Declaration. However, his ardent endeavour only resulted in raising the abductees issues to the forefront of political controversy. Because of the abductees issues and the North Korean nuclear programme that drew people's attention again from October 2002, Japan took a tougher stance against North Korea. Japan aligned with the hardliners within the Bush administration to push North Korea into the corner, expecting the North Korean leader to step back and compromise. From the Japanese perspective, both South Korea and China, advocating the North Korean position, looked suspicious. Instead of putting pressure on North Korea, the two countries continued to talk to and negotiate with North Korean leaders, gave assistance to North Korea without reciprocal returns, and showed sympathy for the rhetoric of the North Korean government. Whenever North Korea provoked its neighbours with missile launches, nuclear tests, and military provocations, Japan took unilateral or multilateral initiatives to adopt sanctions against North Korea. South Korea and China, on the other hand, remained reluctant, or at least hesitant, to take hard-line measures vis-à-vis North Korea. Therefore, a big rift emerged between Japan, on one side, and South Korea and China, on the other, when they dealt with North Korea. From the Japanese standpoint, South Korea played the North Korea game in the Chinese court.

Historical controversy constituted another source of cleavage among the three Northeast Asian countries. During the Cold War period, historical issues were overshadowed by the strategic rivalry between the liberal and socialist camps. It was around the late 1980s when the historical controversy emerged to the fore. Chinese historians had long been working towards bringing justice to the history issue despite the reluctance of the Chinese government (Reilly 2004: 276–94). Furthermore, Chinese and South Korean civil society organisations have coalesced together to internationalise the comfort women issue since the late 1980s. Japanese right wing groups angrily denied the existence of the issue itself. However, the Japanese government, after thorough investigation, acknowledged government engagement in mobilising comfort women and apologised formally. The then Chief Cabinet secretary Kono made a statement of apology in 1992. In 1994, Japanese Prime Minister Murayama announced a declaration where he sincerely apologised on the issue. He also established the Asia Women's Fund to compensate the victims.[4] However, rather than silencing the dissident right wing groups in Japan, repeated apologies by the Japanese authorities agitated the already dissatisfied right wingers in Japan who vehemently resisted the apology, or kowtow, diplomacy to its neighbours (Tamamoto 2007). From the Japanese right-winger's viewpoint, dragging out the shameful history of Japan looked as if it was an attempt to isolate Japan in East Asia while giving advantage only to China. During the Koizumi period, Japanese leaders sympathised with the right wing's claims and took the position that they would not apologise again. Koizumi not only endorsed a history textbook made by the hawkish conservatives, *Tsukurukai*, but also paid homage to the Yasukuni shrine, where 14 A-class war criminals are enshrined. These provocative actions galvanised the Chinese and South Korean public. Whether intended or unintended, Koizumi's action and rhetoric put China and South Korea in the same basket, not because South Korea was seduced by China but because South Korea and China shared similar historical perspectives as victims. President Roh Moo Hyun's declaration of 'diplomatic war' with Japan in March 2005, symbolised antipathy towards Japan, though this was not necessarily an expression of identical historical perspective with China. In 2004, South Korea experienced an unexpected soft clash with China concerning Koguryo history[5] (Chung 2009: 468–83). However, unlike China that immediately put a hold on the issue when South Korea showed anger, Japan conveniently ignored the South Korean request to end the controversy. This led to the unintended coalition between South Korea and China on the historical controversy front. Japan did not fully realise that South Korea was pushed away by Japan's own action rather than pulled by China.

Japan also developed a different approach to the regionalism drive in East Asia. When ASEAN invited the three Northeast Asian nations, South Korea, China and Japan in 1997 for a meeting, not a single nation rejected the proposal. Later this initiative developed into the ASEAN Plus Three (APT) forum. China approached ASEAN more assertively by concluding an FTA framework agreement with it in 2001. Japan tried to secure its own position by doing the same in 2002. The sense of regional rivalry was there. China and South Korea agreed on the APT formula as the core of East Asian Community building. However, Japan assumed that the APT was a disguised attempt to exclude the United States from the region. Accordingly, Japan assertively argued that Australia, New Zealand and India should be included as the members, which resulted in the formation of the East Asia Summit (EAS) (Fukushima 2009: 103–27). At the same time, Japan pursued so called 'value diplomacy', which sounded as if China still remained out of the club. Prime Minister Abe showed interest in forming a league of democracies where Australia, New Zealand and India were integral partners. Also the subsequent Prime Minister Aso drew up the notion of an arc of liberty and prosperity, in which China was fully integrated. Hence, Japan tried to attenuate the East Asian regionalism drive while spearheading the process towards globalising the US–Japan alliance partnership. From the Japanese perspective, South Korea under its progressive political leaders was perceived as a hesitant coalition partner or an opportunistic country to play the role of a 'balancer' between China and Japan. Overall, in the eyes of Japan, South Korea–China relations looked as if they got too close, even to the extent that the two countries were trying to isolate Japan in East Asia.

5. PHASE TWO (2008–2011): STRATEGIC CONVERGENCE BETWEEN SOUTH KOREA AND JAPAN AGAINST CHINA

It is noteworthy that the relations among three East Asian countries have been reshaped in the post-Koizumi and post-Roh period. Japanese Prime Minister Abe took an initiative to ameliorate the relationship with China and South Korea by visiting Beijing and Seoul first before going to Washington (Yahuda 2009: 365–79). Chinese leadership also reciprocated the move by taking a new policy stance towards Japan. Instead of pressuring Japan, which usually results in elevating the voices of right wing groups in Japan, China began following a softer approach to Japan. Fukuda proclaimed a notion of turning the Pacific into another Mediterranean sea of cooperation. By that he tried to balance out the ties with the United States and Asian countries. Aso also remained very careful not to provoke Japan's neighbours. No Japanese prime minister after Koizumi have visited the Yasukuni shrine, learning from their predecessor's turbulent ties with Asian neighbours. After the change of government in Japan from the Liberal Democratic Party to the Democratic Party of Japan, Japanese leaders did not hesitate to restore Asian diplomacy assertively. Prime Minister Hatoyama was a strong advocate of East Asian diplomacy, though his vision of East Asian Community building remains ambiguous. His argument for an equal partnership with the United States raised doubts in the US as to whether Japan was a reliable partner (Funabashi 2009; Green 2010: 3–19). Under Hatoyama's leadership, Japan tantalised the United States by initiating renegotiations about the future of Futenma airbase in Okinawa, which the LDP government decided to relocate in 1996 in an attempt to show a sympathetic attitude towards China. When Hatoyama had a troubled relationship with the US, Ozawa, former DPJ leader, visited Beijing with about 600 powerful political and business leaders. Also, Ozawa worked hard to let the next generation leader, Shizin Ping, meet the Japanese emperor despite a violation of internal rules. However, Hatoyama had to step down because he could not make any progress on the issue of the Futenma base relocation. He failed not only to relocate it to a different country but even to relocate it out of the Okinawa prefecture, even though he had made an oral commitment to do so.

After Naoto Kan had succeeded Hatoyama as prime minister, he initiated a drastic policy shift in two arenas (Park 2011). First, he began arguing the need for a tax increase to deal with the snowballing fiscal deficit. Also, he presented his view that US–Japan alliance was the centrepiece of Japan's diplomacy. An unexpected development regarding the regional situation also expedited his foreign policy reorientation. On 7 September 2010, a Chinese fishing boat collided with a Japanese coastal guard ship in the middle of trying to approach the Senkaku islands. Out of 14 Chinese fishermen who were arrested, Japan kept a captain captive for an extended period of time, which aggravated the relationship between Japan and China. The Chinese leadership did not hesitate to pressure Japan with several available policy tools, including arresting Japanese tourists, stopping the export of 'rare earth', geological material used for producing LCDs, to Japan, etc. Eventually Japan under the Kan leadership stepped back by releasing the captain without pressing charges. However, this radically changed the perception of China among ordinary Japanese. It looked as if a rising China was not hesitant to show its teeth in order to achieve what Beijing refers to as core interests. This threatening face of China led the DPJ regime to tilt more towards tightening the US–Japan alliance. Also, unexpected tragic events on the Korean peninsula alerted the Japanese leadership to the importance of staying with the US. After a South Korean navy ship, Chonan, was sunk by a North Korean submarine in March 2010, North Korea shelled Yeonpyeong island which is part of South Korean territory, resulting in about 17 casualties, including two civilians. This military provocation led to the awareness of the need for tighter South Korean–Japanese military cooperation.

In South Korea, the advent of a new conservative president, Lee Myung-bak, brought about shifts in foreign policy initiatives (Snyder 2009: 85–102). Most of all, President Lee made a realist turn by emphasising a tougher stance towards North Korea. He drastically revised the logic of 'benign engagement' policy by giving priority to national security concerns, which was denuclearising North Korea. The 'benign engagement policy' was based on the idea of awarding the sense of comfort and security by assisting North Korea to get out of economic hardships. It was hoped that North Korea would subsequently come out to the regional or global community with an attitude of reforming the regime. This would eventually and ultimately bring about a denuclearised North Korea. However, despite – not because of – engaging North Korea, Pyongyang developed nuclear weapons and conducted a nuclear testing on 9 October 2006, even when the South Korean government followed a benign engagement policy, and again on 25 May 2009. North Korea has not given up its nuclear weapons programme despite its repeated promises in September 2005 and February 2007. What North Korea really wants seems to be the possession of the nuclear weapons (Cha 2009: 119–38). Instead of a benign, unconditional, engagement policy, the conservative Lee administration has frontloaded denuclearisation as a priority concern.

In addition, in the eyes of South Koreans, the question as to whether China is the most reliable partner to realise the denuclearisation of North Korea has not been solidly answered. Despite rhetorical commitments to the denuclearisation of North Korea, a Chinese priority concern seems to lie in guaranteeing the survival of the North Korean regime (Shambaugh 2003: 44).[6] As Bonnie Glaser points out, Beijing is reluctant to join a multilateral effort to persuade North Korea to give up its nuclear ambition (Glaser and Liang 2008: 167). Also, China's image in South Korea turned wild. In 2004, the unexpected clash between South Korea and China concerning the *Koguryo* issue highlighted the submerged but potentially explosive historical controversies between the two countries (Chung 2009: 468–83).

On the other hand, North Korea's nuclear tests and outspoken desire to directly negotiate with the United States instead of coming back to the Six Party Talks urged South Korea to strengthen its ties with the United States

(Reiss 2006–07: 103).[7] First, in order to cope with an increasing North Korean military threat, including both the conventional and nuclear threat, South Korea is obliged to deepen its security ties with the US. Second, in order to cope with the North Korean requests to directly talk to the US, South Korea needs enhanced coordination and consultation with the US. Presidents Lee and Obama adopted the Joint Vision for the Alliance at a summit meeting on 16 June 2009 with a view to develop the alliance ties into a comprehensive and strategic alliance of bilateral, regional and global scope (*Yonhap News* 2009). President Lee also upgraded its ties with Japan. In 2008, the Korean president and the Japanese prime ministers met, either in a bilateral or in a multilateral setting, at least five times on official occasions.[8] In 2009, the Korean president had six summit meetings with the Japanese prime minister.[9] In a presidential speeches on 1 March (independence movement day) and 15 August (independence day), President Lee did not even mention Japan in 2008 to 2010. However, compared to the previous South Korean government, the Lee administration gave more emphasis on upgrading ties with the US and Japan.

As a result of political reconfigurations in both Japan and South Korea, the foreign policy orientations of Japan and South Korea contain more converging elements than discord. The two countries are in agreement on adopting a hedging strategy towards China, which means deeply engaging China in the economic arena while forging strong alliances with the United States in the security realm (Han 2008: 335–51). In dealing with North Korea, the US and South Korea, together with Japan, rely on a combined strategy of pressure and dialogue. South Korea under Lee is not fascinated by regional community building, compared to the past regime.

6. CONCLUSION

With the rise of China, Northeast Asia turns out to be a region with a dynamic future. The region is dynamic in two senses. Northeast Asia is an engine of economic vitality. At the same time, however, this region is full of uncertainty and instability, especially when it comes to the issue of geopolitics and its global implications. The rise of China poses an immense challenge to the world, because it has the potential to revise the existing rules of global governance. Also, the rise of China defines the regional ramification of power in a sense that it is rapidly challenging the conventional leadership of Japan in the region.

Until the mid 1990s, ASEAN countries firmly seated themselves in a driver's seat of regional cooperation. The inclusion of the Northeast Asian powers in the extended ASEAN process added a new dimension to the regionalism drive. Eventually these three Northeast Asian countries began developing cooperative mechanisms of their own, though they never parted from the ASEAN Plus Three process. Depending on the strategic directions that the trilateral countries take, the East Asian regional and global order is likely to take a different shape. In case the three nations converge in their strategic conceptions, the geopolitical and geo-economic weight of three Northeast Asian countries will be increased.

This chapter has presented a microscopic contour of trilateral ties among South Korea, Japan and China, as well as a telescopic outlook for regional cooperation. The telescopic analysis suggests that cooperation among East Asian countries, including the three Northeast Asian nations, is steadily and constantly on the move. The ties among the East Asian countries are not only associatively cross-linked but also institutionally thickened. However, the microscopic analysis shows that the three Northeast Asian countries do not share same visions or perspectives about the future development of the region.

Analysis of intra-regional geopolitical dynamics endows us with both hope and challenge. The fact that the three Northeast Asian countries develop converging notions of strategies at one time and diverging notion of strategies at other times implies that conflict among the three countries is not inevitable. This is quite different from the Cold War era when strategic cleavages existed between the liberal and socialist blocs. Different combinations of cooperative ties can develop, depending on the issues and situational context. Hence, it opens the potential for future cooperation. But, at the same time, strategic convergence and divergence among the three Northeast Asian countries suggests that the development of regional cooperation in Northeast Asia would not be smooth.

This chapter identified three issues that affect the cooperative potential among the three nations: the North Korea issue, historical controversies and the geographical boundary of East Asian regionalism. Future challenges for the upgrading of regional cooperation structures would also be associated with the following dimensions. First, maintaining friendly ties among three Northeast Asian countries will depend much on whether China will retrieve soft power diplomacy without testing its military muscle in Northeast Asia. If China drifts away from the status-quo orientation towards a revisionist temptation, cooperation among the Northeast Asian Big Three would remain unstable and inconsistent. The second challenge for the three countries in Northeast Asia may be the careful handling of the territorial and historical issues. The Senkaku islands issue will remain a diplomatic trap between China and Japan, while the Dokdo controversy works as a stumbling block for a further deepening of ties between South Korea and Japan. Whether Japan relies on nationalistic pride or places itself in the regional setting will affect the future of ties among Northeast Asian countries. Last but not least, the way that North Korea's nuclear and security situation is handled will gravely affect the future direction of regional cooperation in Northeast Asia. The North Korean issue can be a black hole that ruins every potential for heightening regional cooperation. However, it also contains the possibility of working as a bond that enriches coordination and cooperation among regional neighbours.

NOTES

1. Eventually the United States and Russia joined this institution. Unlike China that utilised APT as a primary organ for regional cooperation, Japan opted for an East Asian Summit where its allies and friends were added up. For the Japanese perspective on the regional multilateralism, refer to Fukushima (2009).
2. Data from South Korean Foreign Ministry, http://www.mofat.go.kr/state/areadiplomacy/asiapacific/index6.jsp?TabMenu=TabMenu4 (accessed: 11 May, 2010).
3. Data from South Korean Foreign Ministry, ibid. The number of Korean students studying in the United States is from the Department of Homeland Security, cited from *Yonhap News* (2010).
4. For the development of the comfort women issue, refer to the home page of the Asia Women's Fund. http://www.awf.ro.jp (accessed: 18 May, 2010).
5. In 2004, the Chinese Academy of Social Science launched a research project called 'Northeast Asia History Project', where they claimed that *Koguryo*, the old dynasty that Korean people regarded as theirs, was a Chinese kingdom.
6. David Shambaugh suggests that halting North Korea's nuclear programme is not the ultimate end that China hopes to achieve (Shambaugh 2003).
7. Mitchell Reiss also remains sceptical about the Six Party Talks by suggesting that sometimes it seems as the sole purpose of the Six Party Talks is to get Pyongyang to show up (Reiss 2006–07).
8. On 25 February, Prime Minister Fukuda attended the inauguration ceremony of the new Korean President Lee Myung-bak and conducted a summit meeting. That was the first summit meeting after President Lee officially assumed his position. On 20 April, 2008, President Lee visited Tokyo on his way back from Washington and had another summit meeting. President Lee and Prime Minister Fukuda met again on 6 July, 2008, when President Lee was invited to the G-8 meeting. On 24 October, 2008, a new Japanese Prime Minister Aso conducted a summit meeting with President Lee on the occasion of the ASEM conference. On 23 December, 2008, President Lee, Prime Minister Aso and Chinese Prime Minister Wen had a three-way summit in Fukuoka, which was the first Northeast Asia Trilateral Summit meeting.
9. Out of them, three occasions were mutual visits and the other three meetings took place in multilateral settings like the G20 meeting in London, ASEAN+3 meeting in Pattaya and the UN meeting in New York.

REFERENCES

Acharya, A. (2009), 'The strong in the world of the weak: Southeast Asia in Asia's regional architecture', in M. Green and B. Gill (eds), *Asia's New Multilateralism*, New York: Columbia University.

Amsden, A. (1992), *Asia's Next Giant: South Korea and Late Industrialization*, Oxford: Oxford University Press.
Arase, D. (2007), 'Japan, the active state: security policy after 9/11', *Asian Survey*, **47**(4), 560–83.
Burnstein, R. and R. Munro (1998), *The Coming Conflict with China*, New York: Vintage.
Calder, K. (1988), *Crisis and Compensation*, Princeton, NJ: Princeton University Press.
Carlie, L. and M. Tilton (1998), *Is Japan Really Changing its Way*, Washington, DC: Brookings Institution.
Cha, V. (2009), 'What do they really want? Obama's North Korea conundrum', *The Washington Quarterly*, **32**(4), 119–38.
Christensen, T. (1999), 'China, the U.S.–Japan alliance and the security dilemma', *International Security*, **23**(4), 49–80.
Chung, J.H. (2008), *Between Ally and Partner*, New York: Columbia University Press.
Chung, J.H. (2009), 'China's soft clash with South Korea: the history war and beyond', *Asian Survey*, **XLIX**(3), 468–83.
Curtis, G. (1988), *The Japanese Way of Politics*, New York: Columbia University Press.
Evans, P. (1995), *Embedded Autonomy: States and Industrial Transformation*, Princeton, NJ: Princeton University Press.
Friedberg, A. (Winter 1993/1994), 'Ripe for rivalry: prospects for peace in a multipolar Asia', *International Security*, **18**(3), 5–33.
Frost, E. (2008), *Asia's New Regionalism*, Boulder, CO: Lynne Rienner.
Fukushima, A. (2009), 'Japan's perspective on Asian regionalism', in M. Green and B. Gill (eds), *Asia's New Multilateralism*, New York: Columbia University Press.
Funabashi, Y. (2009), 'Tokyo's trials', *Foreign Affairs*, **88**(6).
Glaser, B. and W. Liang (2008), 'North Korea: the beginning of a China–U.S. partnership?', *The Washington Quarterly*, **31**(3), 167.
Goldstein, A. (2005), *Rising to the Challenge: China's Grand Strategy and International Security*, Stanford, CA: Stanford University Press.
Green, M. (2010), 'Japan's confused revolution', *The Washington Quarterly*, **33**(1), 3–19.
Green, M. and B. Gill (2009), *Asia's New Multilateralism*, New York: Columbia University Press.
Grimes, W. (2001), *Unmaking the Japanese Miracle*, Ithaca, NY: Cornell University Press.
Haggard, S. (1990), *Pathways from the Periphery*, Ithaca, NY: Cornell University Press.
Han, S. (2008), 'From engagement to hedging: South Korea's new China policy', *Korean Journal of Defence Analysis*, **20**(4), 335–51.
Han, S.H. (2010), 'From engagement to hedging', *Korean Journal of Defence Analysis*.
Japan Aviation Association (JAA) (2008), *Air Statistics 2008*, Tokyo: Japan Aviation Association.
Johnson, C. (1982), *MITI and the Japanese Miracle*, Stanford, CA: Stanford University Press.
Johnston, I. (2003), 'Is China a status quo power?', *International Security*, **27**(4), 5–56.

Kang, D. (2007), *China Rising*, New York: Columbia University Press.
Kang, D. (Jan-Apr. 2009), 'Between balancing and bandwagoning: South Korea's response to China', *Journal of East Asian Studies*, **9**(1), 1–28.
Katzenstein, P. (1978), *Between Power and Plenty*, Madison, WI: University of Wisconsin Press.
Lincoln, E. (1999), *Troubled Times*, Washington, DC: Brookings Institution.
Lincoln, E. (2004), *East Asian Economic Regionalism*, Washington, DC: Brookings Institution.
Mahbubani, K. (2008), *The New Asian Hemisphere: The Irresistible Shift of Global Power to the East*, New York: Public Affairs.
Mearsheimer, J. (Nov–Dec 2005), 'Better to be Godzilla than Bambi', *Foreign Policy*, 145, 47–8.
Park, C.H. (2004), 'Jonsubangwi eso Jokgukbangwi ro [*From Exclusive Defense to Active Defense*]', *Korean Journal of International Studies*, **44**(1), 169–90.
Park, C.H. (2011), 'Policy shifts of the Democratic Party of Japan and unstable party competition in Japan', *Review of International and Area Studies*, **20**(1), 31–59.
Park, J.M. and S.R. Hong (2010), 'East Asian intra-trade and logistics network', *Muyok Sangmu Yonku* [*Trade and Commerce Studies*], **46**(May), 237–61.
Pempel, T.J. (2005), 'Emerging webs of regional connectedness', in T.J. Pempel (ed.), *Remapping East Asia*, Ithaca, NY: Cornell University Press.
Pempel, T.J. (ed.) (2005), *Remapping East Asia*, Ithaca, NY: Cornell University Press.
Pempel, T.J. (2006), 'The race to connect East Asia: an unending steeplechase', *Asian Economic Policy Review*, **1**(2), 239–54.
Reilly, J. (2004), 'China's history activists and the resistance against Japan', *Asian Survey*, **44**(2), 276–94.
Reiss, M. (Winter 2006–07), 'A nuclear-armed North Korea: accepting the unacceptable', *Survival*, **48**(4), 97–109.
Ross, R. and Z. Feng (eds) (2008), *China's Ascent*, Ithaca, NY: Cornell University Press.
Rozman, G. (2004), *Northeast Asia's Stunted Regionalism*, Cambridge: Cambridge University Press.
Shambaugh, D. (2003), 'China and the Korean peninsula: playing for the long-term', *The Washington Quarterly*, **26**(2), 43–56.
Shambaugh, D. (Winter 2004/5), 'China engages Asia: reshaping the regional order', *International Security*, **29**(3), 64–99.
Shambaugh, D. (2005), *Power Shift: China and Asia's New Dynamics*, Berkeley, CA: University of California Press.
Snyder, S. (2009), 'Lee Myung-bak's foreign policy: a 250-day assessment', *Korean Journal of Defense Analysis*, **21**(1), 85–102.
South Korean Ministry of Foreign Affairs and Trade (MOFAT) (2011), *Diplomatic White Paper 2011*, Seoul: MOFAT.
Tamamoto, M. (2007), 'Japan's politics of cultural shame', *Global Asia*, **2**(1), 14–20.
Vogel, E. (1979), *Japan as Number One*, New York: Harper Colophon Books.
Vogel, S. (2006), *Japan Remodelled*, Ithaca, NY: Cornell University Press.
Wade, R. (1990), *Governing the Market*, Princeton, NJ: Princeton University Press.
Woo, J. (1991), *Race to the Swift*, New York: Columbia University.

Woo-Cumings, M. (ed.) (1999), *The Developmental State*, Ithaca, NY: Cornell University Press.
Yahuda, M. (2009), 'Sine–Japanese relationship: partners and rivals?', *Korean Journal of Defense Analysis*, **21**(4), 365–79.
Yonhap News (2009), 17 June.
Yonhap News (2010), 19 January.

PART IV

East Asia and global development

11. China and the changing nature of globalisation

Jeffrey Henderson

1. INTRODUCTION

The re-emergence of China as a global economic and political power is beginning to have major consequences for political economies and societies in many parts of the world. One of the things that characterises the vast majority of research on these consequences, however, is that it operates at the level of the national (for example China and the United States) or world-regional (for example China and Africa) interfaces only. Very little of it seeks to understand the consequences of China's rise for the nature of globalisation, and, through that 'lens', for particular national or sub-national political–economic and social formations.[1] As will become clear below, this is an unfortunate omission for both science and policy. As a consequence, it is this concern that animates the arguments developed in this chapter.

In reflecting on what the rise of China might mean for the nature of globalisation, two propositions will help to guide the subsequent argument. The first concerns the need to take 'the global' seriously as a level of analysis. While this argument has a history of nearly 40 years (Wallerstein 1974), the current form of US-driven globalisation (from the late 1970s/early 1980s) and now China's emerging global presence, serve to underline the need to break from state-centric modes of analysis (and their related expressions: 'international', 'transnational', and so on) in order to deliver the analytic categories necessary for an adequate understanding of the contemporary world and its problems. Global processes and the various forms of power that they incorporate and express have a relative autonomy from those that are spatially bounded (nationally and sub-nationally) in their origins and effects. As such, and among other things, they serve to question the efficacy of traditional, place-specific research and policy agenda.[2]

The second proposition is the need to recognise that globalisation is not a reflection of some idealised, monadic notion of capitalism as much of the globalisation literature seems to assume. Rather it needs to be understood as a consequence of the gradual 'externalisation' of particular national forms of capitalism, in particular historical periods.[3] If we want to know what constitutes a form of globalisation, where it has come from, what might be its dynamics and how it might be changing, we first need to understand the nature of the dominant national capitalism (and its historical, institutional and social origins) that gives that form of globalisation its particular character. I begin with the second proposition, return to the first and from that point I proceed to ask a related question: what might the rise of China and an attendant form of globalisation mean for the analysis and policy practice of 'development'?

2. DOMINANT CAPITALISMS AND GLOBALISATION

2.1 Varieties of National Capitalism

Scientific appreciation of the fact that not all national forms of capitalism are alike goes back at least to Dore's (1973) research on the differences between workplace organisation and control in Japanese, relative to other manufacturing companies, and Johnson's (1982) work on the Japanese political economy more generally. Subsequent to Johnson's work and the growing recognition among many social scientists of the vital roles played by states and other non-market agents in capitalist (as distinct from state socialist) economic development, comparative research on national 'varieties' of capitalism gradually began to emerge from the early 1980s, but particularly from around 1990.[4] Variously concerned with national differences in the sources of competitiveness, in welfarism, economic policy, corporate managerial priorities, economic governance, firm structures, innovation and so on, this literature has evolved in ways that have tended to disconnect it from analyses of the sources and forms taken by the multi-layered processes of globalisation and, as indicated above, vice versa. The view taken here is that globalisation and national capitalisms are far from being constellations of ultimately profit-seeking activity that have emerged as if in separate galaxies. Rather, particular national capitalisms – and in some cases the nature of their social formations also – have been the institutional sources of the predominant driving forces of globalisation in particular historical periods, and have thus tended to provide it with its economic, political and social logics. As a result, globalisation is perhaps best understood not as a reflection of some supposedly universalistic version of capitalism,[5] but rather as an externalisation of a given national form, or related forms, of capitalism.

2.2 Enter the Eagle

Grasped in this way, it is possible to comprehend the fact that gradually since the 1920s, and particularly since the late 1940s, it has been possible to identify the economic, social, political and cultural dynamics of the US form of capitalism as the principal source for the characteristics of contemporary globalisation. Among these dynamics, the following now seem to be particularly important:

- The transnationalisation of private corporate power through investment, consumption and the integration of national economies through global production networks.
- Space–time compression as a consequence of information and communications technology (ICT) revolutions and the evolution of cyber-networks.
- The emergence of neo-liberalism as the dominant economic, social, political and ideological practice.
- The emergence of 'financialisation' as the dominant regime of accumulation.
- The militarisation of US foreign policy.

Projected to the global level, the articulation of these dynamics has given rise to what we might refer to as a 'global neoliberal era' (Henderson 2010). It was in the United States that capitalists, from the 1880s, pioneered the large, multidivisional firm and it was from among their number that modern transnational corporations were forged, particularly after World War II. Not only did US corporations create and dominate what by the 1980s became to be known as the 'new international division of labour' (Frobel et al. 1980), but it was often those same companies (for example in garments, electronics and automobiles) that reduced costs while maintaining control over the highest value-adding functions (for example research and development, innovation, brand names) via multiple layers of subcontracting associated with global production networks (Henderson et al. 2002). Even in the contemporary period, with the challenge of first Japanese, German and other European corporations and, more recently, Korean and now Chinese and Indian ones, it has been the US that has continued to be home to nearly 30 percent (in 2010) of the world's largest corporations.[6] Furthermore, it has been predominantly US corporations, sometimes with the help of the US military, that have driven ICT innovation in first hardware and subsequently software, from Fairchild Semiconductor and the origins of Silicon Valley in the 1950s, through to Apple, Microsoft, Google and beyond, today. In so doing they have been predominantly responsible for creating the cyber-networks that are at the core of the transformation of economic transactions and the daily lives of billions of people across the globe.

Crucially for contemporary globalisation, it was in the United States, in the mid-1970s, that the policy agenda we now refer to as 'neoliberalism' began to emerge (Harvey 2005). From then, through to the present day, neoliberal agendas have been rolled out across much of the world and have involved the reconstruction of the operations of the state and welfare provision via the application of radical free-market doctrines. These have elevated 'the market' (not the state, no matter how democratic the polity) to the dominant role in economic governance and in decisions over the flows of goods and capital (including 'human capital', namely workers) and their prices. Along with this, neoliberalism has helped secure for the private sector, private property and the interests and values associated with them, the dominant role in society, and moreover has relatedly served to legitimate a politics designed to maintain these interests and ends.

Consistent with the expansion of neoliberalism from the 1980s has been the emergence of a new global regime of accumulation: 'financialisation'. Driven forward initially by the Reagan government in the US and the Thatcher government in Britain, financialisation has involved the subordination of all forms of capital in whatever industrial branches and whether productive or not, as well as governments and the daily lives of human beings, to the particular interests and rhythms of finance capital (Williams 2000; Glyn 2006). This subordination has ensured that there has been a direct line from the liberalisation of financial markets in the 1980s to the economic and political turmoil that many parts of the world have endured since 2008.

Complementing the rise of neoliberalism has been a militarisation of US foreign policy (Harvey 2003; Johnson 2004). Beginning with the US and North Atlantic Treaty Organization (NATO) interventions in Bosnia and other parts of the former Yugoslavia in the early 1990s under the Clinton administration, and reaching its zenith in the invasion of Iraq and the ongoing occupation of Afghanistan, there seems to have been an increasing tendency in the US government's foreign relations for military options to quickly displace the search for diplomatic solutions. In recent years this tendency has been most obvious in the US government's relations with developing countries, particularly where opposition to US global power and its particular sense of 'modernity' have been evident.

2.3 Enter the Dragon

If, as I have argued elsewhere (Henderson 2008), we are now witnessing the gradual emergence of a new form of globalisation, consistent with the rise of China and perhaps, eventually, other Asian powers, then it is likely that this form will be fashioned initially from the Chinese form of capitalism, a form that Nee and Opper (2007) refer to as 'politicised capitalism'. If it is, then the coming globalisation is likely to be driven by an emergent 'great power' that in many ways is quite distinct from those that have driven earlier forms of globalisation.

At issue here are not especially China's year-on-year double digit growth rates, or the rapidity with which its industrialisation project has been put into operation and achieved considerable success. Those have been matched by other East Asian economies in earlier periods (Winters and Yusuf 2007; Henderson 2011) and probably by the Soviet Union between the early 1930s and the late 1960s (Krugman 1994). Even the fact that in 2010 it overtook Japan as the world's second largest economy and on current projections is destined to overtake the US as the world's largest economy within the next 20 years (McCurry and Kollewe 2011) is, in itself, important largely because of its symbolic rather than substantive significance, especially given China's low per capita gross national income (GNI) and very high income inequality.[7] More significant than the numeric size of China's economy *per se*, is the extraordinary scale at which labour is being combined with capital to transform raw materials into commodities and, as part of that process, the fact that embedded within China's political economy and society may be considerable potential for innovation (Appelbaum et al. 2011; OECD 2007).

Coupled with the huge scale of resource mobilisation is the particular natures of the 'engine rooms' (the state, capital, corporate forms, labour exploitation and so on) and other features of Chinese capitalism and its social formation that mark it off from any other form that has dominated, or currently has the possibility of dominating, the global economy. Decisive among these would appear to be the following:

- The transnationalisation of state-owned corporate power.
- Governance exercised by an authoritarian, neo-Stalinist state.
- An unusual nationalism, which includes a sense of historic humiliation derived for the experiences of colonisation.
- The significance of race and identity, both internally and externally.
- The projection of an alternative, non-'western' modernisation project.

With the rise of China and the externalisation of its form of capitalism, we are witnessing, for the first time in the history of globalisation, the transnationalisation of state-owned companies on a very large scale. In all the sectors in which Chinese companies are currently, or are becoming, among the world's most active – such as oil, gas, some renewable energies, mining, construction, some financial services (for example asset acquisitions by its sovereign wealth funds), and in countries as disparate as South Sudan, Sri Lanka, Peru, Libya and Greece – it is companies wholly, or at least partially, owned by central government ministries or provincial state governments that constitute the cutting edge of China's economic globalisation strategy.

Consistent with this is the fact that China continues to be ruled by an authoritarian, neo-Stalinist state which is responsible for strategic planning and large swathes of economic co-ordination. In this, the Chinese government and its economic planners have undoubtedly learned a great deal from the development models pioneered by other countries in the East Asian region. In preparation for the economic reforms that began in the late 1970s, Chinese economic planners are reputed to have turned to early examples of how to combine state socialism with private sector activity, such as the debates led by Bukharin in the 1920s Soviet Union and the experience of Hungary's 'new economic mechanism' after 1968 (Fewsmith 1994). Viewing the 'lessons' implied there as inadequate to the task of igniting economic growth in China, they soon turned their attention to the experiences of some of their East Asian neighbours; those that had emerged from the 1950s and 1960s as 'developmental states'. While much debate focussed on the developmental experiences of Japan and Taiwan, it was probably South Korea that attracted most attention. With its very high levels of capital concentration (that is, 30 companies responsible for over 80 percent of GDP by the 1980s, and this concentration rising into the early 1990s) and strategic direction exercised by an authoritarian, militaristic state, it is not hard to see why South Korea, of all the East Asian developmental states, might emerge as a model for Chinese government perceptions of the country's economic future (Kim 1997). This 'demonstration effect' – a form of knowledge transfer between the Northeast Asian region and China – was subsequently complemented by major investment flows from Japanese, Korean, Taiwanese and Hong Kong companies[8] which in the case of the first three have now resulted in China's integration into the world economy via foreign-dominated global production networks.

In contrast to the stamp that US capitalism placed on the current form of globalisation, there are issues that arise from the specificities of China as a social formation that are likely to have considerable resonance as it helps to reconstruct the nature of globalisation. Among the issues of relevance here is the fact that, for the first time in history, a great power is emerging from the ranks of the 'Global South'. As a consequence, and with the sole exception of the United States itself, we have with China a country that is forging the nature of globalisation that was subject to direct colonisation: brutally so in the case of Japan's occupation of Manchuria and its subsequent invasion of other parts of the country between 1931 and 1945. Partly as a result of the sense of humiliation that impacted its national psyche in the wake of colonisation, China has emerged in the post-1945 period with a strong sense of victimhood as a fundamental element in its nationalism (Chang 2001; Gries 2005). While this in itself is not an unusual component of nationalism, it is in the context of a potential great power.

Associated with both these elements is the fact that China will be the first driver of globalisation to be populated by peoples who are non-white. As a consequence the particularities of Han[9] perceptions of race and identity (Dikotter 1992) – and others' perceptions of the Chinese – can be expected to influence social and ultimately political interactions between Chinese corporate and other agents of globalisation and the governments, companies and populations with which they engage. Consistent with the nature of Han identity, China – unlike other rising powers such as India and Brazil – arguably represents an alternative to the Western influenced modernisation project which has 'guided' development – for increasing parts of the globe and for better or for worse – for over five centuries (Jacques 2009).

In conclusion, these features of Chinese capitalism and the country's social formation, as they continue to be externalised, may be giving rise to a new, and qualitatively different, form of globalisation: a Global-Asian Era. If so, what might be the processes of externalisation, and what might be some of their consequences?

3. VECTORS OF TRANSFORMATION

3.1 Context

The process of China's 'global externalisation' is carried along, in practice, through a series of transmission belts or 'vectors'. These vectors are constituted, variously, by a series of cross-border flows – finance, trade, migration, ideas, imagery, knowledge and power – and by institutional issues associated with global and regional governance. Diffused amongst them are elements of Chinese culture and values and visions of modernity. Among the vectors that could be examined to help gauge the impact of China's global externalisation, only two will be mentioned here, both in regard to the developing world and only in very brief outlinc at that.

3.2 Global Production Networks

One vector that encapsulates facets of a number of these cross-border flows and foregrounds the business enterprise as the primary actor in the transformation process is the global production network (GPN). A GPN refers to 'the nexus of interconnected functions and operations through which goods and services are produced, distributed and consumed. Such networks not only integrate firms into structures which blur traditional organisational boundaries – through the development of diverse forms of equity and non-equity relationships – but also integrate national economies (or parts of such economies) in ways which have enormous implications for their well-being. At the same time, the precise nature and articulation of firm-centred production networks are deeply influenced by the concrete socio-political contexts within which they are embedded. The process is especially complex because while the latter are essentially territorially specific, the production networks themselves are not' (Henderson et al. 2002: 445–6).

The 'architecture' of GPNs, the nature of the lead firms and the institutional power that can be mobilised in those locations incorporated into the GPNs have enormous implications for value creation and capture, for employment, wages, labour standards, human rights, technology and knowledge transfers and so on. They have, in other words, enormous implications for the possibilities of industrial upgrading to the benefit of the host economy and society. While prominent and largely privately-owned Chinese companies such as Lenovo, Haier and Huawei are beginning to forge their own production networks outside of China, these are emerging, as yet, only in a very small number of advanced industrial countries. The most globally active Chinese companies in terms of investment and their consequences for economic and social transformation in developing countries are predominantly state-owned companies in the energy, mining and construction sectors. Currently they have a particular presence in Sub-Saharan Africa and include Sinopec in Angola, CREC[10] in the Democratic Republic of the Congo and NFC Africa Mining (NFCA) in Zambia. In the first two of these cases, the companies involved in oil extraction (Angola) and copper and cobalt mining (Congo) are constituted as joint ventures between the Chinese companies and their African state-owned counterparts: Sonangol in Angola and Gecamines in the Congo (Vines et al. 2009; Afdevinfo[11]). NFCA's copper mine in Zambia, however, is entirely Chinese-owned (Haglund 2009).

Irrespective of the equity split, however, it seems clear that the transformational benefits that can be associated with GPN involvements are, at best, unevenly present in these cases. In all of them, sub-contracting seems to be largely confined to other Chinese companies, while with the exception of mining, there seems to be a great reluctance to employ African workers, preferring to use imported (and, effectively 'indentured', that is contractually tied) workers from China (Haglund 2009; Ferreira 2009; Vines et al. 2009). Additionally, the Chinese managers and workers live in separate compounds and have almost no relationship with the local communities, in some cases not even at a petty commercial level, buying food and other supplies. As a consequence, and with the exception of the Congo case, it seems unlikely that knowledge and skill transmissions are part of the developmental contribution these Chinese-led GPNs are making. Additionally, as Lee's (2009) work on Zambia has shown, the Chinese companies that do employ African workers,[12] have imported the neoliberal labour practices now typical in China. They have resisted pre-existing unionisation, broken the formerly secure employment contracts and have instituted the wholesale casualisation of their workforces. Additionally, the Chinese companies studied by Lee are reputed to pay the lowest wages of all the foreign-owned companies in their sectors (Haglund 2009).

Against this background, Chinese involvement in the Congo's copper and cobalt mining industries seems to hold out better prospects for assisting that country's development. While many of the problems identified in the Chinese corporate engagements in Angola and Zambia are likely to be reproduced in the Congo, in forming the Socomin joint venture, CREC and Gecamines agreed to commit 0.5 percent of all investment to training the workforce and on technology transfer, while 3 percent will be spent on social provision (health, education) for the local community. Furthermore, Socomin is specifically required to subcontract 12 percent of its work to Congolese companies and limit its Chinese workforce to 20 percent of the total (Komesaroff 2008). While, in principle, these arrangements may have set a new benchmark for the Congolese Government's future contractual negotiations with foreign mining companies, there seems to be no evidence, as yet, that they are being reproduced elsewhere in Africa.

3.3 Aid

China's emergence as a major actor in terms of aid and related forms of development assistance has underlined the growing questions over the efficacy of foreign aid delivered by the members of the OECD's Development Assistance Committee (DAC). Unlike the majority of Western DAC donors (China is not a DAC member) China's aid-related flows focus on trade, productive investment and infrastructure provision; arguably on enhancing the resources needed to enable low-income countries to move up the development curve. Furthermore, its distinctive approach to development co-operation is sharpening existing debates within the Western donor community. Among other things, its challenge, at least implicitly, has served to compound existing critiques of structural adjustment programmes as dogmatic and inflexible, aid conditionality as creating dependent 'governance states' and western aid as having limited impacts on growth.

Chinese agencies such as the Export–Import Bank (Exim, or the Development Bank), unlike their Western counterparts, primarily deliver assistance through projects. In doing so, they arguably reduce opportunities for corruption and the approach yields quicker and more tangible results. Additionally, Chinese development assistance seems to be seen by recipients as being much more streamlined and effective in reaching its targets, though this may be at the expense of attention to 'good' governance, human rights and the environment. In terms of delivery, China's rationale seems to place it in a distinctive, possibly oppositional relation to Western aid logics and practices. Rather like Japan's and South Korea's development assistance, China's efforts seem to be focussed on the delivery of 'concrete needs' via such things as infrastructure and agriculture without wrapping these up in a package of political or economic reform as is typical of the World Bank and many bilateral donors.

In many ways China's development co-operation seems to problematise the very notion of 'aid' as that has been operationalised in recent decades. 'Aid' has always been a differentiated set of policies and practices (with associated values and assumptions) which, arguably, have been rooted in the differing institutional environments and development experiences of the donor country in question. Just as the world economy is composed of a variety of different capitalisms, so aid engagements are themselves far from monadic. Indeed, they are arguably constituted by a variety of differing 'aid regimes'. Priorities behind the Swedish International Development Co-operation Agency's (SIDA), Britain's Department for International Development's (DfID) or the United States Agency for International Development's (USAID) programmes arguably have much to do with the particular development histories and experiences evident in Sweden, Britain and the US respectively. Similarly the form and content of China's development cooperation seems to be quite distinct from those of most DAC members (though, as noted, with similarities to Japan and South Korea) and, as such, can be seen to represent a new aid regime. If it is, and in as far as it may be capable of generating more positive outcomes relative to those of the largely Western DAC regimes, then it is an aid regime that may be posing a challenge, intellectually and practically, to some of the others. Additionally, the Chinese approach to aid and its consequences may well be an example of why, more generally, traditional approaches to development and the discourses associated with them are inappropriate for understanding the wider implications of China's rise.

Though brief, this reference to two of the vectors through which China is transforming the developing world indicates that it is still far too early to come to firm conclusions about the overall consequences of China's global externalisation. Even though it seems that Chinese aid may be having more positive than negative consequences and the spread of GPNs via the activities of state-owned companies may currently yield a mixed record in terms of positive effects, the evidence seems to suggest the need to proceed with our evaluations on an almost case by case basis. In spite of this caution, however, when it comes to reflection on what might be the appropriate concepts and discourses for assessing economic, political and social change, both within China and in an era of China's global externalisation, I think we are on firmer ground.

4. DEVELOPMENT, TRANSITION OR TRANSFORMATION?

In the foregoing discussion I have relied on the term 'transformation' rather than 'development' to grasp the processes and consequences of change both within China and externally.[13] This has been deliberate as I believe that the rise of China is highlighting how inadequate the discourses of 'development' are to the task. They are so, in part, because they remain imbued with the essentially 19th century Western notions of 'progress' and 'modernisation' (Wallerstein 2001) and these continue to have important consequences for analytic schemes and affiliated policy agendas. Additionally, the definition of 'development' (at least in English) is itself problematic. *The Concise Oxford Dictionary*, for instance, indicates that the term refers to a gradual unfolding, fuller working out, growth, stage of advancement, more elaborate form of the object in question, as well as other meanings inappropriate to social-scientific analysis. As a result, without significant definitional clarification, it seems that the term has multiple, mutually exclusive meanings that render it too imprecise to be useful as an analytic concept for understanding historical change, particularly of the sorts with which this chapter has been concerned.

If the notion of 'development' and its attendant discourses are inadequate or inappropriate to the task of grasping the consequences of China's rise for globalisation and the developing world, then what might be the alternatives? One possibility is the notion of 'transition'. While having a certain longevity in the historical and social sciences, transition discourses have become particularly popular in the media and politics, as well as in scientific circles over the last 20 years or so in commentaries on political and economic change in the former, and still existing, state socialist countries. While initially transition discourses were largely mobilised in regard to a number of Central and Eastern European countries subsequent to their historical ruptures of 1989 to 1991, recently they have begun to be mobilised to assist the comprehension of changes afoot in China (Pei 2006), Vietnam and similar Southeast Asian countries. In principle, they could be mobilised for analyses of change in the developing world more generally.

As with the notion of 'development', the term 'transition' is also problematic. It is so because it imposes particular ways of thinking and seeing the processes of 'development' which are equally inappropriate. As *The Concise Oxford Dictionary* indicates, 'transition' is a passage, change, from one place or state or act or set of circumstances to another. The sense the term conveys, then, is of movement from a known starting point to a *known* end point. Thus while a discourse of transition is a legitimate way of understanding processes of historical change whose consequences and legacies are now settled – as for instance in the transition from feudalism to capitalism in Europe – this is not the case when we are dealing with contemporary processes where we ourselves are living through the period of historical change. In those circumstances – and this is true of contemporary China and the whole swathe of the developing world – to adopt a discourse of transition is, in effect, to assume that we can predict the future and allow our predictions (albeit unconsciously) to influence our analyses of the change process. Clearly, this is a methodologically dubious way of proceeding that is likely to lead to implausible analyses and inappropriate policy responses.

In rejecting both these discourses, I would argue that the most appropriate analytic lens for analysing the rise of China and its consequences for globalisation and developing world is one associated with the notion of 'transformation'. It is so because, as *The Concise Oxford Dictionary* indicates, the verb 'to transform' refers to making especially considerable change in the form, outward appearance, character, disposition, and so on of the element in question. While economic, political and social transformation must include changes in content as well as form it seems clear that, at least in English, the term 'transformation' signals a process with a known starting point, but with an *unknown* (and thus no pre-defined) end point. Employing a discourse of transformation, then, allows for the possibility of serious but, crucially, open-ended reflection on the dynamics and consequences of political–economic change.

Adopting a discourse of transformation for the analysis of political–economic and related changes in China, the developing world and in the nature of globalisation seems particularly appropriate for a number of reasons. First, unlike transition-type discourses such as those informed in various ways by neoclassical economic theory and modernisation theory, those focused on transformation should be better equipped to avoid premature theoretical closure, and thus many of the pitfalls of earlier and current policy engagements with economic and social development, like the International Monetary Fund/World Bank 'structural adjustment' agenda. Second, and relatedly, transformation discourses should encourage analysts to transcend the Eurocentrism that continues to inform Western social-scientific analyses of the Global South and other parts of the non-Western world. Taken together these intellectual innovations suggest that the adoption of transformational analysis may lead to a substantial re-think in some of the fundamentals of development policy and practice, perhaps even legitimating the idea that developing countries should be encouraged and supported to find their own routes to economic success, drawing on their own histories, cultures and internal resources, with or without the benefits of China's global externalisation.

NOTES

1. For partial exceptions see Breslin (2007) and Hung (2009).
2. As, for instance, in area studies and development studies.
3. While I am aware that, in practice, the dynamics of historical change are often driven by processes that combine elements that are endogenous and exogenous to a given territorial space, for analytic purposes it is necessary, in the first instance, to hold these separate from one another. Manuel Castells effectively captures this methodological tactic in his depiction of globalisation as a dialectic between the 'space of places' and the 'space of flows' (Castells 2000; Castells and Henderson 1987).
4. Among the key contributions, see: Zysman (1983), Esping-Andersen (1990), Whitley (1999), Coates (2000), Dore (2000) and Hall and Soskice (2001).
5. As Gary Runciman reminds us, the unvarying core of capitalism is merely 'a mode of production in which formally free labour is recruited for regular employment by ongoing enterprises competing in the market for profit' (Runciman 1995: 33).
6. 139 of the leading 500, by revenue, according to *Fortune*, http://en.wikipedia.org/wiki/Fortune_Global_500 (accessed 7 July 2011).
7. China's GNI per capita was US$2,940 in 2008 compared with, for instance, US$6,970 in Malaysia, US$7,350 in Brazil, US$21,530 in South Korea, US$38,210 in Japan, US$42,440 in Germany and US$47,580 in the US (Henderson 2011, Table 1.1: 3). In 2004, according to Gini coefficient calculations, income inequality in China was 0.45 (Chen 2007) compared (in the mid-2000s) with 0.38, 0.34, 0.32, 0.31 and 0.28 for the US, Britain, Japan, South Korea and France respectively (Henderson 2011).
8. Prior to decolonisation in 1997, flows from Hong Kong were regarded as 'foreign' investment.

9. The Han Chinese constitutes about 90 percent of China's population. The rest are composed of a variety of ethnic groups who emanate predominantly from the north and west of the country.
10. A joint venture between the China Railway Engineering Corporation and Sinohydro.
11. http://www.afdevinfo.com/htmlreports/org/org_68389.html (accessed May 6, 2011).
12. She studied NFCA in Zambia and the textile company, the Tanzania–China Friendship Mill in Tanzania.
13. This section is informed by the analysis in Henderson (2011) and Henderson and Nadvi (2011).

REFERENCES

Appelbaum, R.P., R. Parker and C. Cao (2011), 'Developmental state: nanotechnology in China', *Global Networks*, **11**(3), 298–314.

Breslin, S. (2007), *China and the Global Political Economy*, London: Palgrave Macmillan.

Castells, M. (2000), *The Information Age: Economy, Society and Culture, Volume I: The Rise of the Network Society*, 2nd edn, Oxford: Blackwell.

Castells, M. and J. Henderson (1987), 'Techno-economic restructuring, socio-political processes and territorial development: a global perspective', in J. Henderson and M. Castells (eds), *Global Restructuring and Territorial Development*, London: Sage Publications.

Chang, M.H. (2001), *Return of the Dragon: China's Wounded Nationalism*, Boulder, CO: Westview Press.

Chen, J. (2007), 'Poverty and income inequality in China', PhD thesis, Manchester Business School, University of Manchester.

Coates, D. (2000), *Models of Capitalism*, Cambridge: Polity Press.

Dikotter, F. (1992), *The Discourse of Race in Modern China*, Hong Kong: Hong Kong University Press.

Dore, R. (1973), *British Factory, Japanese Factory: The Origins of National Diversity in Industrial Relations*, Berkeley and Los Angeles, CA: University of California Press.

Dore, R. (2000), *Stock Market Capitalism – Welfare Capitalism: Japan and German Versus the Anglo-Saxons*, Oxford: Oxford University Press.

Esping-Andersen, G. (1990), *The Three Worlds of Welfare Capitalism*, Cambridge: Polity Press.

Ferreira, M.E. (2009), 'China in Angola: just a passion for oil?' in C. Alden, D. Large and R. Soares de Oliviera (eds), *China Returns to Africa: A Rising Power and a Continent Embrace*, London: Hurst.

Fewsmith, J. (1994), *Dilemmas of Reform in China: Political Conflict and Economic Debate*, Armonk, NY: M.E. Sharpe.

Frobel, F., J. Heinrichs and O. Kreye (1980), *The New International Division of Labour: Structural Unemployment in Industrialised Countries and Industrialisation in Developing Countries*, Cambridge: Cambridge University Press.

Glyn, A. (2006), *Capitalism Unleashed: Finance, Globalization and Welfare*, Oxford: Oxford University Press.

Gries, P.H. (2005), *China's New Nationalism: Pride, Politics and Diplomacy*, Berkeley and Los Angeles, CA: University of California Press.

Haglund, D. (2009), 'In it for the long term?: Governance and learning among

Chinese investors in Zambia's copper sectors', *The China Quarterly*, **199**, 627–46.
Hall, P.A. and D. Soskice (eds) (2001), *Varieties of Capitalism: The Institutional Foundations of Comparative Advantage*, New York: Oxford University Press.
Harvey, D. (2003), *The New Imperialism*, Oxford: Oxford University Press.
Harvey. D. (2005), *A Brief History of Neoliberalism*, Oxford: Oxford University Press.
Henderson, J. (2008), 'China and global development: towards a global-Asian era?', *Contemporary Politics*, **14**(4), 375–92.
Henderson, J. (2010), 'Neoliberal globalization', in N. Young (ed.), *The Oxford International Encyclopaedia of Peace, Volume III*, New York: Oxford University Press.
Henderson, J. (2011), *East Asian Transformation: On the Political Economy of Dynamism, Governance and Crisis*, London: Routledge.
Henderson, J. and K. Nadvi (2011), 'Greater China, the challenges of global production networks and the dynamics of transformation', *Global Networks*, **11**(3), 285–97.
Henderson, J., P. Dicken, M. Hess, N. Coe and H.W.C. Yeung (2002), 'Global production networks and the analysis of economic development', *Review of International Political Economy*, **9**(3), 436–64.
Hung, H.F. (ed.) (2009), *China and the Transformation of Global Capitalism*, Baltimore, MD: Johns Hopkins University Press.
Jacques, M. (2009), *When China Rules the World: The Rise of the Middle Kingdom and the End of the Western World*, London: Allen Lane.
Johnson, C. (1982), *MITI and the Japanese Miracle: The Growth of Industrial Policy, 1925–1975*, Stanford, CA: Stanford University Press.
Johnson, C. (2004), *Sorrows of Empire: Militarism, Secrecy and the End of the Republic*, New York: Metropolitan Books.
Kim, E.M. (1997), *Big Business, Strong State: Collusion and Conflict in South Korean Development, 1960–1990*, Albany, NY: State University of New York Press.
Komesaroff, M. (2008), 'China eyes Congo's treasures', *Far Eastern Economic Review*, **171**(3), 38–41.
Krugman, P. (1994), 'The myth of Asia's miracle', *Foreign Affairs*, **73**(6), 62–78.
Lee, C.K. (2009), 'Raw encounters: Chinese managers, African workers and the politics of casualisation in Africa's Chinese enclaves', *The China Quarterly*, **199**, 647–66.
McCurry, J. and J. Kollewe (2011), 'China overtakes Japan as world's second largest economy', *The Guardian*, 14 February.
Nee, V. and S. Opper (2007), 'On politicised capitalism', in V. Nee and R. Swedberg (eds), *On Capitalism*, Stanford, CA: Stanford University Press.
Organisation for Economic Development and Co-operation (OECD) (2007), *OEDC Reviews of Innovation Policy: China-Synthesis Report*, Paris: OECD.
Pei, M. (2006), *China's Trapped Transition: The Limits of Developmental Autocracy*, Cambridge, MA: Harvard University Press.
Runciman, W.G. (1995), 'The "triumph" of capitalism as a topic in the theory of social selection', *New Left Review*, 210 (March–April), 33–47.
Vines, A., M. Weimer and L. Wong (2009), *Thirst for African Oil: Asian National Oil Companies in Nigeria and Angola*, London: Royal Institute of International Affairs.

Wallerstein, I. (1974), *The Modern World System, Volume I: Capitalist Agriculture and the Origins of the European World Economy in the Sixteenth Century*, London: Academic Press.

Wallerstein, I. (2001), *Unthinking Social Science: The Limits of Nineteen-Century Paradigms*, 2nd edn, Philadelphia, PA: Temple University Press.

Whitley, R. (1999), *Divergent Capitalisms: The Social Structuring and Change of Business Systems*, Oxford: Oxford University Press.

Williams, K. (2000), 'From shareholder value to present-day capitalism', *Economy and Society*, **29**(1), 1–12.

Winters, A.L. and S. Yusuf (eds) (2007), *Dancing with Giants: China, India and the Global Economy*, Washington, DC: World Bank.

Zysman, J. (1983), *Governments, Markets and Growth: Financial Systems and the Politics of Industrial Change*, Ithaca, NY: Cornell University Press.

12. China's developmental experience: lessons for the Asia-Pacific

Minglu Chen and David S.G. Goodman

1. INTRODUCTION

At the end of the March 2011 session of the National People's Congress of the People's Republic of China (PRC) the Premier, Wen Jiabao, was asked by a journalist if China's development during the last 30 years had lessons for other countries. He replied that 'It is not right to draw an analogy between China and other countries'. This answer may have been somewhat predictable at the time given that the questioner also asked whether China's case was instructive in the light of the changes that some North African countries were then experiencing (*China Daily* 15 March 2011: 4).

Others within the PRC during the last few years have been less modest about the successes of the PRC since it started opening to the world and its process of reform in 1979. Deng Zhenglai, of Fudan University, has written about 'China's Living Wisdom': a triumphalist argument that links the last 30 years of dramatic growth with the long traditions of Chinese civilisation (Deng 2010). This is not an uncommon view within the PRC where many people now talk very positively about 'The China Model' or 'The Beijing Consensus' to describe the economic successes of China's growth, its growing international influence, and the possibility of a still greater role in international affairs (Yu 2006; *Renmin luntan* 2008).

Outside the PRC these two terms have their origins in observations of the same phenomena. China's 30-year economic growth pattern has been dramatic: a sustained 9–10 per cent of GDP per annum, despite the Asian Financial Crisis of the late 1990s and the Global Financial Crisis of the late 2000s, compared (for example) to Mexico's economic growth over the same three decades of 0.9 per cent of GDP per annum. And all achieved under the aegis of a ruling Communist Party. Those two characteristics are the starting point for any description of the China Model. In its international context the China Model is also sometimes referred to as the Beijing Consensus, in contrast to the earlier Washington Consensus – based on democratic capitalism and distinctly neoliberal development policies – that dominated the 1990s. To quote Joseph Cooper Ramo (the phrase's 2004 populariser) writing even before the Global Financial Crisis of 2008:

> The Beijing Consensus offers hope for the world. After the collapse of the Washington Consensus, the breakdown of WTO talks, the implosion of Argentina's economy, much of the world was uncertain what a new paradigm for development ought to look like. (Cooper Ramo 2004: 60)

There is a fairly widespread assumption not simply that the PRC has had a specific recipe for development, but that other countries may copy its model, or at the very least learn lessons from its experience. In many ways the economic growth of the PRC since 1978 seems to have directly challenged theories of economic development. The key challenge to theories of modernisation, as previously understood, is that the PRC's experience seems to suggest that authoritarian politics and economic restructuring can co-exist. Certainly in many ways from the standpoint of 1978 the most remarkable feature of the PRC's development does seem to have not been simply the continuation of Chinese Communist Party (CCP) rule but its adaptability (Shambaugh 2009). This has even led some commentators to argue that China's democratic centralism is not just 'decent' but at least as preferable as liberal democracy as a system of governance (Angle 2005): the contrast is often made between liberal democracy and effective 'responsible government' (Li 2009).

China's rise is certainly a challenge. As many countries in the Asia-Pacific have discovered over the last few decades, not least as foreign direct investment has been diverted towards the PRC, China's rise has meant that the rest of the world has had to adjust. China's rise may also pose a challenge to ideas of modernisation and economic development, but not necessarily so. The degree of purchase obtained by the China Model rests on the extent to which China's experience is seen to be presenting an alternative path that others may follow, and not simply seen to be the result of unique circumstances. From that perspective the China Model rapidly becomes of little use to the developing Asia-Pacific. There are essentially three problems: there is very little agreement about what constitutes the China Model; China's development of the last three decades is for the most part the result of highly specific circumstances; and where there are lessons to be learnt there is little in the experience of the developing Asia Pacific to suggest that those lessons can readily and generally be begun to be replicated.

2. THE IDEA OF A CHINA MODEL

The notion that there might be a China Model is very seductive. The PRC has had spectacular growth rates for 30 years and has transformed the country. The Beijing Olympics and Shanghai Expo, not to mention the high speed rail network and the development of international standard universities, have all been tangible manifestations not only that China has reached a level of wealth and technical competence that can increasingly match the more developed countries of the world, but also that it is possible for a less developed country to become one of the wealthiest. The economy is now the second largest in the world and almost every other country (Mexico and Canada are notable exceptions) has the PRC as their largest trade partner. At the same time it is clear that the idea of the China Model does not come ready-wrapped as an off-the-shelf blueprint. On the contrary, both inside and outside the PRC the topic of what constitutes the China Model is a topic of hot debate, with no agreement.

Within the PRC, discussion of the China Model and a Beijing Consensus developed rapidly following the publication of Joseph Cooper Ramo's pamphlet on *The Beijing Consensus* in 2004. For the most part, though, until 2009 this discussion focussed on trying to work out what the rest of the world meant by the terms. This all changed with the publication of Peking University's Professor Pan Wei's edited volume on *The China Model: Reading 60 Years of the People's Republic of China*. This volume contains Pan's influential and much quoted chapter on 'The China Model: An Analysis of the Economy, Politics and Society in the Chinese System' (Pan 2009a, 2009b).

Pan's argument is essentially a mixture of historical determinism and the superiority of doctrines of responsible (as opposed to democratic) government. China is the inheritor of superior traditions of economic, political and social systems that 'serve the people'. Pan rejects the 'false' division between democracy and autocracy, and stresses responsibility instead. In his words 'The West emphasizes rights, but China emphasizes responsibility . . . the primacy of responsibility forms the foundation of the "China Model"' (Pan 2009b). Pan was embraced by the Party-state. His edited volume was selected by the PRC General Administration of Press and Publications to appear in its *Classic China International Publishing Project* to represent China internationally. Pan himself was sent off to Confucius Institutes around the world to talk about the China Model, and spoke at the British House of Commons (Yang 2011). Clearly this was less an attempt to export revolution (or even a model of development) than a project to explain China's growth and to ensure its acceptable exceptionalism to the rest of the world.

China in the twenty-first century may still have a ruling CCP but is nonetheless more pluralist than might be otherwise expected. Pan Wei's work has been the subject of much debate within the PRC. Perhaps the most trenchant criticism has come from Yang Jisheng. He has attempted to ensure the politics of his argument by playing the nationalist card. 'Foreigners', he argues, who have talked about the China Model must necessarily be flawed in their assessment:

> These foreigners cannot possibly understand China within such a short period of time. Read their writings and you'll find that they have entirely avoided very real contradictions in China, choosing only to see China's brighter and fresher surface. They are far removed from the reality in China.

The idea of the China Model, in his view, essentialises China's historical experience and misunderstands the dynamics of the present. He then moves from this analysis of what the China Model might be on the ground to concentrate on the discourses of its development. Here, he identifies a very strong trope that others have also found in the literature (Zhao 2010: 419): the theme not simply of an alternative to American capitalism, but also of anti-westernisation both inside and outside the PRC. Yang makes his point clearly:

> The praise for the 'China Model' today recalls for me the praise some academics in the West in the 1930s showered on the Soviet Union. The background at the time was that the West faced economic crisis while the Soviet Union outshone everyone. Today the countries of the West once again face economic crisis, and China shines above them. History has already shown that those academics who praised the Soviet Union were historically short-sighted, and I wish scholars today would not follow in their footsteps. (Yang 2011)

All the same, the positive interpretation of the idea of the China Model has considerably more support from the Party-state than any more critical writings. In March 2011 an article elaborating positively on the China Model was published in the theoretical journal of the CCP (*Seeking Truth*). Zhang Weiwei emphasised Pan Wei's historical determinism and took it even further:

> China is a 'civilization-type nation' and moreover it is the only country of such a type in the world. Why? Because China is the oldest [nation] in the world with a history as a unified nation. China is the only country in the world to have 5,000 years of unbroken civilization. China is the only nation where a millennia-old civilization fully coincides with the morphology of a modern state. In order to illustrate this concept, I can give you a very accurate comparison. It is as though ancient Rome was never dissolved, and continued to the

> present day, making the transition to a modern nation-state, with a central government and a modern economy, incorporating traditional cultural elements, having a massive population in which everyone speaks Latin.

He then identifies eight ways in which China's society, decision-making, economics, social development, international relations, system of governance, and culture are all 'essentially the product of China's deep history' promoting 'harmony' and 'non-ideological politics' (Zhang 2011).

Discussion of the China Model outside the PRC shares some of the concerns of the debate within China less to portray a workable blueprint than to explain China's development in the last 30 years, though inevitably some of the commentary blurs distinctions between the two. Joseph Cooper Ramo, for example, when outlining the idea of the Beijing Consensus states quite explicitly 'China's path to development and power is, of course, unrepeatable by any other nation' though he emphasises the significance of China's impact and emulation effect for much of the world (Cooper Ramo 2004: 5).

Other than identifying that there has been rapid economic growth it is almost impossible to find agreement about what constitutes the China Model. There is agreement that there has been economic reform, but not about the nature of that reform, especially those aspects surrounding the roles of the state and private enterprise in economic development. Moreover, while some contrast the economic reform with a lack of political change others argue that political reform has also been central to the successes of the last three decades.

The China Model is inherently neo-liberalist says David Harvey (Harvey 2007: Ch. 4). The China Model is the very antithesis of neoliberalist capitalism says Giovanni Arrighi (Arrighi 2007). The China Model combines economic reform with no political change says Martin Jacques (Jacques 2009: 12). The China Model would not have been sustainable, says Suisheng Zhao, without political reform alongside the economic restructuring that has taken place (Zhao 2010: 424). The China Model is based on privatisation above all else, argues Steven Halper (Halper 2010: 11; 209). The China Model is often mistaken for privatisation, says Barry Naughton, stressing instead the continued role of the state, and the roles that a whole series of public–private partnerships play in successful economic development (Naughton 2010: 451).

3. UNREPLICABLE SUCCESS

Interestingly, despite the apparent differences between these various accounts of the China Model, both within and outside the PRC, they do point to a clearer understanding of the developmental experience of the last three decades (Chen and Goodman 2012). In the first place, this is only a model in terms of a device for explaining China's development. It is not a model in terms of principles that might be adapted anywhere else, let alone universally, despite any rhetorical flourishes to the contrary. Secondly, there are three features that together form the unique foundation on which the PRC's developmental success of the last 30 years has been based: its size and scale; its pre-1979 experience of state socialism; and its developmental trajectory since 1979.

A significant feature of China's success is the size and scale of the country, and for that matter the economy. Much has been made of China's growth and its status as the second largest aggregate economy (by PPP). The growth and the achievements are spectacular. At the same time, having the largest population in the world does mean that China has always been a large economy, and that the impact of fairly small changes in individual income may be magnified in terms of the aggregate economy. It was the world's largest aggregate economy until 1830 and only ceased to be so when industrialisation meant that GDP per capita in Europe and North America grew disproportionately. Even so, from 1830 to 1978, when China's economic growth was low, China never slipped below being the fourth largest economy in the world (Maddison 2007: 47). One consequence is that government expenditure can grow quite considerably, assuming the state's extractive power.

The scale of China also helps explain how there can have been an annual growth rate of 9–10 per cent in GDP for 30 years with relatively little inflation. There have at times been inflationary pressures, and as in other economies these have been mediated through interest rate management and control of money supply. In China's case, though, the notion of a national growth rate masks the lack of an integrated economy, or perhaps more accurately the slow pace of economic integration for China's economic regions. There are 13 poorly integrated economic regions, with communications still difficult north to south, and even to some extent east to west even despite the obvious river systems (Yellow River in the north, Yangtze River in the south) (Keng 2001). This lack of integration explains, for example, China's need to import coal despite having the Ordos, the world's largest and best quality coalfield in the north, statistically able to meet all national needs (Goodman 1999). A national average annual growth rate of 10 per cent per annum masks a process in which first one economic region (centred on Guangdong) grew at rates well in excess of the national average for a few years, to be followed by others in turn expanding at similarly rapid rates.

China's size and continental scale means also that it has a vast domestic market that to date has been little developed. Development has been concentrated for the most part on the eastern seaboard, where the initial export-oriented industries of the reform era were located. The opening up of the interior is an obvious and long-standing challenge (Goodman 2004) with the prospect that China may ape the developed countries of the world and generate a larger proportion of world GDP than its share of world population: a goal still to be achieved. The structures for this were put in place at a fairly early stage of the PRC's reform development with the introduction of fiscal federalism (Montinola et al. 1995: 50).

A second significant set of circumstances contributing to the PRC's economic success is the history of state socialism before 1979. The reform era does not represent China's let alone the PRC's first attempts at modernisation and industrialisation. In particular, in both politics and economics the state socialism of the previous 30 years bequeathed useful legacies, though not sometimes without their costs, that led to the later success. In economics, as Naughton has detailed (Naughton 2010: 437) but as others have also argued (Nolan 2004), state socialism before 1978 bequeathed both the structures of a modernising state and considerable slack in economic capacity. Almost everyone can quote the PRC's high economic growth rates since 1978. Less well known, but equally important, was the average annual growth rate during 1952–1978 of 6 per cent per annum (Maddison 2007: 96). There was dramatic variation within this period (Great Leap Forward, Cultural Revolution) but overall growth delivered the development of a modernising state, especially through heavy industry, transport and communications, welfare and education, and particularly in urban China. Development before 1978 had been labour-intensive and inefficient in terms of productivity. The changes at the end of the 1970s brought an approach based on capital-intensive investment and the more economically efficient use of labour. The result was domestic capacity for economic growth, alongside (not inconsiderably) an attractive market for world investment and a large supply of cheap, low-skilled labour, at a globally low price.

The political legacy of state socialism is no less important. National unity, political stability, and even to some extent authoritarian politics, all contribute to the state's ability to create a framework in which rapid development can take place. The PRC's experience before 1978 resulted in a unified and centralised political system, with an organisational hierarchy – based on the CCP – that was able to build and take advantage of the opportunities presented by the realisation that modernising states do not need to micro-manage to be effective (Goodman 1985: 218). This legacy is important in organisational terms for the Party-state as a whole, and for the individual – cadre, entrepreneur, worker – who is well-schooled in the rules of the authoritarian system (Shambaugh 2009).

The third set of factors contributing to China's unique experience since 1978 all relate to the trajectory of its development since 1978. There is a developmental aspect to the PRC's economic experience of reform that is often overlooked. Reform proceeded tentatively immediately after 1978 and economic growth required a number of kick-starts before momentum was established. Even then, there have been adjustments in direction (particularly in the management of state–economy relations) albeit within the general commitment and framework of reform and economic growth (Huang 2008). Equally as important, as already noted, the reform era was not written on a blank sheet of paper. There are three key characteristics of the reform era's economic evolution after 1978 that need to be kept firmly in mind: the Party-state's management of policy experimentation; the CCP's alliance with business; and the role of the overseas Chinese, especially in the first two decades of growth.

While commentators outside China are fond of referring to the flexibility and pragmatism that seems to characterise the PRC's development experience, they sometimes miss the dynamics of policy experimentation that occur. There is considerable local autonomy but it too is subject to the Party-state's monitoring and approval. Contrast the experiments conducted in Shenzhen to establish a special economic zone in the early 1980s (Vogel 1989), with those to establish 'big society, small government' in Hainan in 1988 when the latter achieved provincial status (Feng and Goodman 1995). Shenzhen has been a runaway success from the Party-state's point of view, with the policy of special economic zones spreading and developing to much of China. The experiments in Hainan on the other hand led nowhere and were brought to an end by Beijing. The CCP and the Party-state more generally have shown themselves to be tremendous learning organisations (Li 2006). This need not be a unique feature of development in China though one suspects that when coupled with the continuation and enhancement of its hierarchical authoritarianism – which is necessary in order to maintain organisational discipline – there would be few countries able to emulate this aspect of reform.

Clearly the role of the CCP has been central to the PRC's development during the last three decades, and not simply because it has restored its own political order and created a new stability. As Bruce Dickson makes clear, in the process the CCP has also created a strategic alliance with the new entrepreneurs whose emergence it has encouraged

> the party has integrated itself into the private sector . . . encouraged its members, including party and government officials, to 'plunge into the sea' of the private

> sector, and recruited growing numbers of successful entrepreneurs into the party. These red capitalists represent the integration of wealth and power that is at the heart of crony communism in China. This integration is a key element of the so-called 'Beijing Consensus': the ability to achieve economic growth without accompanying political reform. Red capitalists own the largest firms and are more likely to participate in China's formal political institutions. As such, they are more inclined to support the status quo in which they have prospered than seek fundamental political reform. Indeed, red capitalists are part of the status quo, not challengers on the outside looking in. Most red capitalists were already in the CCP before joining the private sector, giving them an even stronger stake in the current political system. In short the integration of political and economic elites in China may serve to sustain the existing authoritarian political system rather than pose a direct challenge to it. The CCP's strategy of integrating itself with the private sector, both by encouraging current party members to go into business and co-opting entrepreneurs into the party, continues to provide dividends. This is a key element of the CCP's strategy for survival and so far it is working. (Dickson 2008: 238)

The pace of reform, though sustained, has not been even. This is not too surprising. The politics of cultural revolution left many scars so that individuals – in both leadership positions and at the base of the social hierarchy – were sometimes loathe to use their initiative or to act differently, as they were now being asked to do. The CCP itself has at times been anxious about how to proceed, as in 1978–1979 once a decision to reform had been taken; in 1989 as popular protest seemed to get out of hand; and in 1992 when faced by sudden apparent self-doubt. Economic reform started in the countryside and only came to urban China in and after 1984. Global interactions have certainly played their role in this unevenness as China has become more economically integrated with the rest of the world.

One of these global interactions was the important role played by the Chinese diaspora in the early years of reform. Much was made in the 1980s of China's increased integration with the region and the global economy. The vehicle of this integration was often overseas Chinese, who though now resident in other countries were prepared to work with their former 'home place' for mutual benefit. Speaking the same language, understanding local customs and practices, and above all able to deliver introductions and connections to local notables and economic leaders, they played a vital role particularly at that time in China's economic development (Bolt 2000).

4. LESSONS OF DEVELOPMENT

Clearly, then, there are unique features of the PRC's developmental experience since 1978 that make emulation, especially in the sense of a model, impossible. China's size and scale, the role of the CCP, the legacy of state socialism, and the economic networks provided by the Chinese diaspora have together created a heady mix for economic success. At the same time, this is not the whole story, and alongside these unique features of development there are other aspects from which less comprehensive lessons might be drawn. Barry Naughton in his recent analysis of China's economic success since 1978 highlights six aspects that he sees as crucial to the successes achieved to date and which could each be taken as a possible lesson to others (Naughton 2010: 451).

The first is that public ownership has not been abandoned and has proved itself 'reasonably efficient'. Indeed the PRC now has a mixed industrial system. It remains a market-based developmental system where non-government-owned firms dominate in the sectors where competition is encouraged, but government ownership dominates industries regarded as strategically important for economic development or social stability: transport, energy, pharmaceuticals, finance, communications, mining. It is a balanced as well as a mixed system where Party-state direction monitors and may change the balance (ibid.: 442).

The second is that competition is encouraged in all sectors except those designated as strategic and remains more important than ownership. Naughton gives the example of the restructured telecommunications industry in China where three companies, albeit still state-owned companies, replaced the former state monopoly. He contrasts the quality of service produced with Mexico where weak regulation and a lack of competition has produced high prices, poor service, and the world's richest man (ibid.: 445). The commitment to competition in a large national market makes a difference, argues Naughton

> In contrast to smaller economies, China's political system is forced to acknowledge multiple interest groups and contenders for power. Chinese leaders act as if their hold on power is always somewhat tenuous, and depends on good economic performance. There are always multiple candidates waiting in the wings, ready to step up to the demands of power. The contrast is great with a political system which is capable of being united in the interest of a single, narrowly defined clique, as in the case of Marcos in the Philippines. Highly ineffective policies and extreme corruption typically lead to serious challenges to individual leaders. China is not less prone to bad policy or corruption than other countries, but the degree of both is arguably held in check by the challenge of political competition. (p. 445)

The third feature is that public ownership is used to exploit market power and to generate revenues for investment and public goods' creation. Naughton emphasises this developmental state aspect of the PRC's economy. He notes the rising profits of state-owned enterprises especially during the last five years, and far from being alarmed by this argues that it reinforces the Party-state's ability to manage the structuring of the economy, especially its management of competition and its ability to ensure that competition is maintained.

Naughton fourthly emphasises the importance of a strategy of investment-led growth. Unlike in a highly privatized or idealised neo-liberal economy it is seen as desirable to invest ahead of demand and create capacity that can be used later. This too is part of the government management of structuring the economy. At the same time it is important for growing the middle-class base of support for the future of the regime. Investment ahead of demand, for example, has created the infrastructure in roads, rail and air for increased people and goods movement. The only limit to such pre-investment must be that it goes to increase productivity (ibid.: 451).

The fifth feature of economic development is that the state sector has been and remains able to create growth and revenue opportunities outside the state sector. Once again there is not simply a mix of the public and the no-government but also a directed attempt at balance in development. The non-government sector contributes to the public in terms of taxation but it may also benefit through investment.

The final aspect of the PRC's economic development highlighted by Naughton as a possible lesson is that managers of state-owned enterprises are subject to market forces despite their position in non-competitive (for the most part) enterprises. Their incentives to better economic performance come from tying their remuneration to their company's performance in maximising asset value, efficiency and performance, in a system established by the state body responsible for overseeing state-owned enterprises. These comments led Naughton inevitably to the observation:

> It cannot be said that China has had no political reform; rather, the political reforms that have taken place have created a newly effective authoritarian hierarchy. The result is a system in which market incentives and administrative supervision and surveillance are both unusually strong. The system is pulled taut. Officials and managers have lots of authority and strong temptations, but they are also subject to strong surveillance and draconian punishments. (p. 457)

Marketisation and competition, and the state's role in ensuring both, lie at the heart of this analysis. Privatisation and the private sector certainly exist but they play much less of a role than is usually assumed. Privatisation is often used as a shorthand for marketisation in China (and non-government enterprises are often referred to as 'private') but there are important distinctions between the two in explaining the success of the PRC's economic development.

The first is that privatisation implies ownership relationships that could not be applied to the PRC until the legal recognition of property rights in 2006 and the introduction of insolvency legislation in 2008. While state and collective sector assets may have been assigned away from the original company responsible for their development, it has been rare for their ownership, as opposed to control over their use and disposal, to pass to individuals. Moreover, while there have been private enterprises since 1984, for the most part these enterprises have been structurally confined to the small-scale, deprived of access to land, labour and resources in order to grow. A significant feature of the growth of the PRC economy has been the development of a wide range of hybrid public–private companies that have emerged from the restructuring of state-owned enterprises, the evolution of collective and town and village enterprises, and the development of private enterprise, and their various sometimes extremely complex interactions. In these circumstances, control and management of resources is more important than ownership (Goodman 2008a: 29).

The second reason for not describing change in terms of privatisation is that this suggests the withdrawal of state management of the economy. While it is clearly the case that economic enterprise management is no longer a function of government departments, as Naughton details, the state retains a central role in economic management that extends way beyond the macro-economic controls exercised by nation-states acting as regulators. In the case of the PRC there is still a large state-owned enterprise industrial sector. Numbers are uncertain but there are about 155 central government state-owned enterprises, and about 143,000 in total subject to all levels of jurisdiction. State-owned enterprises may be but are not necessarily share-based. Those that are in designated strategic industries – transport, energy, mining, pharmaceuticals, finance – cannot go bankrupt. Moreover, the state retains its role in strategic economic planning, not least by monitoring and adjusting the public–private balance in the mixed economy, and by ensuring and managing competition.

At the same time, as Naughton's analysis emphasises, the principle of the sanctity of market forces has been introduced into the public sector. State-owned enterprises are required to operate within the market and, as already noted, their managers are judged by their performance in that regard. Competition and its maintenance is an essential part of the PRC development strategy. Alongside marketisation this has meant that there has been a high degree of both governmental decentralisation and local autonomy in enterprise management, which are also significant markers of China's recent developmental experience. The PRC now has a world-high 70 per cent of total governmental expenditure managed by sub-central jurisdictions (Landry 2008: 3) and enterprise management is judged on results, whether in state-owned or private enterprises, or any of the extensive varieties of hybrid public–private companies (Dickson 2008: 40–41).

One corollary of this introduction of market forces has been the growth of a consumer society and a significant increase in the middle classes. While attention almost necessarily focuses on the emergence of the super rich in the PRC's reform era, the continuing and substantial growth of the numbers of the middle classes may be of considerably more long-term significance for the PRC. The PRC certainly had middle classes before; professionals and managers were essential to the modernising project of state socialism. Now, however, with the growth of economic and technological activities of all kinds, the middle classes have continued to expand still further. These middle classes increasingly have more real disposable income which now goes to house purchase and development, education, as well as more lifestyle choices including leisure time activities: activities and expenditure which are seen by both the middle classes and the Party-state as creating a community of interest. Official sources estimate that the middle classes (defined in income terms) currently constitute about 11 per cent of the population (those earning more than 60,000 yuan a year) but estimate that the middle classes will grow to 20 per cent of the population by 2020 (Goodman 2008b).

5. THE APPEAL OF CHINA

In an article in the *Wall Street Journal* during the middle of 2010 a noted China Studies scholar asked the reader to guess which country it was where

> GDP grew at 11% annually for almost 10 years. The authoritarian, one-party state promoted rapid industrialization by relocating workers to coastal urban areas. The government welcomed foreign-direct investment and courted companies through tax exemptions and other benefits. Seventy-five percent of the top 100 largest domestic firms' assets belonged to the state sector. The government's savings rate doubled in less than a decade, while the agricultural share of employment fell by more than one-third over the same period. (Huang 2010)

Despite the obvious parallel with contemporary China the description is of Brazil under military rule from 1965 to 1974. It is a useful warning shot across the bow of those who would describe a China Model. There is clearly a danger in either triumphalism or, as the examples of the developing countries of the world have long provided evidence, in assuming that modernisation can be readily codified and easily transplanted. The applicability of the lessons learnt from the PRC's developmental experience during the last three decades to the countries of the Asia-Pacific, or indeed more generally, has to be limited. Only India has the scale to operate structurally in a similar manner to the PRC. With the obvious remaining exceptions of Vietnam, the Democratic People's Republic of Korea and Cuba, few countries have experienced state socialism and a ruling Communist Party (or equivalent) for the last 30 years.

Even the more specific lessons about measures and policies that might be learnt from China are likely to be limited in their impact. There have been three key development characteristics in China's recent experience. One is the development of a substantial middle class, not simply as a matter of economic expansion but also as part of a state project to establish a social base. The second is investment in infrastructure, borne out of concerns about the negative impact of the global financial crisis but embraced *inter alia* as an instrument to counter the previously disappearing welfare provision. The third is the state's operation of a mixed economy. This is an economy that runs on a public–private mix, with the state keeping a firm hand on the tiller to ensure what it considers to be the appropriate balance to that relationship. State-owned and private enterprises have different roles to play in the developing economy, as do the range of hybrid enterprises that come from their interaction. None of these is a dramatically innovative idea: elements have been implemented elsewhere and where they have not until now it is because local conditions and political configurations make such possibilities unlikely.

At the same time, it is not hard to see the appeal of the idea of the China Model to developing countries worldwide. China has maintained stable government and become an international economic force within four decades of having been close to being a pariah state. It has also become more of an independent voice in international affairs, especially independent of the USA. In the process it has also tapped into a dominant discourse of modern nationalism: there has been a cultural shift designed to restore its place in the world. The Brazilian Ambassador to the PRC in 2007 highlighted this aspect of international relations in an article in China's leading journal of Latin American Studies (de Castro Nueves 2007: 9). The test of the appeal of the Beijing Consensus can be seen in the case of Mexico: all but in a trade war with the PRC for much of the last decade their political relationship is nonetheless very close, especially in international forums such as the United Nations (Carrillo et al. 2011).

REFERENCES

Angle, S.C. (2005), 'Decent democratic centralism', *Political Theory*, **33** (4), 518–46.

Arrighi, G. (2007), *Adam Smith in Beijing: Lineages of the Twenty-First Century*, London: Verso.

Bolt, P.J. (2000), *China and Southeast Asia's Ethnic Chinese: State and Diaspora in Contemporary Asia*, New York: Praeger.

Carrillo, B., M. Chen and D.S.G. Goodman (2011), 'Beyond asymmetry: cooperation, conflict and globalisation in Mexico–China relations', *The Pacific Review*, **24** (4), 187–215.

de Castro Nueves, L.A. (2007), 'Zhongguo de jueqi: Baxi (huo Lading Meizhou) guanjiao' ['China's rise seen from a Brazilian (and perhaps a Latin American) perspective'], *Lading Meizhou Yanjiu* [*Journal of Latin American Studies*], **29** (2), 35–7.

Chen, M. and D.S.G. Goodman (2012), 'The China Model: one country, six authors', *Journal of Contemporary China*, **21** (72), 51–75.

Cooper Ramo, J. (2004), *The Beijing Consensus*, London: The Foreign Policy Centre.

Deng, Z. (2010), 'The "living wisdom:" a theorisation of China's development', 20 August, Fudan Institute for Advanced Study in Social Sciences.

Dickson, B.J. (2008), *Wealth into Power: The Communist Party's Embrace of China's Private Sector*, Cambridge: Cambridge University Press.

Feng, C. and D.S.G Goodman (1995), *China's Hainan Province: Economic Development and Investment Environment*, Perth, WA: University of Western Australia Press.

Goodman, D.S.G. (1985), 'The Chinese political order after Mao: "socialist democracy" and the exercise of state power', *Political Studies*, **33** (2), 218–35.

Goodman, D.S.G. (1999), 'King coal and Secretary Hu: Shanxi's third modernisation', in Hans Hendrischke and Feng Chongyi (eds), *The Political Economy of China's Provinces: Comparative and Competitive Advantage*, London: Routledge.

Goodman, D.S.G. (ed.) (2004), *China's Campaign to 'Open Up the West': National, Provincial and Local Perspectives*, Cambridge: Cambridge University Press.

Goodman, D.S.G. (2008a), 'Why China has no new middle class: cadres, managers and entrepreneurs', in David S.G. Goodman (ed.), *The New Rich in China: Future Rulers, Present Lives*, London: Routledge.

Goodman, D.S.G. (ed.) (2008b), *The New Rich in China: Future Rulers, Present Lives*, London: Routledge.

Halper, S. (2010), *The Beijing Consensus: How China's Authoritarian Model will Dominate the Twenty-First Century*, New York: Basic Books.

Harvey, D. (2007), *A Brief History of Neoliberalism*, New York: Oxford University Press.

Huang, Y. (2008), *Capitalism with Chinese Characteristics: Enterpreneurshp and the State*, Cambridge: Cambridge University Press.

Huang, Y. (2010), 'Chinomics: the fallacy of the Beijing consensus', *The Wall Street Journal*, 20 June.

Jacques, M. (2009), *When China Rules the World: The Rise of the Middle Kingdom and the End of the Western World*, London: Allen Lane.

Keng, C.W.K. (2001), 'China's future economic regionalization', *Journal of Contemporary China*, **10** (29), 587–611.

Landry, P.F. (2008), *Decentralized Authoritarianism in China: The Communist Party's Control of Local Elites in the Post-Mao Era*, Cambridge: Cambridge University Press.

Li, L.C. (2006), 'Embedded institutionalization: sustaining the rural tax reform in China', *Pacific Review*, **19** (1), 126–57.
Li, L.C. (ed.) (2009), *Towards Responsible Government in East Asia: Trajectories, Intentions and Meanings*, Oxford and London: Routledge.
Maddison, A. (2007), *Chinese Economic Performance in the Long Run: 960–2030 AD*, Paris: OECD Publishing, Development Centre Studies.
Montinola, G., Y. Qian and B.R. Weingast (1995), 'Federalism, Chinese style – the political basis for economic success in China', *World Politics*, **48**, 233–61.
Naughton, B. (2010), 'China's distinctive system: can it be a model for others?', *Journal of Contemporary China*, **19** (65), 437–60.
Nolan, P. (2004), *Transforming China: Globalization, Transition and Development*, London: Anthem Press.
Pan, W. (ed.) (2009a), *Zhongguo moshi – jiedu Renmin gonghe guo de 60 nian* [*The China Model: Reading 60 Years of the People's Republic of China*], Beijing: Zhongyang bianfan chubanshe.
Pan, W. (2009b), 'The China Model: an analysis of the economy, politics and society in the Chinese system', in Pan Wei (ed.), *Zhongguo moshi – jiedu Renmin gonghe guo de 60 nian* [*The China Model: Reading 60 Years of the People's Republic of China*], Beijing: Zhongyang bianfan chubanshe.
Renmin luntan (2008), 'Beijing gongshi yu Zhongguo Mushi' ['The Beijing consensus and the China Model'], *Renmin luntan* [*People's Forum*], **12**, 20–23.
Shambaugh, D. (2009), *China's Communist Party: Atrophy and Adaptation*, Berkeley, CA: University of California Press.
Vogel, E.F. (1989), *One Step Ahead in China: Guangdong under Reform*, Cambridge, MA: Harvard University Press.
Yang, J. (2011), 'How I see the "China Model"', *Yanhuang Chunqiu*, January.
Yu, K. (2006), 'Zhongguo mushi: jiedu' ['Understanding the China Model'], *Zhongguo yuanyang quanwu gongbao* [*Maritime China*], **1**, 21–7.
Zhang, W. (2011), 'The analysis of a miracle: the China Model and its significance', *Qiushi* [*Seeking Truth*], 22 March.
Zhao, S. (2010), 'The China Model: can it replace the Western model of modernization?', *Journal of Contemporary China*, **19** (65), 419–36.

13. China's move to high-tech innovation: some regional policy implications

Richard P. Appelbaum and Rachel Parker[1]

1. INTRODUCTION

China has emerged as a major economic player in recent years. Even as the United States, Europe and Japan are plagued with sluggish economic growth and growing financial strains, China continues with double-digit growth and sizeable surpluses of foreign revenues, surpluses that are ploughed back into growth-inducing infrastructure projects. The United States in particular, as of this writing (August 2011), appears to be politically gridlocked over the appropriate vision for government: should it be investing in future economic growth, or avoiding economic involvement altogether, letting the market determine economic outcomes? This is in part a question about the role of the state in fostering economic development, and in broad terms about industrial policy. Such a question is not a matter of great contention in China, which is investing heavily across the Chinese economy, particularly in high-tech sectors. The Chinese government is placing its bets that heavy public investment in targeted areas, focusing especially on supporting research and development, will pay off in a big way: it will make China less dependent on foreign firms and their technologies as the key source for innovative ideas, products and markets. China, in other words, appears to be moving increasingly towards uncoupling itself, at least in part, from dependence on others.

In this chapter, we first examine the steps China has recently taken to 'leapfrog development' through a series of government programmes intended to foster indigenous innovation. We examine the ways in which these programmes serve to define a *de facto* industrial policy that is contributing toward high-tech development in China, briefly comparing China's approach with that of the US. We then critically examine the claim that China is becoming a political as well as economic superpower, before turning to a discussion of China's global and regional future.

With regard to the former, we focus on US–China relations, in particular the reaction of the US government and leading businesses to what is often perceived as the Chinese threat. With regard to regional issues, we examine some of the tensions between China and its neighbours; tensions that are fuelled by China's growing economic and military power, as well as hunger for natural resources from fish to petroleum. We conclude with some speculations about China's future if current trends play out.

2. CHINA: AN EMERGING GLOBAL HIGH-TECH POWER

China's economic growth is the result of state policies aimed at fostering high-tech development, with the ultimate goal of achieving 'indigenous innovation' capabilities that reduce China's dependence on foreign firms for both employment and technology. In its Five-Year Plans and 15-Year Plans, China is effectively pursuing industrial policies designed to make China a high-tech world player, by aiming 'at the forefront of world technology development, intensify[ing] innovation efforts, and realis[ing] strategic transitions from pacing front-runners to focusing on "leap-frog" development in key high-tech fields in which China enjoys relative advantages'.[2] The plan to accomplish these goals is laid out in China's Long and Medium Term Scientific and Technological Development Plan Guidelines for the period 2006–2020 (hereafter MLP), issued in December 2005. The MLP called for China to invest heavily in research and development in advanced technologies, calling for China to become an 'innovation-oriented society' by 2020 and a world leader in science and technology by 2050 (Appelbaum and Parker 2008; Parker et al. 2009, Appelbaum et al. 2011).

Given the country's limited resources, however, it also concluded that China should 'do what it needs and attempt nothing where it does not' (*you suo wei, you suo bu wei*),[3] concentrating its public investments where a high payoff was deemed most likely. Four 'science megaprojects' (nanotechnology, development and reproductive biology, protein science, and quantum research) were therefore singled out as key areas for funding, along with five 'frontier technology' programmes, 13 'engineering megaprojects' and 11 'key areas' (Appelbaum et al. 2011: 43). China's plans for 'leapfrogging development' involve moving directly into high-impact emerging technologies, rather than merely building on its successes with low-wage/low- to intermediate-technology exports. Leapfrogging thereby bypasses the more traditional step-by-step movement up the value chain, and requires state investment in areas where firms are unable or unwilling to invest. Niosi and Reid (2007), for example, have identified nanotechnology and biotechnology as two fields that less developed countries – China included – might be able to use as foundations for catching up. Specifically looking at patent trends, they observe that China is well positioned to use these two fields as platform technologies to leapfrog development.

China has, in effect, adopted a set of policies aimed at making the country a high-tech global power. The country is well situated to make such an effort. By August 2011 China had amassed an estimated US$3 trillion in foreign reserves[4] to invest in high-tech development initiatives; roughly half of these were invested in US Treasuries, contributing to an extraordinarily high degree of financial interdependence between the two countries. China has placed its bets largely on the creation of a national innovation system that will result in indigenous innovation in leading-edge areas of science and technology, which are seen as key to national prosperity. Both the 11th and 12th Five-Year Plans (2006–2010, 2011–2015) view innovation as the centrepiece of China's economic strategy, the means to address the country's significant social, environmental, global competitive and national security challenges. To take one example in which China has been particularly successful at branding successful indigenous innovation, Huawei, a privately owned maker of routers and switches, mandates in its charter that a minimum of 10 percent of its sales revenue be devoted to research and development for exploratory and pre-competitive technology.[5] With more than two-fifths of the company's employees working on R&D at least part of the time, it is no coincidence that Huawei has been the leader for six consecutive years in terms of patent applications (Parker et al. 2009).

While China's leadership does not call for abandoning its export-led industrial growth, it regards this strategy as insufficient by itself: not only have the largest profits remained with the multinationals that are manufacturing in China, but the degree of technology transfer – especially with the most advanced technologies – has proven to be limited. China's development strategy now calls for a three-pronged approach: to continue to foster exports, its domestic market and promote the growth of high-technology industries. To achieve these goals, the Chinese government, at all levels, is making substantial investments in infrastructure, universities and high-tech industrial parks. The importance of these efforts is evidenced by the fact that state planning lies with the Chinese Communist Party (CCP), which exerts its influence through co-ordinating bodies – Leading Groups created within the State Council that are usually chaired by a vice premier or higher level figure who also belongs to the CCP Central Committee Politburo or its Standing Committee, China's *de facto* governing body.[6]

China's spending on R&D grew from 0.6 percent of its GDP in 1996 to 1.5 percent in 2010, approaching that of the European Union (1.7 percent). Government policy calls for reaching US levels (2.9 percent) by 2020 (Grueber and Studt 2009). One industry forecast of R&D spending describes China's R&D spending during the past decade as 'history-making', since it 'exceeds and challenges both the US and Europe in terms of the intellectual property it generates and the financial and infrastructure commitments it continues to make in science and technology endeavours'.[7] The study points to such indicators as China's growing share of research publications in virtually every scientific category, its increased success rate in generating domestic patents through its State Intellectual Property Office (SIPO), its rapid growth in international research collaboration, and its growing workforce of scientists and engineers.

The return of overseas Chinese scientists and engineers (so-called 'sea turtles') and extensive overseas collaborations, has also proven to be sources of strength (Suttmeier 2008). Overseas Chinese scientists are increasingly returning home, attracted by what they perceive as China's growing opportunities for conducting research, often in hopes of launching a financially successful high-tech venture.[8] The Chinese government is reinforcing this return migration. Initiatives such as the 'Thousand Talents Programme', launched by the CPC Central Committee in January 2009, resulted in the return of several hundred scientists and engineers from the US, Japan, Britain, Germany, France and other advanced industrial economies by September of that year. A survey of more than 600 Chinese returnees reported that nearly three out of four believed they were doing better professionally by virtue of having come back to China.[9] Heads of the Life Science departments at China's two leading universities (Peking and Tsinghua) were recruited from prominent positions at leading US universities (Northwestern and Princeton).

One study on the state's role in Chinese development concludes that the government 'engages in huge and ever-increasing investments in infrastructure, institution- and human capital building, R&D, and in other areas, on a scale unequalled anywhere else in the world [generating] a network of systemic external economies [which] decisively enhance the competitiveness, productivity and profitability of both public and privately owned/controlled industrial enterprises' (Gabriele 2009: 3, 17). And a recent study by researchers at Georgia Tech's Technology Policy and Assessment Centre bullishly concludes, 'China is rapidly heading to rival the United States as the principal driver of the world's economy. . . . One might well predict that China will surpass the United States in technology-based competitive capabilities within a decade or two' (Porter et al. 2009: 20).

In comparison, the US also has a form of industrial policy – one that is hidden, unacknowledged, and arguably less effective at the present time than that of the Chinese. Sociologist Fred Block argues that the US has what he terms a 'hidden developmental state' based on his observation that, under the auspices of 'competitiveness policy', US Congress 'periodically passes legislation that bolsters and expands the developmental capacities of the US state, but this happens with little public debate or discussion' (Block 2008: 2). The US National Nanotechnology Initiative (NNI), launched in 2000, is one example. The NNI has channelled billions of US dollars into nanotechnology R&D since its inception. While the US has not developed a unified high-tech industrial strategy – like that of Japan or China where there are single ministries in charge of industrial issues – the NNI is a rare case in the US where federal policy is far more integrated. As Motoyama et al. (2011) comment, 'The NNI demonstrates the emergence of a new mechanism for policy and financial planning, targeting a key emerging technology that has achieved substantial funding with strong bipartisan support' (pp. 116–17).

The US approach differs from China's approach in that the former is aimed primarily at the basic research end of the research–development–commercialization continuum, while the latter encompasses a broader range of activities, including (and in particular) commercialization. US government support for the commercialization of high-tech applications is largely limited to two programmes, the Small Business Innovation Research and Small Business Technology Transfer programmes, which together provide a sort of federal venture capital fund amounting to roughly US$2 billion annually, spread out across a number of federal agencies (Motoyama et al. 2011). While it is beyond the scope of this chapter to do so, we elsewhere argue (Appelbaum and Parker 2012) that the unwillingness of the US government to explicitly engage in some form of industrial policy, subject to public debate and discussion, significantly disadvantages US innovators and entrepreneurs relative to countries, such as China, that are willing and able to use public resources for fostering cutting-edge technological developments.

3. DOES ECONOMIC GROWTH CONFER SUPER-POWER STATUS?

China's economic clout is accompanied by an increased willingness to assert political power, as seen in China's significant role at the December 2009 Copenhagen climate change summit, or the fact that the G20 (in which China is prominent) is already arguably replacing the G8 as the world's primary economic forum (see chapters by Dobson, and Hong and Fang). Nobel Prize-winning economist Robert Fogel (2010) even predicts that the Chinese economy will account for two-fifths of the world's GDP in 2040, with a per capita income of US$85,000, more than double that predicted for the EU. However, there remain a number of doubters about China's future prospects (Pei 2009; Scissors 2011). Following the economic turbulence that roiled world markets following the downgrading of US government securities, a *Beijing Times* commentary pointed to four 'uncertainties' about China's future: continued reliance on massive public fixed-asset investments such as the intelligent power grid and high speed rail (plagued by high costs and low usage), said to be the main guarantor of a minimal 8 percent annual GDP growth; the shaky economic condition of many small and medium-sized enterprises; inflation (estimated at nearly 7 percent in July 2011); and signs of slowing economic growth in China's major cities.[10]

Economists view China's over-reliance on investment at the expense of consumption as a major drag on future economic growth (Lardy 2006). Although state planners are now trying to reverse this, it remains unclear how well they will succeed. China's one-party state can stifle the very innovation that party leaders have made central to its economic planning. Areas targeted by state planners for heavy investment may prove ill-advised at best, if not outright disastrous (Chang 2010). China's state-owned enterprises, which still account for an estimated two-fifths of GDP, tend to be bureaucratic and conservative, while the emerging private sector generally remains small, under-capitalized and generally risk-averse. China's universities and laboratories continue to suffer from a hierarchical structure that stifles innovation and creativity, remaining highly dependent on foreign technology despite the push for indigenous innovation. Misconduct in science is another problem: given the enormous pressures to publish in scientific journals, quantity often trumps quality, and plagiarism and other forms of fraud are widespread.[11]

As many as two-thirds of China's population lives in rural areas, still mired in poverty and lacking in safe drinking water, healthcare and adequate education. Unemployment has grown; one government report estimates that some 20 million lost their jobs during the 2008 economic downturn, while as many as 40 percent of college graduates will not find work (Ernst 2009). And a rapidly aging population (partly the result of China's one-child policies) will prove a growing burden, whose costs will come up against those of public investment in growth-inducing projects. The country's reliance on cheap, 'old coal' energy sources has resulted in significant environmental damage, intolerable pollution levels in major cities, shortages of potable water and considerable land degradation. And a growing number of mass protest incidents – estimated at 127,000 in 2008 (the most recent year for which figures are available) – pose a potential threat to stability.[12]

According to Suttmeier (2008), who has long tracked China's emergence as a technology leader, the very notion of a 'science superpower' needs to be recast: instead of emerging as a national superpower, China is better equipped to become a leading presence in global networks of research and innovation. It is important also to bear in mind that China is surrounded by strong regional rival powers, such as Japan, India and Russia. It also has less powerful, but economically rising, neighbours, including Indonesia, Vietnam and South Korea. China's geopolitical and military influence is therefore likely to be constrained, regardless of its economic strength (Pei 2009).

4. SOME THOUGHTS ABOUT CHINA'S GLOBAL AND REGIONAL FUTURE

4.1 Introduction

At present, China and its trading partners, such as the US, are highly interdependent. The US trade deficit with China accounts for a significant portion of China's foreign account surplus, an arrangement that has proven beneficial for both parties, notwithstanding occasional protests from both sides. For China, the surplus has helped to finance the massive investments in science, technology and infrastructure that underlie China's rapid economic growth. For the US, it has kept inflation low for some time now by providing consumers with an endless stream of low-cost goods. The downsides for both parties are also obvious: for China, a vast supply of funding for speculative investments in housing, office space and infrastructure that is fuelling a bubble economy; on the US side, the continuing loss of manufacturing jobs. Yet while American blue collar workers may have suffered as a result, Americans as consumers have benefited. Moreover, China's sizeable holdings of US Treasury securities – approaching US$1.2 trillion as of May 2011, and accounting for nearly a quarter of all foreign US Treasury holdings – give China a vested interest in the continued stability of the dollar, and the US an interest in China's continuing economic growth and stability.[13]

Nonetheless, it is useful to speculate on how China's rise might play itself out, if current trends continue into the next decade or so. Our speculation is based on the assumption that China will successfully transition from a growth strategy based largely on export-oriented industrialization, to one in which an increasing array of local products are sold to a rapidly-expanding Chinese middle class numbering in the hundreds of millions – indigenous brands that are designed, marketed, manufactured and sold by Chinese firms rather than by foreign multinationals. In short, China will make the classic emerging economy transition from export-oriented industrialization to import-substitution industrialization. Such an economic future could have significant foreign policy implications.

4.2 China and the US: Differing Approaches, Great Power Rivalry

US businesses and policy-makers have typically viewed China's economic and political ascendance with some alarm. During the closing years of the Clinton administration, the Project for the New American Century (PNAC) – an influential neo-conservative think tank that advocated a reassertion of US power in world affairs – called for 'raising US military strength in East Asia [as] the key to coping with the rise of China to great-power status' (PNAC 2000: 19). Among other concerns, the report cited China's early build-up (in the 1990s) of naval power seen as 'greatly improving China's ability to attack US Navy ships' (PNAC 2000: 65). Conservative writers associated with PNAC continue to issue warnings about a rising China, although they went largely unheeded during the George W. Bush administration, in part because the US military was fully engaged elsewhere. Official US policy towards China during the Bush years remained generally moderate, an approach that reportedly earned Bush high marks in China.[14] Then Treasury Secretary, Henry Paulson, writing in the influential journal *Foreign Affairs*, cited 'the inextricable interdependence of China's growth and that of the global economy', and called for 'strategic economic engagement' with China.[15] Yet despite calls for engagement and frequently moderate tones, US policy has also been wary of China.

In 2000, when the PNAC reported its above concerns about China's economic and military ascendance, US Congress created the US–China Economic and Security Review Commission (USCESRC), with a mandate to 'monitor, investigate, and submit to Congress an annual report on the national security implications of the bilateral trade and economic relationship between the United States and the People's Republic of China'.[16] The USCESRC's work is directed to eight areas: proliferation practices, economic transfers, energy, US capital markets, regional economic and security impacts, US–China bilateral programmes, WTO compliance and the implications of restrictions on speech and access to information in China. It holds hearings throughout the year, taking testimony from dozens of policy-makers, business people, labour leaders, military experts and academics. Its initial report, issued in 2002, concluded 'China's leaders view the United States as a partner of convenience, useful for its capital, technology, know-how and market . . . In time we will learn whether China is to become a responsible world power or an aggressive, wealthy dictatorship' (USCESRC 2002). Its most recent report (USCESRC 2010) continues to express strong concerns on numerous fronts, most notably economic (unbalanced trade relations, the sizable Chinese holdings of US debt, the undervalued Chinese yuan), military security (China's growing air and weapons capabilities) and growing regional influence.[17] The turn towards indigenous innovation is of special concern, especially 'China's pursuit of policies that rely on trade-distorting government intervention intended to promote China's domestic industries and protect them from international competition' (USCESRC 2010: 4).

In addition, the US Chamber of Commerce minces no words in denouncing China's drive for indigenous innovation, claiming it 'is considered by many international technology companies to be a blueprint for technology theft on a scale the world has never seen before' (McGregor 2010: 4). The title of the Chamber's report, *China's Drive for Indigenous Innovation: A Web of Industrial Policies*, provides a clear statement of the difference between the Chinese and US approach to economic growth. As described above, China has a clear industrial policy, in which extensive public resources are used to foster high-tech development in selected areas. The very phrase 'industrial policy' is anathema to current political discourse in the US, where market forces alone are regarded as capable of sending the correct signals and allocating resources to innovators and entrepreneurs. The choice of the phrase 'web of industrial policies' in the Chamber's subtitle suggests a shadowy, sinister network of Chinese governmental policies and programmes. According to the Chamber report, China's industrial policy ecosystem includes:

- A domestic patent regime allowing the use of 'junk patents' that can be employed to retaliate against foreign companies inside China which have filed intellectual property rights (IPR) violation lawsuits against Chinese companies outside of China
- Compulsory certification and standards requirements that slow or block the entry of foreign products into the China market
- Requirements for the disclosure of technology secrets and other proprietary information that serve to exclude foreign products from major Chinese markets
- An uneven and lax enforcement of IPR protection. (McGregor, 2010: 22)

The US Chamber of Commerce, the USCESRC and many economists regard China's industrial policy approach as both unfair to foreign competition and unwise for China: unfair because it is seen as in restraint of trade and possibly in violation of WTO principles, and unwise because it will lead to government bureaucrats placing bets on the wrong industries. The Chinese, on their part, have expressed their own concerns with the country that is at the same time seen as their biggest rival and closest partner. Lee's (2011) analysis of articles by members of the Chinese Academy of Social Sciences found some common themes: a belief that the US, as a superpower, will seek to maintain its power in the face of Chinese competition; that the US will try to spread its democratic values, thereby threatening China's one-party leadership; and – perhaps paradoxically – that the US's commitment to democracy can result in unpredictable (indeed, irrational) policy reversals that lead to increased hostility toward China. As a result, Chinese strategists view with some alarm current US strategic thinking in Asia, a situation that presumably could be rebalanced were China to assert its muscle more effectively in the region.

4.3 China: A Rising Regional Power?

As a marker of China's economic ascendance, its leaders have embarked on a programme of military modernization that has 'expanded China's ability to operate outside its borders and reach US regional allies, such as Japan, as well as US forces in the region' (USCESRC, 2010: 5). US and European multinationals, eager for market access, may well be playing a role in this modernization, since 'foreign aviation manufacturing firms, such as Boeing and Airbus, are compelled to provide technology and know-how offsets in return for market access' (USCESRC 2010: 5). China's semi-official public unveiling of its J-20 Stealth fighter, when images of the aeroplane appeared on Chinese internet during a January 2011 visit by US Defence Secretary Robert Gates, has amplified these concerns. During the last two decades, China has 'developed a variety of solid-fuel ballistic missiles, fourth generation aircraft, submarines, military satellites, anti-satellite weapons, airborne early warning systems, cruise-missiles and other advanced weaponry systems' (Evron 2010: 1). China planned to test its first aircraft carrier (an aging Soviet carrier bought in 1998) sometime during 2011, and was reported to be designing its own carriers based on the former Soviet model. While China has assured its neighbours that the carrier was intended only for peaceful uses, it was widely viewed as challenging US naval supremacy in the region, as well as reinforcing China's increasingly confrontational role in regional territorial disputes.[18] Yet the effectiveness of this military build-up, at least to date, remains unclear. China's military remains severely hampered. Making technological breakthroughs does not necessarily translate into successful field deployment. According to Evron

(2010), China's military equipment is likely to be plagued by limited operational utility, inefficiency, unmet targets, poor quality, inadequate supplies of systems and spare parts, and in general weak support. As a consequence, China's leadership appears to have concluded that its military presence should for the time being be restricted to the East Asia region.

Overlapping territorial jurisdictions have embroiled China in disputes with its neighbours with some frequency. In 2010 China was embroiled in a highly public dispute with Japan, when the Japanese coastguard detained a Chinese fishing ship captain (the crew was released) after the Chinese boat collided with a Japanese boat in disputed waters. China retaliated by briefly halting the shipment of rare earth elements to Japan. China is by far the world's largest producer of such elements (currently over 90 percent for many of them) and Japan the world's largest consumer. Rare earths are essential in the material production of numerous clean energy (for example wind turbines, solar photovoltaic cells), electronics and other strategic high-tech industries. Such conflicts are not only about nationalist sentiments, they also have to do with vital resources, from fishing rights to energy (Schofield et al. 2011).[19] Seismic surveys have led to maritime territorial disputes because they are conducted for purposes of oil and gas exploration, vital (and scarce) resources for the region's growing economies. While such disputes have made it nearly impossible to derive an accurate assessment of undersea oil reserves in the Gulf of Thailand and the East and South China Seas, China believes that such reserves are substantial – a belief that accounts for the conflicting maritime claims and conflicts that trouble the region.[20] China today imports around 80 percent of its oil (even though it is the world's fifth largest oil producer), while Japan imports over 95 percent. For both countries, the vast majority of its oil imports are still sourced from the Middle East, and the tankers carrying this oil must pass through at least one of Southeast Asia's narrow choke-point sealanes, most importantly the Straits of Malacca. Protecting sealane trade routes is therefore vital, especially given net oil imports to the region are expected to triple between 2008 and 2030, at which time as much as three-quarters of Southeast Asia's energy requirements will be provided by imports.

5. CONCLUSION

To the extent that China becomes less dependent on foreign multinationals as sources of investment and innovation, and foreign markets as consumers of made-in-China products, China will be increasingly free to act as a great power, using its economic and political influence to attempt to shape world events in its own interest. Will China begin to uncouple its economy from that of the US in particular, selling designed-in-China brands to its own growing middle class, and moving it lowest-cost production offshore, as wages rise at home? With its large population and territory, and a Communist Party elite determined to maintain its power through a combination of economic growth and authoritarian rule, China is in a position to increasingly 'go it alone', relying on its growing internal market, natural resources and technological capability. China is already flexing its muscles globally, moving production offshore to East Asia, Latin America and Africa, investing in roads, factories and natural resource extraction. Its leaders, concerned about protecting sealane trade routes – and mindful of historical geopolitical enmities – are developing China's military power, particularly its naval and air capabilities.

When China surpassed Japan as the world's second largest economy in 2010, its leaders downplayed this achievement. When this long-awaited moment arrived, Chinese Commerce Ministry spokesperson Yao Jian simply noted that 'China is a developing country. The quality of China's economic development still needs to be raised. It needs more effort to improve economic quality and people's lives'.[21] Yet despite such claims, the 'Middle Kingdom' – after conceding technological, economic and political leadership to western powers for some five centuries – is clearly on the verge of reasserting its historic place among nations.

How will the US and China's neighbours, respond? If the US engages in China bashing, blaming its economic challenges on China, China will respond both defensively and assertively. China's advances in science and technology can be seen as a threat to US dominance, or as part of a global science and engineering effort to solve common problems. By the same token, China's disputes with its neighbours can escalate into open conflicts or be resolved through co-operation. There are signs that China sees it as in its interest to pursue a more co-operative regional path. At the 2011 Association of Southeast Asian Nations (ASEAN) Regional Forum summit in Bali, steps were taken to ease tensions when China and Southeast Asian states agreed on guidelines to more effectively implement the 2002 Declaration on the Conduct of Parties in the South China Sea. The guidelines, while not fully resolving territorial issues, point the way towards future co-operation in oil and gas exploration, maritime environmental protection, scientific research, navigation safety, and other areas. While China's motivation to co-operate with its neighbours may in part reflect its desire to send a signal to the United States that regional problems can be solved without outside interference, it is also a measure of China's growing regional economic ties. China's growth trajectory seems clear. How it plays out geopolitically will depend in large part on the response of others.

NOTES

1. The material is based upon work supported by the National Science Foundation under Grant No. SES 0531184. Any opinions, findings, and conclusions or recommendations expressed in this material are those of the author and do not necessarily reflect the views of the National Science Foundation. It was conducted under the auspices of the UCSB's Centre for Nanotechnology in Society (www.cns.ucsb.edu).
2. National High-tech R&D Programme (863 Programme), ChineseEmbassy.Org www.bg.chineseembassy.org/eng/dtxw/t202501.htm (accessed: 16 August 2011).
3. This theme was taken from the then CCP General Secretary Jiang Zemin's report to the 15th CCP Congress in 1997.
4. *New York Times*, 8 August 2011.
5. See Huawei, Research and Development, R&D Investment, December 2009 http://www.huawei.com/corporate_information/research_development.do (accessed: 16 August 2011).
6. Research interview conducted at the Chinese Institute of Physics, Beijing, 25 July 2007.
7. *Battele*, '2010 Global R&D Funding Forecast' (December 2009) www.rdmag.com/uploadedFiles/RD/Featured_Articles/2009/12/GFF2010_ads_small.pdf (accessed: 16 August 2011).
8. *New York Times*, 7 January 2010.
9. *New York Times*, 18 January 2010.
10. *People's Daily*, 11 August 2011.
11. *New York Times*, 18 January 2010.
12. *Wall Street Journal (Asia)*, 14 June 2011.
13. It is worth noting that Japan's holding of US Treasury securities is almost as large as China's (in May 2011, Japan's holdings totalled US$912 billion); China and Japan together accounted in that month for 46 percent of all foreign holdings (US Federal Reserve Bank, http://www.federalreserve.gov/, accessed: 16 August 2011).
14. *CN Reviews*, 8 August 2008; *Los Angeles Times*, 15 January 2009.
15. *Foreign Affairs* (2008, September/October), http://www.foreignaffairs.com/articles/63567/henry-m-paulson-jr/a-strategic-economic-engagement (accessed: 16 August 2011).
16. US–China Economic and Security Review Commission, http://www.uscc.gov/about/facts.php (accessed: 16 August 2011).
17. On the plus side, the report also applauds China's 'green energy policies and efforts to promote alternative energy sectors' (USCESRC 2010: 8).
18. *CNS News*, 27 July 2011.
19. China is the world's largest fish-producing country, accounting for a third of the world's total fish production, including a sixth of all captured fish.
20. Estimates vary widely. For example, China estimates as much as 213 billion barrels of oil lies beneath the South China Sea; assuming a 10 percent recovery rate (the industry standard), this would yield 21.3 billion barrels. The US Geological survey, on the other hand, puts the figure of recoverable oil at only 1.6 billion barrels (Schofield et al. 2011).
21. *Canadian News*, 17 August 2010, http://www.cbc.ca/news/world/story/2010/08/17/china-economy.html (accessed: 16 August 2011).

REFERENCES

Appelbaum, R.P. and R.A. Parker (2008), 'China's bid to become a global nanotech leader', *Science and Public Policy*, **35**(5), 319–34.

Appelbaum, R.P. and R.A. Parker (2012), 'The Chinese century? Some policy implications of China's move towards indigenous innovation', in B.H. Harthorn and J. More (eds), *The Social Life of Nanotechnology*, London: Routledge.

Appelbaum, R., R.A. Parker, C. Cao and G. Gereffi (2011), 'China's (not so hidden) developmental state: becoming a leading nanotechnology innovator in the twenty-first century', in F. Block and M.R. Keller (eds), *State of Innovation: The US Government's Role in Technology Development*, Boulder, CO: Paradigm Publishers.

Block, F. (2008), 'Swimming against the current: the rise of a hidden developmental state in the United States', *Politics and Society*, **36**(2), 169–334.

Chang, G. (2010), 'Hard sciences require freedom too', *New York Times Blog*, 18 January, accessed 16 August 2011 at www.roomfordebate.blogs.nytimes.com/2010/01/18/will-china-achieve-science supremacy.

Ernst, D. (2009), *Asia's Challenges in the Global Crisis: A Catalyst for Change?*, Honolulu, HI: East West Centre.

Evron, Y. (2010), 'China's military build-up in the early twenty-first century: from arms procurement to war-fighting capability', S. Rajaratnam School of International Studies working paper series no. 218, Singapore.

Fogel, R. (2010), 'Why China's economy will grow to US$123 trillion by 2040', *Foreign Policy*, 4 January.

Gabriele, A. (2009), 'The role of the state in China's industrial development: a reassessment', *IDEAS: Economics and Finance Research*, 5 April.

Grueber, M. and T. Studt (2009), 'Emerging economies drive global RT&D growth', *R&D Magazine*, 22 December.

Lardy, N.R. (2006), 'China: towards a consumption-driven growth path', Institute for International Economics Policy Briefs in International Economics no. PB06-6, Washington, DC.

Lee, J. (2011), 'China's America obsession', *Foreign Policy*, 6 May.

McGregor, J. (2010), *China's Drive for Indigenous Innovation: A Web of Industrial Policies*, Washington, DC: US Chamber of Commerce.

Motoyama, Y., R.P. Appelbaum and R. Parker (2011), 'The National Nanotechnology Initiative: federal support for science and technology, or hidden industrial policy?', *Technology in Society*, **33**(1–2), 109–18.

Niosi, J. and S.E. Reid (2007), 'Biotechnology and nanotechnology: science-based enabling technologies as windows of opportunity for LDCs?', *World Development*, **35**(3), 426–38.

Parker, R., C. Ridge, C. Cao and R.P. Appelbaum (2009), 'China's nanotechnology patent landscape: an analysis of invention patents filed with the state intellectual property office', *Nanotechnology Law and Business*, **6**(4), 524–39.

Pei, M. (2009), 'China's not a superpower', *The Diplomat Magazine*, 29 December.

Porter, A.L., N.C. Newman, J.D. Roessner, D.M. Johnson and X.Y. Jin (2009), 'International high-tech competitiveness: does China rank #1?', *Technology Analysis and Strategic Management*, **21**(2), 173–93.

Project for the New American Century (PNAC) (2000), *Rebuilding America's Defences: Strategy, Forces, and Resources for the New Century*, Washington, DC: Project for a New American Century.

Schofield, C., I. Townsend-Gault, H. Djalal, I. Storey, M. Miller and T. Cook (2011), *From Disputed Waters to Seas of Opportunity: Overcoming Barriers to Maritime Co-operation in East and Southeast Asia*, Seattle, WA: National Bureau of Asian Research.

Scissors, D. (2011), *The United States vs. China: Which Economy is Bigger, Which Is Better?*, Washington, DC: The Heritage Foundation.

Suttmeier, R.P. (2008), 'The discourse on China as science and technology superpower: assessing the arguments', presented at the International Symposium on China as a Science and Technology Superpower, China Research Centre of the Japan Science and Technology Centre, 9–10 December, Tokyo.

US–China Economic and Security Review Commission (USCESRC) (2002), *2002 Annual Report*, Washington, DC: USCESRC.

USCESRC (2010), *2010 Annual Report*, Washington, DC: USCESRC.

14. A Northeast Asian model of ODA? Comparing Chinese, Japanese and Korean official development assistance

James Reilly

1. INTRODUCTION

World politics is undergoing a historic transition. Rising powers such as Brazil, Indonesia, South Africa, Turkey and India are challenging longstanding institutional arrangements, international norms and practices. Permanent membership on the United Nations Security Council, leadership of the International Monetary Fund and World Bank, rules over global trade and responsibilities for climate change are all being contested. In the realm of official development assistance (ODA), a growing pluralism among aid donors and approaches has emerged as the most significant challenge to Western aid orthodoxy in decades. In response, the Organisation for Economic Co-operation and Development's Development Assistance Committee (OECD-DAC) is striving to reshape international norms defining effective and appropriate ODA. Yet the DAC process faces a contradiction between being more inclusive by welcoming new members, collaborating with aid recipients, and collaborating with non-DAC members, while also being more exclusive by codifying and promulgating selective norms on ODA. Contestation over normative content and pervasive hypocrisy by major aid donors further undermine DAC norms. This chapter explores one aspect of this ongoing contestation; the alternative approach to development assistance employed by Japan, South Korea and China.

Having finally secured entry into DAC in January 2010, South Korea pledged: 'Korea will formulate an original Korean assistance model that transmits the country's successful development experience aligned to the recipient country's national development strategies'.[1] In 2010, Chinese Premier Wen Jiabao also announced the successful creation of a model of development aid with Chinese characteristics (Wen 2010). In fact, China and Korea's aid programmes are not only similar; they also parallel Japan's earlier approach to ODA. Commonalities include prioritizing economic growth, preference for subsidized loans rather than grant aid, infrastructure-centred programmes, support for a state-led development model, the pursuit of 'mutual benefit' and a reluctance to tie aid provision to political or social conditions. In all three countries, large government agencies work closely with domestic corporations in designing and delivering aid projects.

These similarities across three distinct regime types can be traced back to their economic development strategies. All three states responded to the challenge of 'late development' with a single-minded emphasis upon rapid economic growth through industrialization and transformation. They strategically directed foreign aid into investments in basic infrastructure while avoiding dependence and donor conditionality. Strong, autonomous state agencies guided economic development through selective support for market actors and mechanisms in pursuit of state-defined objectives. Most importantly, these strategies worked. First Japan, then South Korea followed by China grew rapidly, enabling them to move quickly from foreign aid recipient to donor. Their economic success fostered confidence in challenging neo-liberal models of economic development, and shaped their approaches to providing development assistance abroad. These examples suggest that domestic economic experience, rather than regime type, plays a crucial role in shaping foreign aid strategies.

This chapter begins by outlining key DAC norms on ODA and contestation around these norms, and then reviews the developmental state model in East Asia. Subsequent sections examine how domestic economic development influenced aid programmes in Japan, South Korea and China. I conclude by considering how the Northeast Asian model of ODA may impact international norms on aid.

2. 'A SILENT REVOLUTION' IN AID NORMS

A norm is simply a set of collective expectations about appropriate behaviour for a given identity. Norms tend to be more powerful if they are logically consistent across a set of ideals, institutionalized (included in official documents; embedded within formal institutions) and consistent with actual practice. As the self-proclaimed 'venue and voice' for 24 of the world's leading bilateral aid donors, who collectively provided US$129 billion in ODA in 2010, the OECD's Development Assistance Committee (DAC) has actively sought to shape international norms defining effective and appropriate aid.[2] This effort culminated in the 2005 Paris Declaration on Aid Effectiveness, endorsed by 91 countries, followed by the 2008 Accra Agenda for Action. The DAC insists:

> The Paris Declaration and Accra Agenda for Action are founded on five core principles, born out of decades of experience of what works for development, and what doesn't. These principles have gained support across the development community, changing aid practice for the better. *It is now the norm* for aid recipients to forge their own national development strategies with their parliaments and electorates (*ownership*); for donors to support these strategies (*alignment*) and work to streamline their efforts in-country (*harmonisation*); for development policies to be directed to achieving clear goals and for progress towards these goals to be monitored (*results*); and for donors and recipients alike to be jointly responsible for achieving these goals (*mutual accountability*).[3]

The effort to put aid recipients in the driver's seat, to move 'from donorship to ownership', is the most significant normative shift articulated in Paris and reaffirmed in Accra. Yet the DAC norms still support donor-imposed conditions on aid recipients.[4] To combat 'excessive fragmentation of donor activities', the Paris Declaration urges donors to enhance country-level collaboration.[5] The DAC also seeks a results-based approach to aid and urges greater transparency. Most fundamentally, the DAC definition of what counts as ODA reflects an ideal that aid should advance the economic interests of developing countries and their citizens, not enrich wealthy donor states. ODA must be concessional and promote the economic development and welfare of developing countries. All loans must include a grant element of at least 25 percent. Export assistance, military aid, cultural promotion and market-based transactions are excluded.[6] The DAC urges that most aid be directed to least developed countries (LDCs) and that such assistance should essentially be in the form of grants (OECD-DAC 2008). The DAC strongly discourages tied aid: the requirement that a certain percentage of aid funds be used to purchase services or items from the donor country, particularly for aid to LDCs.

While the DAC has no enforcement capacity, it has sought to leverage its moral weight in urging new DAC applicants and even non-DAC members to follow these norms.[7] Aid recipients have also been encouraged to adopt parallel statements, such as Laos' 2006 Vientiane Declaration on Aid Effectiveness.[8] However, scholars have widely documented the extent to which actual aid flows reflect donors' economic, strategic and ideological interests. The United States' aid, for instance, targets strategically important states, while France and Australia overwhelmingly give to their former colonies (Alesina and Dollar 2000). Even Sweden's aid correlates more closely with its trade relations than with humanitarian needs (Schraeder et al. 1998). Domestic interests and a growing 'securitization' of foreign aid are also key drivers (Woods 2005; Lancaster 2006). As Bueno de Mesquita and Smith (2009: 310) contend: 'OECD members have little humanitarian motivation for aid giving'. Optimism about aid's contribution to ending poverty in our time has also been challenged by virulent attacks on the aid industry and the effectiveness of aid (Sachs 2005; Moyo 2009). The most important challenge has come from a group of so called 'emerging donors' outside of the DAC orthodoxy.

Although being a heterogeneous group, non-DAC donors tend to focus on 'development effectiveness' rather than 'aid effectiveness', prefer a partnership or 'mutual-benefit' approach to aid, prioritize basic infrastructure (roads, energy, telecommunications) and other productive sectors, and apply a less bureaucratic and more practical approach to aid delivery (Davis 2008; McCormick 2008). Woods (2008: 1206) argues that a 'silent revolution' is emerging as emerging donors pose a 'serious challenge to the existing multilateral assistance regime'. The most significant challenge arises from the economic development model employed in Northeast Asia.

3. LESSONS AND LEGACIES OF STATE-LED DEVELOPMENT IN EAST ASIA

The developmental state approaches employed in Japan, South Korea in the 1960s to 1970s, and China in the 1980s to 1990s share certain common features. Strong, autonomous government agencies provided tariff protection, tax concessions, preferential capital allocation and 'administrative guidance' to support strategic sectors of the economy. Indicative state planning existed alongside market mechanisms such as competition and market-based prices. The focus was on export-oriented growth, rapid industrialization and quick transitions from light to heavy industry, and then into high-tech and service sectors. State support was directed to new and higher-tech infant industries while simultaneously assisting in the decline of mature industries such as agriculture and textiles. Natural resources, where available, were exploited in support of growth. The state invested heavily in basic infrastructure while enacting social and political reforms designed to manage wages, regulate working conditions and address social inequities in order to ensure political and social stability (Woo-Cumings 1999; Wade 2004; Chang 2006; Lee 2008; Kang 2010). Above all, the model required a steadfast dedication to rapid economic development. As Korean President Park Chung-Hee (1970: 32) declared: 'my chief concern was economic revolution. One must eat and breathe before concerning himself with politics, social affairs and culture'.

Despite substantial costs and ongoing contestation over these strategies, all three countries emerged with a dominant consensus that their economic policies were successful. As they began to provide development assistance to other states, these lessons and legacies shaped their aid programmes. The ideological foundation of the developmental state is that economic development necessarily precedes social or political reforms, and often justifies their delay. Imposing external conditions unnecessarily weakens the recipient state. Instead, recipient states should be strengthened in order to shape their own unique path toward growth. This economic emphasis also justifies a 'win–win' approach to aid provision, particularly if the donor is itself in the midst of economic development. Close integration between the states and large firms in East Asia easily translated into a preference for tied aid, in which Japanese, Korean or Chinese firms could gain economic advantage while delivering valuable infrastructure projects. These elements were first evident in Japan's aid programme.

4. JAPAN AS NUMBER ONE

Japan, like South Korea and China, began its growth process as a major aid recipient. The United States provided Japan with a total of approximately US$5 billion in assistance between 1946 and 1951. Japan also received 34 loan projects worth about US$860 million from the World Bank, only fully repaid in 1990; a year after Japan emerged as the world's largest bilateral aid donor. Japan's aid programme began in 1954 as part of its reparations to Asian countries following World War II, and indeed up until 1972 some 98 percent of all Japanese aid was directed to the Asia-Pacific (Koppel and Orr 1993).

Japan's formal launch of its 'economic co-operation' programme in 1961 coincided with Prime Minister Ikeda Hayata's 1961 plan to double Japan's national income in a decade. Following the 1985 Plaza Accord, which led to the revaluation of the Japanese yen, Japan emerged in 1989 as the world's largest aid donor, and remained so until 2002 (Woods 2005). As the aid levels rose, so did scholarly attention to Japan's 'narrow, mercantilist model of foreign assistance' (Ensign 1992: 175). Rix (1980) emphasized the importance of bureaucratic factors, Yasumoto (1986) noted the importance of rationalist, strategic objectives, Orr (1990) focused on foreign pressure and Arase (1995) highlighted the influence of domestic commercial interests. One of the most important elements, however, was Japan's own economic development experience.

Japanese officials and scholars argued that their successful state-led developmental model was 'normal' and so embodied important lessons for other developing states (Lee 2008). As Japan's Ministry of Finance's Committee on Asia-Pacific Economic Research declared in 1990: 'It is necessary that what Japan used to do should be done by the Asian NIEs (newly industrialized economies); what the Asian NIEs used to do should be done by ASEAN countries' (cited in Lee 2008: 524). Japan also began to promote the state-led economic development model within multilateral banks and other international forums (Katada 2004).

Having become an aid donor early in its own economic development process, Japan defended the legitimacy of a mutual-benefits approach to aid. As Prime Minister Yoshida Shigeru explained: 'since the Burmese did not like the word investments, we used the word reparations as they wished, but for us it was investments. Through our investments Burma would develop and it would become a Japanese market, and so our investment would return' (cited in Edström 2009: 19). Over the next few decades, aid continued to be explicitly regarded as a legitimate arm of national policy designed to advance Japan's economic and commercial interests (Rix 1980; Arase 1995).

Japan's aid was also grounded, or at least justified, by the assumption that economic development must come first in developing countries (Hook and Zhang 1998). Japan thus supported authoritarian regimes without imposing political or social conditions, providing, for instance, some US$2.2 billion to Burma under General Ne Win's military regime (1962–1988). By 1987, Japan's ODA covered 20 percent of Burma's national budget, constituting 71.5 percent of all foreign aid to Burma (Oishi and Fumitaka 2003). Up until 1990, Japan's Ministry of Foreign Affairs (MFA) resisted imposing conditions on recipients as undue interference in their internal affairs (Takamine 2006). When the West began to impose structural adjustments upon African aid recipients in the mid-1980s, Japan expanded its support for African infrastructure and production assistance. This shift, Lee (2008: 511) argues, 'was closely linked to Japan's commitment to the state-led economic development alternative'.

Japan's aid programme reflected key elements within its own domestic economy. For instance, private investment, market-rate loans and concessional loans were all integrated under the rubric of 'economic co-operation' (Koppel and Orr 1993). Japan directed its aid toward large-scale infrastructure projects, an approach that benefitted Japanese construction firms looking to gain a foothold overseas. Concessional loans were prioritized, in part because ODA drew from the postal savings of Japanese citizens and so had to be repaid in full (Koppel and Orr 1993). Japanese aid officials also defended the loans as usefully enforcing market-based discipline among recipients (Hook and Zhang 1998). Like South Korea, and later China, Japan delivered its aid through a single agency, the Japan International Cooperation Agency (JICA), designed to meet these multiple political and economic objectives.

In response to international and domestic criticism, Japan issued a new ODA charter in 1992 pledging to reduce the level of tied aid, broaden aid distribution, prioritize support for poorer countries, and emphasize social and political objectives (Government of Japan 1992). Yet quantitative studies revealed that Japan continued to provide substantial aid to lower–middle income countries in Asia, prioritize economic infrastructure and prefer yen loans over grant aid (Hook and Zhang 1998). Even though Japan's aid programme has changed significantly in recent decades, Japanese scholars and officials continue to question DAC norms and defend Japan's distinct approach to aid provision (Jerve 2007). Japan's most significant influence on aid norms, however, emerged through one of its largest aid recipients: South Korea.

5. SOUTH KOREA AS A MODEL

Like Japan, the Republic of Korea (ROK, or South Korea) was a major recipient of US aid after World War II, particularly following the Korean War (1950–53). When US aid began to falter by the early 1960s, President Park Chung-Hee turned to Japan. From 1971 to 1974, Japan delivered one-quarter of all of its foreign aid to South Korea (Kim 2010). In total, from 1945 until the early 1990s, South Korea received some US$13 billion in overseas aid. The early grant aid helped meet subsistence needs and finance South Korea's balance of payments deficits. Following the introduction of the first Five Year Plan in 1962, South Korea used concessional loans to augment state investments in education and infrastructure. As South Korea grew rapidly, aid loans were directed toward heavy and chemical industrialization, and then to economic restructuring and industrial modernization (Lumsdaine and Schopf 2007).

In 1995, South Korea graduated from the World Bank's lending list, and the following year it joined the OECD. By 2000, Korea had left the DAC's list of aid recipients. The strategic use of foreign aid was seen as critical for South Korea's success. The Ministry of Foreign Affairs and Trade (MOFAT) declares: 'Korea shares with other East Asian newly industrialized countries the unique experience of overcoming national poverty and achieving economic growth in just a few decades. Effective use of the enormous amount of foreign aid was crucial to Korea's sustained economic growth.'[9] Much like China and Japan, South Korea began providing aid early in its economic development process. By the end of the 1960s, South Korea had developed a robust technical training programme for experts from developing countries, even though its own gross domestic product (GDP) per capita in 1969 was only US$210 (Söderberg 2010). In 1982, it established the International Development Exchange Programme (IDEP) to train developing country officials and experts, followed five years later by the Economic Development Co-operation Fund (EDCF) to provide bilateral concessional loans (Lumsdaine and Schopf 2007). Today, two ministries dominate Korea's aid programme: MOFAT is responsible for grants, training programmes and subscriptions to multilateral development banks that are implemented by the Korea International Co-operation Agency (KOICA). The Ministry of Strategy and Finance (MOSF), along with the Export–Import Bank of Korea (Korea EXIM Bank) are responsible for South Korea's concessional loans, which are implemented by the EDCF (Jerve and Selbervik 2009). Both KOICA and the EDFC are closely modelled on their Japanese counterparts (Söderberg 2010).

Describing South Korea as a model for poverty reduction, Park Kang-ho explains that 'sharing [Korea's] successful development experience with developing countries is the most effective means of assistance' (Park 2010: 1). South Korea dedicates approximately 30 percent of its bilateral grant aid to technical co-operation, training some 4,000 people from developing countries annually. In 2009, the South Korean government and the United Nations Development Programme (UNDP) established a Policy Centre on Global Development Partnerships in Seoul to transfer Korea's development experience and knowledge to developing countries (Park 2010). The Knowledge Sharing Programme administered by the Ministry of Finance's Korea Development Institute (KDI) claims to 'offer advantageous perspectives stemming from its own economic history, providing a blueprint for a smoother economic transition to economic advancement' (Jerve and Selbervik 2009: 27).

Compared to other DAC donors, South Korea's aid has a relatively low ratio of ODA to GDP, a high percentage of concessional loans relative to grants, a high percentage of tied aid, a strong regional bias (focused on Asia), and a wide distribution of aid recipients relative to the size of its aid programme (Chun et al. 2010). As a 2008 DAC review noted: 'A feature of the Korean development system is the large use of concessional loans, partly explained by Korea's own positive experience as a recipient of loans, and the profoundly held belief that this instrument imposes essential fiscal discipline on the recipient country' (OECD-DAC 2008: 14). In 2007, among DAC donors, only Japan's grant ratio (portion of grants in total bilateral aid) of 51.3 percent was lower than Korea's 68.2 percent, the DAC average being 88.3 percent that year (Jerve and Selbervik 2009).

Moreover, South Korea tends to reserve its grants for economically and strategically significant countries. As a result, in 'Korea, the poorer the recipient country is, the higher is the tendency to use concessional loans' (Chun et al. 2010: 792). As Kim (2010) notes, between 1987 and 1999, South Korea directed over half (55.5 percent) of its bilateral loan assistance to support for economic infrastructure, a figure up to 75.3 percent by 2009. As of 2008, an estimated 98 percent of South Korean bilateral aid was either fully or partially tied (OECD-DAC 2008). Like Japan and China, South Korea's aid is also closely aligned to its strategic priorities. While the percentage of Asia in South Korea's overall ODA declined from 72.6 percent in 2001 to 52.2 percent in 2008, aid to both Asian and African continues to prioritize countries of strategic and/or economic significance (Chun et al. 2010). In South Korea, as in Japan, 'aid works as a vanguard for their investors in the developing countries' (Park and Lee 2008: 19).

South Korea's efforts to join the international aid community have, like Japan, generated pressures to conform to DAC norms. As part of its accession to DAC, the Korean government pledged to increase its ODA/GDP ratio to 0.15 percent by 2012 and to 0.25 percent by 2015, while increasing grant aid and reducing tied aid. While Lumsdaine and Schopf (2007) see the pledges as part of an ongoing evolution in South Korea's aid programme toward more coherence with DAC norms and practices, the process remains uncertain. Like Japan, a nominal reduction in tied aid may end up as more of a redefinition exercise rather than removing reliance upon Korean firms and products in the aid programme (Chun et al. 2010: 60). President Lee Myun-bak's 'resource diplomacy' also reflects a renewed determination to use aid for strategic purposes (Nishino 2008). Like their Japanese counterparts, South Korean scholars have also criticized DAC norms as inflexible, weighed down by jargon, and embedded with high transaction costs for recipients (Chun et al. 2010). Similar tensions are evident in the world's largest 'emerging donor', China.

6. CHINA'S AID PROGRAMME: LESSONS LEARNED

China is one of the world's most experienced providers of foreign assistance, with an aid programme dating back to 1950. In 1964, Premier Zhou Enlai announced eight principles of Chinese aid.[10] At loggerheads with both the Soviet Union and the United States, China then rapidly expanded its aid programme in support of new nations 'fighting against colonialism and hegemony', or *fanzhi fanba* (Shang 2010). By 1973, aid spending reached 2.1 percent of China's GDP, taking up an astonishing 6.9 percent of total government expenditures, this even exceeding China's own educational budget (Bräutigam 2009: 41). Clearly, the programme's scale was unsustainable. A 1975 State Council conference signalled a scale down in assistance by urging that aid recipients rely on themselves in developing their economies (Yang 2009). In July 1979, Deng Xiaoping told a Politburo working group: 'we must ensure that both the donor and the recipient country can receive benefits' (cited in Bin 2008: 36).

In reviewing the early aid programme, Chinese scholars are surprisingly critical. As Peking University professor Sun Luxi (2007: 9) argues: 'The individuals who designed China's aid policies primarily considered political and security interests, but ignored economic interests. Because of this, China's true national interests suffered.' Furthermore, these historical errors justify China's shift to a more pragmatic approach, and: 'China's new approach to aid reduces the fiscal burden on our country, and supports our own economic development. Strengthening trade, education, and other cooperative programmes through [our] foreign assistance enables our country and our enterprises to receive greater economic benefits.'

As part of this pragmatic shift, China began to accept foreign aid from non-socialist states. The largest bilateral aid donor was Japan. In 1978, China pledged to import US$10 billion worth of Japanese technology and capital equipment over the next eight years, to be paid for by exporting Chinese oil and coal to Japan. Japan's first round of yen loans (1979–1983) was 330 billion yen (US$1.4 billion) (Wan 2006). Japanese loans funded the construction of railways and ports to ensure the export of coal and oil back to Japan, and then to hydroelectric and thermal power plants, telecommunications, highways and fertilizer plants, forming the backbone of China's modernization. As Deborah Bräutigam explains:

> China saw all of these tactics as *beneficial* for China's development. Japan and the West could use their modern technologies to exploit natural resources that Chinese technology could not yet unlock. China could pay for this investment later, with the resources that were uncovered. The subsidies and aid used by the West and Japan to wrap their naked hunger for China's markets meant that China was getting a discount on finance the country needed for its modernization. (Bräutigam 2009: 51)

Even as China's approach to aid evolved over time, Beijing's ideology remained remarkably consistent (Strauss 2009). The first of Zhou Enlai's eight principles is to 'emphasize equality and mutual benefit'. China's win–win rhetoric today echoes this ideal: the 2006 White Paper on China's Africa Policy uses the phrases 'mutual' or 'mutually' 20 times in 11 pages.[11] As Sun Luxi (2007: 9) contends: 'China's new approach to aid reduces the fiscal burden on our country, and supports our own economic development. Strengthening trade, education, and other co-operative programmes through [our] foreign assistance enables our country and our enterprises to receive greater economic benefits.' Zhai Dongsheng (2010: 92) adds: 'The Chinese government and the Chinese people do not need to look down on aid recipients, using a "master" perspective to understand aid recipient countries and citizens. Our national perspective is one of equality . . . the relationship is one of equality and of practical mutual benefit.'

Chinese leaders insist that economic growth should be the core objective. As Li Rougu, the outspoken President of China Export–Import Bank, told the 2007 World Economic Forum: 'The solution to all kinds of development challenges is to have economically sustainable growth . . . Everything should be focused on development, which is the overriding need' (cited in Davis 2007: 78). Liu Guijin, China's special envoy for Africa, similarly explained: 'Development needs to come first; then standards, rights and rules will fall into line. Standards need to be worked out by Africans; not imposed by outsiders' (cited in Wissenbach 2007). China rejects the imposition of political or economic conditions – with the exception of non-recognition of Taiwan – as interference in recipients' domestic affairs. This reflects one of Premier Zhou Enlai core principles, reiterated in China's 2011 White Paper on Foreign Aid, to 'respect sovereignty and never attach conditions'.[12]

China's emphasis on mutual benefit and economic growth justifies blurring the lines between aid and business. China explicitly requires that only Chinese companies complete the infrastructure projects funded by its concessional loans (Kobayashi 2008). Competitive bidding occurs within China, overseen by the Ministry of Commerce. Funds are dispersed directly to Chinese firms, which then implement the aid project. Unlike its substantial debt forgiveness since 2000, China has offered no concession toward the DAC norm of untying its aid.[13] Underpinning China's divergence from DAC norms is a profound scepticism toward claims of altruism and disinterested benevolence. As Ding and Yang (2008: 59) argue:

> Western donors . . . provide foreign aid with specific strategic, political, economic, and humanitarian objectives. To achieve these goals, donors set additional conditions to directly influence the countries in need of aid . . . Regardless of whether the aid is tied or untied, the donor country can always manipulate the type of aid offered, the amounts provided in different categories, and use the inclusion of other political or economic conditions in order to exert influence over developing countries. Setting conditions for democracy, human rights, legal reforms, and good governance . . . these are all ways for the donor countries to exert pressure upon recipients and influence their political development.

7. CONCLUSION

The similarities between China, South Korea and Japan's approach to ODA suggest that there is a relationship between approaches to economic development at home and delivery of development assistance abroad. All three countries achieved rapid economic development, including urbanization, industrialization, technological adaptation and innovation, and high growth rates. Despite significant differences, they adopted similar strategies, including a single-minded focus upon rapid economic growth rates, heavy investment in infrastructure, intensive extraction and reliance on natural resources, a key role for the state in the economy, and a reliance upon external capital investment at early stages of the growth while resisting becoming overly dependent upon foreign assistance.

Having become aid donors relatively early in their economic development process, all three countries applied many of these aspects of their own economic strategy into the provision of foreign aid. All three directed a significant percentage of aid to infrastructure construction. They preferred to provide loans instead of grants, arguing that this builds up recipients' self-reliance, and provides access to low-cost capital to support investment into expensive infrastructure projects. The overarching objective is to enable rapid economic growth, which in turn will provide the resources necessary to address evolving social, environmental and political challenges. As developing states, first Japan, then South Korea and now China, all argued that aid can legitimately advance the interests of both the donor and recipient. These approaches and assumptions vary in significant and consistent ways from the international norms promulgated by the DAC. To this degree, there does appear to be a distinct Northeast Asian model of ODA.

While distinct, the Northeast Asia model is hardly static. As Japan and then South Korea entered into the elite circle of wealthy, industrialized states, they began to seek the affirmation of other developed nations. Over time, Japan and then South Korea began to shift aspects of their aid programme to reflect more closely the dominant norms of the international aid community. These changes have invariably been limited and contested, and in the case of South Korea, are still ongoing – but nonetheless, still reflect a significant effort to strike a different tone in their aid programme. This raises a compelling question for subsequent research: to what degree will China's aid programme begin to conform to DAC norms and practices? In recent years, China has expanded its co-operation with other bilateral and multilateral donors, established a dialogue with the OECD in Beijing, and repeatedly insisted that it is a responsible actor in global affairs (Reilly 2012). While China certainly has an interest in at least appearing to conform to international norms on ODA, the path blazed first by Japan and then South Korea suggests that an alternative route is also open.

The DAC's decision to base the Fourth High Level Forum on Aid Effectiveness in Busan, South Korea highlights the influence that Northeast Asian donors are beginning to have upon the global debate over development assistance. As OECD Secretary-General Angel Gurría and DAC Chair Brian Atwood acknowledged in their April 2011 *Call to Action*: 'We currently are witnessing the emergence of a new development landscape'.[14] The powerful examples of development success from Northeast Asia, and the voices of Northeast Asian donors, will likely remain one of the most important factors reshaping this landscape.

NOTES

1. See: http://www.odakorea.go.kr/eng/include/glance.php (accessed 4 July 2011).
2. See: http://www.oecd.org/document/49/0,3746,en_2649_34447_46582641_1_1_1_1,00.html (accessed 4 July 2011).
3. See:http://www.oecd.org/document/18/0,3343,en_2649_3236398_35401554_1_1_1_1,00.html (accessed 10 June 2011), emphasis added.
4. *Paris Declaration*, p 3; *Accra Agenda*, p. 20. Both available at: http://www.oecd.org/document/18/0,3343,en_2649_3236398_35401554_1_1_1_1,00.html (accessed 10 June 2011).
5. *Paris Declaration*, p. 2.
6. See: http://www.oecd.org/dataoecd/21/21/34086975.pdf (accessed 10 July 2010).
7. For instance, the Special Session with Non-DAC Providers of Development Assistance of the Working Party on Aid Effectiveness, held in Paris on 27 November 2007 (Davis 2008).
8. Available at: www.rtm.org.la/documents/VientianeDeclaration__feb07.doc (accessed 12 July 2010).
9. See: http://www.odakorea.go.kr/eng/include/glance.php (2 July 2011).
10. They are: emphasize equality and mutual benefit; respect sovereignty and never attach conditions; provide interest-free or low-interest loans; help recipients develop independence and self-reliance; build projects that require little investment and can be accomplished quickly; provide quality equipment and material at market prices, ensure effective technical assistance; pay experts according to the local standard of living. Cited in Ministry of Foreign Affairs, 'Build a new international order on the basis of the Five Principles of Peaceful Coexistence' (17 November 2000), at: http://www.fmprc.gov.cn/eng/ziliao/3602/3604/t18016.htm.
11. See: http://english.peopledaily.com.cn/200601/12/eng20060112_234894.html.
12. *China's Foreign Aid*, Information Office of the State Council (April 2011), available at: http://www.gov.cn/english/official/2011-04/21/content_1849913.htm.
13. For China's debt forgiveness data, see: *China's Foreign Aid*, p. 8.
14. See: http://www.oecd.org/dataoecd/6/59/47628081.htm?contentId=47628082#spring.

REFERENCES

Alesina, A. and D. Dollar (2000), 'Who gives foreign aid to whom and why?', *Journal of Economic Growth*, **5**(1), 33–63.

Arase, D. (1995), *Buying Power: the Political Economy of Japan's Foreign Aid*, Boulder, CO: Lynne Reinner Publishers.

Bin, K. (2008), 'Yi li xuanzhe yu zhongguo duiwai yuanzu de bianhua' ['The choice between justice and virtue, and changes in China's foreign aid'], *Xiangchao* [*Hunan Tide*], (August), 34–7.

Bräutigam, D. (2009), *The Dragon's Gift: The Real Story of China in Africa*, Oxford: Oxford University Press.

Bueno de Mesquita, B. and A. Smith (2009), 'A political economy of aid', *International Organization*, **63**(2), 309–40.

Chang, H.-J. (2006), *The East Asian Development Experience: The Miracle, the Crisis and the Future*, London: Zed Books.

Chun, H.-M., E.N. Munyi and H. Lee (2010), 'South Korea as an emerging donor: challenges and changes on its entering OECD/DAC', *Journal of International Development*, **22**, 788–802.

Davis, P. (2007), 'China and the end of poverty in Africa: towards mutual benefit?' report submitted to Diakonia and Eurodad, accessed 1 February 2011 at //www.eurodad.org/uploadedFiles/Whats_New/Reports/Kinarapport_A4.pdf.

Davis, P. (2008), 'Aid effectiveness and non-DAC providers of development assistance', background document for Third High Level Forum on Aid Effectiveness in Accra, Ghana, accessed 23 June 2011 at www.ipc-undp.org/publications/southlearning/penny.pdf.

Ding, S. and W. Yang (2008), 'Xifang guojia duiwai yuanzhu: zhengce mubiao jiqi shixian' ['Western countries' foreign aid: policy goals and their realization'], *Shijie jingji yu zhengzhi* [*World Economics and Politics*], **6**(2008), 59.

Edström, Bert (2009), 'Japan and the Myanmar conundrum, Institute for Security and Development Policy', Institute for Security and Development Policy Asia Paper, October, accessed at http://pwvb.rit-alumni.info/japan_and_the_myanmar_conundrum_-_final.pdf.

Ensign, M. (1992), *Doing Good or Doing Well: Japan's Foreign Aid Programme*, New York: Columbia University Press.

Government of Japan, Ministry of Foreign Affairs (1992), *Japan's Official Development Assistance, 1992*, Tokyo: Association for Promotion of International Co-operation.

Hook, S.W. and G. Zhang (1998), 'Japan's policy aid policy since the Cold War: rhetoric and reality', *Asian Survey*, **8**(11), 1051–66.

Jerve, A.M. (2007), 'Asian models for aid: is there a non-western approach to development assistance', Chr. Michelsen Institute Report 2007 no.12, Bergen, Norway.

Jerve, A.M. and H. Selbervik (2009), *Self-Interest and Global Responsibility: Aid Policies of South Korea and India in the Making*, Bergen, Norway: Chr. Michelsen Institute.

Kang, N. (2010), 'Globalisation and institutional change in the state-led model: the case of corporate governance in South Korea', *New Political Economy*, **15**(4), 519–42.

Katada, S.N. (2004), 'New courses in Japan's aid policy: more humanitarian and more nationalistic', in S.N. Katada, H.W. Maull and T. Inoguchi (eds), *Global Governance: Germany and Japan in the International System*, Burlington, VT: Ashgate.

Kim, S. (2010), 'A bridge over troubled worlds? – an ethical case of South Korea's aid', presented at Development Studies Association UK Annual Conference, 5 November, London.

Kobayashi, T. (2008), 'Evolution of China's aid policy', Japan Bank for International Co-operation working paper, no. 27, Tokyo.

Koppel, B.M. and R.M. Orr (1993), 'A donor of consequence: Japan as a foreign aid power', in B.N. Koppel and R.M. Orr (eds), *Japan's Foreign Aid: Power and Policy in a New Era*, Boulder, CO: Westview.

Lancaster, C. (2006), *Foreign Aid: Diplomacy, Development, Domestic Politics*, Chicago, IL: University of Chicago Press.

Lee, Y.W. (2008), 'The Japanese challenge to neo-liberalism: who and what is "normal" in the history of the world economy', *Review of International Political Economy*, **15**(4), 506–34.

Lumsdaine, D. and J.C. Schopf (2007), 'Changing values and the recent rise in Korean development assistance', *The Pacific Review*, **20**(2), 221–55.

McCormick, D. (2008), 'China and India as Africa's new donors: the impact of aid on development', *Review of African Political Economy*, **35**(115), 116–28.

Moyo, D. (2009), *Dead Aid: Why Aid is Not Working and How There is a Better Way for Africa*, New York: Farrar, Straus and Giroux.

Nishino, J. (2008), *A New Era in South Korean Foreign Policy?*, Tokyo Foundation Report, 31 March, accessed 25 June 2011 at www.tokyofoundation.org/en/articles/2008/a-new-era-in-south-korean-foreign-policy.

OECD-DAC (2008), 'Development cooperation of the Republic of Korea: DAC special review', accessed 16 September 2010 at www.oecd.org/data oecd/53/50/42347329.pdf.

Oishi, M. and F. Fumitaka (2003), 'Can Japanese aid be an effective tool of influence: case studies of Cambodia and Burma', *Asian Survey*, **14**(6), 890–907.

Orr, R.M. (1990), *The Emergence of Japan's Foreign Aid Power*, New York: Columbia University Press.

Park, C.H. (1970), *The Country, The Revolution, and I*, 2nd edn, Seoul: Hollym Corp.

Park, K.-H. (2010), 'Korea's role in global development', Brookings Northeast Asia Commentary 36, February.

Park, B. and H.S. Le (2008), 'Does Korea follow Japan in foreign aid: relationships between aid and foreign investment', International Centre for the Study of East Asian Development working paper series 2008-8, April.

Reilly, J. (2012), 'A norm-taker or a norm-maker? Chinese aid in Southeast Asia', *Journal of Contemporary China*, **21**(73).

Rix, A. (1980), *Japan's Economic Aid: Policy-Making and Politics*, New York: St. Martin's Press.

Sachs, J.D. (2005), *The End of Poverty: Economic Possibilities for our Time*, New York: Penguin Press.

Schraeder, P.J., B. Taylor and S.W. Hook (1998), 'Clarifying the foreign aid puzzle: a comparison of American, Japanese, French, and Swedish aid flows', *World Politics*, **50**(2), 294–323.

Shang, C. (2010), '"Wenge" shiqi zhongguode duiwai yuanzhu' ['Chinese foreign aid in the era of the "Cultural Revolution"'], *Dangshi wenhui* [*Party History Digest*], 2, 56–7.

Söderberg, M. (2010), 'Challenges or complements for the west: is there an Asian model of aid emerging?' in J.S. Sörensen (ed.), *Challenging the Aid Paradigm: Western Currents and Asian Alternatives*, Basingstoke: Palgrave Macmillan.

Strauss, J.C. (2009), 'The past in the present: historical and rhetorical lineages in China's relations with Africa', *China Quarterly*, 199 (September), 777–95.

Sun, L. (2007), 'Cong guojia liyi shiyexia kan zhongguo jianguo yilai de duiwai yuanzhu zhengce' ['Viewing China's foreign aid policy since China's establishment from the perspective of national interests'], *Shidai jinrong* [*Current Finance*], **11**(356), 8–12.

Takamine, T. (2006), *Japan's Development Aid to China: The Long-running Foreign Policy of Engagement*, New York: Routledge.

Wade, R. (2004), *Governing the Market: Economic Theory and the Role of Government in East Asian Industrialisation*, Princeton, NJ: Princeton University Press.

Wan, M. (2006), *Sino-Japanese Relations: Interaction, Logic, and Transformation*, Stanford, CA: Stanford University Press.

Wen, J. (2010), 'Wen Jiabao dui woguo duiwai yuanzhu zuo zhongyao jianghua' ['Wen Jiabao makes an important speech on China's foreign aid'], *Renmin ribao* [*People's Daily*], 14 August, accessed 2 February 2011 at http://cpc.people.com.cn/GB/64093/64094/12440589.html.

Wissenbach, U. (2007), 'Partners in competition? The EU, Africa and China', conference summary proceedings, European Union, 28 June, accessed 13 October 2010 at www.iese.ac.mz/lib/cdoc/base/fd_1534.pdf.

Woo-Cumings, M. (ed.) (1999), *The Developmental State*, Ithaca, NY: Cornell University Press.

Woods, N. (2005), 'The shifting politics of foreign aid', *International Affairs*, **81**(2), 393–409.

Woods, N. (2008), 'Whose aid? Whose influence? China, emerging donors and the silent revolution in development assistance', *International Affairs*, **84**(6), 1205–21.

Yang, H. (2009), 'Zhongguo duiwai yuanzhu de huigu yu fazhan' ['Reflections and development of China's foreign aid'], *Xuexi yukan* [*Study Times*], 439 (November), 40–42.

Yasumoto, D. (1986), *The Manner of Giving: Strategic Aid and Japanese Foreign Policy*, Lanham, MD: Lexington Books.

Zhai, D. (2010), 'Duiwai yuanzhu de shenzhen daode yuanze' ['The cautious moral principles of foreign aid'], *CEOCIO*, (5 April), 92.

PART V

Societal perspectives

15. The rise of an empire: EXPO 2010 as a symbol of the ambiguity of Chinese modernisation

Simen Andersen Øyen

1. INTRODUCTION

Seldom before has the world seen a modernisation process as intense as China's and few countries have experienced similar high economic growth rates over an extended period of time. Simultaneously, the United States' economic dominance is in decline. The country has large economic problems and the wars they are currently engaged in are, for the first time since their Revolutionary War, financed on credit – mainly with loans from China. China has not developed the cultural industries and top universities that the USA has. It also lacks the many non-governmental organisations that generate much of America's soft power. However, the Chinese path to modernity and economical growth represents a viable alternative to the Western approach. This modernisation carries Chinese characteristics and is more compressed in time and intense than similar development stages in the West. Events such as the World Exhibition in Shanghai 2010 (EXPO) and the Olympics in Beijing 2008 are typical examples of how the Chinese government would like to present itself, but they reveal processes of political contestation and tension, new forms of disciplinarian process, disadvantages related to this development such as corruption, and so on as well. They also indicate a shift from 'hard' authoritarianism to a new and 'softer' authoritarianism, an element which constitutes some of its appeal to developing countries especially in Africa and South America.

In its early stages, the Chinese modernisation process was characterised by an import of Western technology without the cultural and political values that accompany it. The internet and internationalisation of communication are illustrative here. However, apparently, Western technology cannot be disentangled from the social and cultural matrix in which it is embedded. Through imported cultural products, Western ideas and ideals reach through to the Chinese people. Yet, to a higher degree than ever before, this is a two-way process. Consequently, China can tell us something about how the matrix of control and freedom is played out more generally in societies that undergo major structural transformations and how this tends to take a transnational form. An understanding of the economic and political development and modernisation of China will be decisive for our ability to analyse regionalism, trade and foreign policy ties, and global power structures. At a more general level, these questions can be analysed structurally and in light of China's geopolitical and economic interests, as well as the degree of influence China can mobilise in the achievement of these interests. However, one must also take into account the cultural, economic and political development in China. This chapter will investigate the Chinese modernisation process – both its soft power potential and its tensions – by seeing EXPO as emblematic for this process.

2. THE CHINESE MODERNITY

As a result of economic liberalisation, increasing social and cultural variation, and urbanisation, China is undergoing modernisation and individualisation processes structurally similar to what we have seen in the West. The individualisation that has occurred in the transition to a modern consumer society has resulted in the individual being freer to choose amongst a greater range of historical possibilities for self-realisation (Beck and Beck-Gernsheim 2002). In this, the contemporary consumer society is paradigmatic of the market's individualisation of society through consumer choice and how it creates identity (Bauman 2007). This provides an atomised conception of political individuals, springing from the conditions characteristic of late modern Western society. This is a tendency which makes possible the claim that the individual in today's Western society is the fundamental element in social reproduction – at the cost of the family and other collective structures. In contrast to the individual in so-called pre-modern societies, the modern individual does not inhabit an assigned permanent identity or social function – except, perhaps, that of a consumer. The modern identity is open, unfinished and differentiated, meaning that it is not determined by assigned roles or primary socialisation, but rather creates itself in a plurality of faceted value and cultural spheres. This development should be seen as a consequence of the neutralisation of tradition and communities of shared values on the one hand, and the differentialisation of social functions on the other (Honneth 2004). These sociological individualisation processes have structural similarities to the ongoing socio-economic development in China, especially with regards to urban environments, while it still retains certain unique cultural expressions which arise in the meeting between the authorities and the populace, patterns of dominance, elite structures, power relations and social movements (Yan 2009).

Chinese modernity, the country's form of capitalism and its political development, is influenced by commerce and new connections with the world at large through trade relations, diplomacy, tourism, migration, and academic and cultural exchange. While the authorities are consciously attempting to make themselves more compatible – and therefore more effective in their cooperation – with the West, the government's interaction with the Chinese populace provides historically and culturally unique processes of change which will have a severe impact on the global political and economic development. A common assumption about the political development in China is that the economic growth and liberalisation in this country should lead to a parallel political liberalisation. An increasingly cultured middle class, seeing their economic influence grow, would demand democratic reform, establishment of a constitutional system and the abolishment of the authoritarian government (Hansen and Thøgersen 2008). This is the direction South Korea, Singapore and Taiwan have taken. These countries began with market liberalisation and have since adopted a constitutional government and developed political systems with democratic characteristics. This view is based in a discourse about civil society which assumes that it acts on behalf of citizens against oppressive states. This is a historical construction produced in the wake of developments in the political systems of South Korea, Singapore and Taiwan, and after the fall of the former Eastern European nations in 1989. The comparison of China with these neighbouring countries can be justified due to China's political and economic liberalisation which can be described as the new authoritarianism, developed in the 1980s. Inspired by their industrialised neighbours' notion of authoritarianism, China has achieved a rapid economic growth at the same time that a strong and authoritarian centralised political power has been maintained (Saich 2004; Hansen and Thøgersen 2008). At the same time, the consequences of privatisation and the restructuring of the economy parallel those that can be observed in the West. Processes of individualisation and social differentiation are perhaps the most visible consequences of this development. With the introduction of 'socialism with Chinese characteristics' and the state-controlled market economy, a culture of consumption and a pleasure-based individualism has appeared – especially associated with the urban culture of the eastern metropolises of Shanghai, Shenzhen, Xiamen, Tsingtao, and so on. This individualism has retained some of the traditional collectivist aspects, in which loyalty to the family and groups are still strongly held values. This is mainly due to a lack of a social security net and manifests socio-economic variations: especially in the countryside, the family remains an important social element and a source of social security in which an individual's needs are, in large, subordinate to family and group interests. These areas have retained production and, with that, income tied to the family's common agricultural enterprise (Hansen and Thøgersen 2008). In the context of individualisation processes, one must also address the issue of the Chinese network culture, or guanxi culture, in which shame or 'losing face' takes primacy over the individualistic concept of guilt. Mayfair Yang (1994) has done an exhaustive study of guanxi culture in modern China. Her perspective is that this network culture will contribute to the development of a Chinese economic system founded on principles fundamentally different from the principles guiding western economies: the instrumental aspects of gift giving and service exchange also contain emotional aspects in which loyalty to those closest to you is a central element. Similar points have been made in that the economic success can be attributed to traditional Chinese society in which collectivism, collective identities, respect for old people and an emphasis on harmony are the major means to resolve social conflicts (see amongst other Kristoffersen 2010).

Consequently, China represents a unique path to modernity and capitalism and hence the development in this country has to be analysed in the context of a concept of multiple modernities (Eisenstadt 2000) and a concept of multiple forms of capitalism (see Jeff Henderson's chapter) where development must be seen in a cultural and historical context which is characterised by parallel developmental tendencies. The Chinese version of capitalism can be described as delivering rapid economic growth while maintaining state control through, amongst others, state-owned companies. Seen socially, Chinese capitalism resembles some features of the Manchester capitalism of the early 1800s. Just as Manchester was the centre for textile production, China today is a centre of industrial production, though more varied, and technologically it is capitalism from the 20th and 21st centuries. China's forceful capitalist expansion is accompanied by similar problems from those experienced in 'Manchester capitalism', such as rapidly increasing differences of income and the state expropriation of agricultural land for industrial use. This has led to a fermenting social unease which the authorities could find difficult to control. In discussions like these it is common to distinguish between capitalist systems in which corporations are mainly dependent on banks for financing, such as in Germany and Japan (the Rhineland model), and systems which have a pronounced shareholder perspective, thereby having developed more sophisticated legal protections for investment, and so better developed finance markets, such as in the USA and Great Britain (the Anglo-Saxon model). However, this distinction is not exhaustive. Capitalism as a distinct cultural and economic programme, with all its institutional implications, spread from Western Europe to the rest of the world, providing the groundwork for continually dynamic cultural and institutional patterns. This has allowed for regional and local variants and is closely connected to the development of multiple modernities. This strand of the discourse primarily maintains that several parallel modernities in different civilisations have appeared which do not necessarily coincide with the Western form of modernity. Each civilisation inhabits its own form of modernity. This approach to the question of modernity implies a certain understanding of modernity's nature, in which modernity must be seen as a specific civilisation, with specific institutional and cultural characteristics. In contrast to the view of modern society as the natural culmination of human organisation so far, modernity is described as a differentiated development in the direction of parallel but different patterns of modernity, a process much like the crystallisation and expansion of the large religions: Christianity, Islam, Buddhism and Confucianism (Eisenstadt 2000).

3. FROM UNILATERALISM TO MULTILATERALISM: THE APPEAL OF CHINESE MODERNITY

There are especially two implications of these investigations which are interesting in light of the question of how China is shaping events outside its own borders. Firstly, China modifies the thesis that claims the end of the nation-state's sovereignty. It is presumed that the nation-state as a legal–economic structure has lost effectiveness with the rise of a series of global economic organisations such as GATT, the WTO, the World Bank and IMF, G-7 (or G-20), BIS, OECD, and so on; regional alliances such as the EU, NAFTA and MERCOSUR, as well as multinational corporations. This increasing and tightening inter-governmental cooperation limits and reduces the national legal structures' possibilities for governance, and is increasing in influence. However, the nation-state remains the most important element in the political legitimisation of these international organisations, and these organs remain tied to national entities. The nation-state is therefore not neutralised as a political entity, especially regarding trade volume, financial movement, research and development. It is perhaps more accurate to speak of a regionalisation rather than a globalisation according to such a perspective. In this, the Chinese system is particularly illustrative due to the large portion of state-owned companies and state control in research and development, for instance in the green technology sector.

Secondly, questions regarding soft power and especially the attractiveness of the so-called Beijing Consensus, as opposed to the Washington Consensus, deserve our attention. The Chinese socio-economic development model, in which a new or semi-authoritarian government is combined with a market economy, is more dynamic and to a larger degree recognises political and cultural differences. This recognition can be understood and seen, for instance, with regards to how China is providing concessionary loan and debt relief without economic and political stipulations, such as demands related to economic deregulation or human rights. In other words, this can be regarded as a way to build soft power as well as being in accordance with a principle of non-interference. It is a presupposition of this approach to modernity that each country should find the path best suited to its own culture and traditions in contrast to enforcing the expansion of market force reforms on developing countries, such as those implemented by institutions like the IMF, World Bank and the US Treasury department. In other words, liberal democracy and extended market reforms is not the only path to modernity and economic development. China seeks to portray its path to modernity, wealth and stability as an alternative to the Western approach. The EXPO can be considered a recent indication of such a representation. China's growing economy, its ability to combine a gradual opening of the economy, a large state sector and authoritarian rule is a major source of its increasing appeal in the developing world. China's ability to shape the preferences of other countries through the attraction of its cultural stability and its ability to set the rules of international organisations through, for instance, its attempts to integrate other Asian governments in global organisations such as the WTO, but also by reducing the 'rule-setting hegemony' of the countries of the OECD – especially the US and the EU (Dosch 2010) – is an indication of such an appeal and an increasing soft power potential. This soft power approach to political values and foreign policies springs from the manner in which the Chinese started to put national interest before moral judgements and ideological considerations, and how they explored ways of using financial assets and international law to challenge US power rather than seeking to match its supremacy in conventional terms. This international soft power is mainly exercised through a non-confrontational diplomacy and by strengthening non-military cooperation, not by confronting the USA's role as a security provider.[1] China wants to build an image of a responsible and peacekeeping stakeholder in the international system, where its distinct style and approach to relationship building emphasises the importance of state sovereignty and non-interference – except for the 'one China' policy that requires recipient governments to sever diplomatic ties with Taiwan and recognise Taiwan as part of China's sovereign territory (McGiffert 2009). Some of China's appeal lies in the changing of global governance structures and alterations in the economic and political relationship between the US and China. The US is the largest export market for China, having also the greatest trade deficit with them.[2] As such, the fate of China and the US is inexorably intertwined. In the course of the last 15 years, China has become the United States' most important trade partner, but also competitor. This rivalry is not just based on the fact that Chinese products push others out of the American market and generate a growing trade deficit, but also because Chinese products increasingly outcompete the American in the United States' own export markets. An important shift is the US becoming an importer of capital instead of an exporter, as was the case during the rebuilding phase after the Second World War. China has, to a large degree, taken over the United States' former position. Compared to China, the USA is in danger of taking on the character of a developing country: the export of agricultural products and the import of industrial goods. This is a problem which goes much deeper than can be rectified through the revaluation of the Chinese Yuan (Skarstein 2010). However, there are signs of change in this interdependent relationship due to China's proximity to the achievement of a global economic independence. By diversifying towards new and growing trade agreements, mainly with countries in Asia, Latin America and Africa but also with Russia and the EU, China is pushing its economic independence forward.

It is China's ambition to shape regional policy through regional institutions such as the Asia-Pacific Economic Cooperation, ASEAN Regional Forum, the East Asia Summit, the Shanghai Cooperation Organization, and so on, China places emphasis on shared Asian values as expressed in the Bangkok Declaration.[3] Concerns as to the stability of North Korea is of special interest and here China and the United States have a common strategic interest in ensuring that there is no conflict on the Korean peninsula, and that North Korea does not become a full nuclear power. This raises questions as to whether China's economic reforms are transferable to North Korea, and whether China's role is compromising one of the country's most important foreign policy principles: that of non-interference (Saich 2004). In the Middle East and in African countries, soft power is important to solidifying energy relationships, ensuring access to viable energy resources and raw materials. This is accomplished through, amongst other means, low-interest loans, aid programmes and providing large contingents of soldiers for United Nations peacekeeping missions. Beijing has also sought to strengthen these relationships by promoting regional economic integration and security mechanisms, emphasising the role of the United Nations, participating in humanitarian missions, providing concessionary loan and debt relief, increasing cultural and academic exchange programmes such as the establishing of Confucius Institutes, and expanding Chinese media (Leonard 2008). In this context, the development of the social sciences in China – especially the major think tanks such as the Shanghai Academy of Social Science – is an important part of the country's soft power. However, this socio-economic development model and path to modernity that the Chinese government wants to represent as an influencing tool for the outside world comprises patterns of dominance, elite structures, power relations and social movements which are likely to have strong social and cultural impacts – including for the countries that might be tempted to adopt this model. EXPO in Shanghai 2010 is symptomatic of these aspects of modernisation – both the soft power potential and the social tensions – and as two indications of this pattern of change we will look at protest movements and protest actions, as well as the social civilising campaigns initiated by the authorities before and during this event.

4. THE 'CIVILISING' OF CHINA

An indication of the thoroughgoing modernisation and disciplinary processes in China is the ongoing, state-initiated civilising of the Chinese populace. This civilising is also illustrative of the Chinese soft authoritarianism. The Chinese civilising process has always been an element of Chinese society, but is now taking a new, conscious direction as a result of China's increased commerce with the West after the country's reform and opening at the beginning of the 1980s. Projects such as the Olympic Games in Beijing and the EXPO in Shanghai acted as catalysts for this western form of civilising; for example a civilising process that has changed in character parallel to the socio-economic changes that China has been experiencing since the beginning of the 1980s. In general, much like the corresponding Western development with its social and cultural shift from external and physical control to an emphasis on self-control and self-restraint, it is a developmental tendency which spreads from the social elite to the greater populace, arising from the interaction between the authorities and elite structures on the one side, and the general populace on the other. However, it also has a significant transnational component where, for instance, the growing number of Chinese who travel, work and study abroad has extended the interaction with foreign societies and cultures and thereby contributed to societal change in China.

During the EXPO, Shanghai wanted to stand out as a modern metropolis without social problems or obvious signs of poverty. The city has been going through major construction and building over the last few years. However, not only have poor areas been renovated, the Chinese people have also been renovated; enormous campaigns with the intent to civilise people have been initiated. One campaign which has caused debate is the government's attempt to prohibit people from wearing pyjamas in public. It is not uncommon while walking in Shanghai to observe somewhat older Chinese padding about the neighbourhood wearing only their pyjamas. In the spring and summer, they wear thin, colourful pyjamas. In the winter, they use insulated pyjamas. The authorities instigated a number of directives, and during the EXPO signs everywhere were proclaiming: 'Do not go outside wearing pyjamas, become a World Expo civilised person'.[4] The problem of wearing pyjamas in public was seen as an issue that affected the whole country's honour. Volunteers encouraged people who wear pyjamas in public to go home and change into something more appropriate. Children were also recruited for this campaign in order to apply pressure on their parents to break this 'bad habit'. At the same time, the issue was frequently discussed in various Chinese internet forums, showing that people were split in their opinions about the campaign. Some thought the practice was charming, others found the authorities' actions to be too aggressive. Those who were against the public wearing of pyjamas suggested that it destroyed China's international image and that it was uncivilised. The sitting party chairman in Shanghai, Yu Zhengshen, stated that the campaign contributed to the reestablishment of the city's public appearance and maintained that the public wearing of pyjamas was a bad habit. Those against the campaign meant that demanding that city citizens refrain from wearing pyjamas in public was tantamount to demanding that they cease being Shanghainese (Øyen 2009/2010).[5]

These anecdotal expressions and seemingly trivial governmental campaigns, which were seen by visitors to Shanghai before and during the EXPO, can be understood as expressions and indications of deep-lying processes of modernisation and civilising and, as such, can contribute to the understanding of cultural change in China. These campaigns are all-encompassing and concern everything from smoking bans in public places and restaurants, to how to queue for the subway trains. These centrally controlled civilising processes, defining an improvement in general behaviour, occur on various levels, and many of them are unique to China. There is a series of governmental organs responsible for these campaigns; amongst others these are the Shanghai Language Committee and the Central Secretariat for Civilized Behaviour. Corresponding processes were initiated in connection with the arrangements for the Olympic Games in Beijing in 2008. For example, the authorities declared the 11th of each month to be an official day of presentable queuing. This date was chosen since two ones can resemble two people standing in line (Galtung 2009).

These examples of campaigns directed towards the prohibition of wearing pyjamas in public are signs and markers of the extensive modernisation processes and their multiple character. The western process of civilisation has focused on the guidance of the individual through an increased degree of emancipation and self control (Elias 2000). The campaigns prior to and during the EXPO in Shanghai can illustrate that similar civilising processes are occurring in China today. These are processes which are a result of increased commerce and new connections with the West, but which take a unique cultural characteristic. They are made possible by an authoritarian and centralised state apparatus and are much more temporally compressed than the similar processes which occurred in the West. But this is not to say that these disciplinary processes are one-directional. While the authorities take conscious steps to become more compatible with the West and make commerce with the West more effective, their interaction with the populace gives rise to patterns of change bearing unique historical and cultural characteristics. The Chinese people do not allow themselves to be dictated to by the authoritarian state.

5. INTERNET-BASED PROTEST ACTIONS AND THEIR TRANSNATIONAL CHARACTER

China is an authoritarian state. The majority of political decisions are made within the frame of the one party system. But this does not prevent the Chinese people from protesting. However, today's protests are concerned less with democratisation and political liberalisation, focusing primarily on the darker sides of the Chinese market economy. This is in contrast to the 1980s, when protests were centred around the ideals of democracy and freedom imported from the West. Today there are new forms of activism: movements tied to environmental and consumer issues, the struggle against corruption and the fight for the improvement of civil rights for all, from ethnic minorities and homosexuals to animals and home owners (Lagerkvist 2006).

The inhabitants of Shanghai were divided in their attitude towards the EXPO. Their viewpoints varied from uncritical enthusiasm to different forms of protests and civil disobedience. The forced evictions in connection with the construction work prior to the EXPO caused particular opposition. For instance, demonstrators in Xizang Street in the district of Luwan, the location of a large construction site, threw garbage and objects in the trees along the pavement. They also filled a wall with posters demanding that the construction work must stop.

These types of protests regarding forced eviction are usually called nail-house protests and they have become an international symbol for opposition towards the Chinese modernisation process since they can be directly tied to the economic growth and need for commercial expansion. These types of protests began in the 1990s and occur weekly over the whole of China today. They concern forced eviction, the name referring to nails which have rooted themselves deep in the planking, no longer being able to be hit with a hammer. Families refuse to move in order to give room for property development before they have received proper compensation. The best known example was the owner of a house in Chongqing in 2007. He refused to abandon his house to make way for a skyscraper. The contractor dug a 10 metre deep pit around the house, and pictures of the lonesome house perched atop a pinnacle of earth in the middle of a building site made their way around the world (Mertha 2009).

One of the largest protest actions in China in modern times is related to the preparations for the EXPO. On 6 March 2006, the government started the planning and construction of a high speed train from Shanghai to Hangzhou which was supposed to be completed in time for the opening of the EXPO in 2010. In January and February of 2007, demonstrations began against these planned constructions. After a variety of protests ranging from demonstrations to petitions and the distributing of pamphlets, and after the mayor of Shanghai and the leader of the project, Chen Liangyu, were convicted of corruption, the project was postponed for an indefinite period. Other protests were of more symbolic and individual character. In connection with the EXPO, the government initiated large campaigns to end pirate taxis. On 14 October 2009, a young man from Henan district was accused of driving an illegal taxi. However, it was established later that the police had provoked and created this incident. The man who was accused cut off several fingers as a symbolic gesture to show he was innocent. This received a great deal of attention in the media and on internet-based fora. The man was finally cleared of all charges, and a committee was appointed to insure that this would not happen again.

The role of the internet is of special interest for understanding political change and its transnational character. The Chinese government's censorship of the media is extensive, but the internet has the advantage of being more accessible and less controllable, hence functions as a channel for expression and influence to a higher degree than the traditional media. At the same time this development provides new opportunities and conditions for governmental control and propaganda. Many of the cases of internet-based protests have a transnational dimension, such as 'anticnn.com' which was launched in order to problematise the tendentious Western media's coverage of the Tibetan uprising in March 2008 where Western media for instance used photos from Nepal to illustrate an alleged clash in Tibet. They presented photographs of a clash between police and monks in Nepal, as though they were from Tibet. This transnational aspect is also illustrated by the hacking of Japanese internet sites in response to both the Japanese Prime Minister Junichiro Koizumi's visit to the Yasukuni Shrine and Japanese textbooks' misrepresentation of the massacre of Nanjing during World War II (Yang 2009). Especially in 2004 and 2005 non-state actors performed cyber attacks on official Japanese web sites, including the official Yasukuni Shrine web site, by defacing or crashing them.

The transnational dimensions of protest movements in China today are complex, but can overall be characterised by how non-state activists direct their protests towards foreign states or corporations and how they focus on transnational issues such as environmental and health problems or international political relationships like the Sino–Japanese relations. Chinese diasporic activists and dissident communities also contribute to this transnational activism: veterans of the 1989 movement, the Falun Gong, the Tibetan exile community and Uyghurs are some examples. Online activism has a structural affinity to social movements in Western societies, being concerned with personal autonomy and self-realisation, the change from state-centric to transnational activism, and the degree to which new information technologies enable local actors to participate in global politics (Boas and Kalathil 2003).

With this the internet is an element in the formation of the characteristically Chinese protest repertoire (Tilly 2004). Traditionally, signs, pamphlets, chanting slogans, singing songs, issuing open petitions and distributing leaflets have had a central function, while demonstrations, large groupings or coalitions, critical writing in the media, and occupation of public spaces have been possible only to a small degree. This must be seen in connection with the difficulties of enacting ideological or system-critical protest under an authoritarian regime. One characteristic form of expression in the Chinese protest repertoire is the political big-character poster (*dazibao*) which has been used since the time of the emperors. An important trigger for the Cultural Revolution was a poster written by the philosophy teacher Nie Yuanzi, who proposed that the universities were in the hands of bourgeois anti-revolutionaries. Big-character posters were also central in the social movement that appeared around the Democracy Wall in 1978 in Beijing. Some of these posters expressed criticism of the Communist party rule and advocated democracy, such as Wei Jingsheng's demand for 'the fifth modernization'. In December 1979, posters of this type at the Democracy Wall were banned. It appears that today the internet can easily play the same role as the Democracy Wall did previously. Blogs and web forums can function as electronic big-character posters, because the internet allows to a greater degree than other media for the mobilisation of large groups in forms of activism in a way that had not been possible before and because protest movements tend to originate as a result of information first published on blogs, internet-based petitions, web forums, electronic bulletin boards, and so on. By that it provides for the possibility of anonymous will and opinion formation which can reach a broader public (Goldsmith and Wu 2006).

This will and opinion formation can temporarily compensate for and balance a lack of institutionalised checks and balances. The Chinese socio-economic development with its rapidly growing economy is characterised by a transitional phase from a planned economy to a market economy. Its socio-economic model in a context of soft authoritarianism is appealing especially to the developing world but it is progressing without the sufficient economic infrastructure such as evaluative and controlling organs, trade organisations, or public institutions and markets which are independent of the state and large corporations. The authorities are accused of being controlled by their own interests without adequate public recourse to complaint organs or institutional channels capable of questioning the authorities. Especially relevant is the problem of a lack of checks and balances with regards to corruption, and this is of special interest in relation to soft power and the expansion and integration of the Chinese socio-economic development to other parts of the world. The internet has had a special role in this in China. Two cases of corruption in which public internet participation was decisive can illustrate this. One case is from Nanjing in 2008. A photo of a public servant was published on the internet. The photo showed that he was wearing an unusually expensive wrist watch and was smoking cigarettes costing approximately US$38 per pack. This led to speculation of corruption and a comprehensive internet-based debate was triggered, partially on http://www.tianya.cn. Because of the public vigilance this public servant was investigated and sentenced to 11 years in jail. The other case is from Guangxi province and dates back to November 2009 when the diary of a manager in the state-owned tobacco company, China National Tobacco Corporation, was published online. In addition to containing detailed depictions of extra-marital affairs, there were descriptions of how he had received bribes of up to 100,000 RMB. He is now being investigated. Both were exposed by non-state actors who are part of a web-based public sphere. This illustrates how the state and the individual are in constant negotiation and change in China. These cyber protests are genuine responses to government corruption and corrupt officials, but they also have a coefficient effect in accelerating the government to rethink approaches to governance. The government is receptive and instrumentalises these new forms of protest into the formation of legitimacy, that is, in how this can serve to ease popular dissatisfaction before it rises to the level of demonstrations, thereby increasing state stability. While the Party-state previously interpreted this kind of critique as attempts to undermine the authorities' control, there is now a greater acceptance for the possibility that public attention on social, political and economic problems can contribute to better leadership through providing a healthy pressure on the political system.

With these processes of change new forms of disciplinary processes also follow, where the new liberal disciplinary processes are equally effective as the authoritarian one, precisely because of their foundation in an apparently autonomous individual's self governance. The individual is disciplined to govern themselves. The general tendency in China indicates a shift from repressive displays of power to disciplinary displays of power, from hard control to soft control. Central to this new regime is the shift to softer forms of control which focus on self discipline, indirect leadership, effective planning and the development of constitutional government. The new principles for this new direction were brought forth at the 16th Congress of the CCP in September 2004 and embraced this soft model. The political line with weight on soft power also has its foreign policy equivalent with China's emphasis on nation building and events such as the EXPO and the Olympics.

6. THE RISE OF A SOFT EMPIRE

After nearly 30 years of self-imposed exile, China has increasingly interacted with the outside world since the 1980s, and the internal societal changes mediated by this interaction – Western modernity and globalisation, regionalism and so on – have started to influence societies outside China, especially through soft power mechanisms. The Chinese government portrays its development path as an alternative to Western modernisation. It is presented as a scientific development, the goal being the establishment of a harmonious society seeking to balance the pursuit of economic growth with social welfare. However, the negative consequences of China's emphasis on economic growth, such as environmental degradation, income inequality, social polarisation, regional disparities, and so on have engendered social unrest. This is also an indication of the tensions, antinomies and contradictory elements inherent in the political and cultural programme of Chinese modernity.

Dynamic, transnational and multidimensional interaction reflects the conditions of growing complexity in the age of globalisation. Social activism in China responds to these complex conditions. In this context, China is especially interesting since it is a state undergoing extensive structural change, thereby providing an opening for an understanding of how control and freedom, power structures, protest movements and heterodoxies more generally develop in a society. To understand these processes, a methodological pluralism is needed as a fundament from which to balance a socio-cultural understanding with a conception based in a parallel development we observe, and have observed, in the West: there is a structural affinity between Chinese modernity and Western modernity but the actual development in China is culturally and historically unique. Processes of individualisation and increasing social and economic diversity – that run parallel to modernisation, industrialisation and expanding market economies – have provided growth conditions for the appearance of separate interest groups and social movements. The interaction between the government and social and economical elites on one side, and the general populace on the other side, is indicating new forms of patterns of dominance, power relations and a shift from 'hard' authoritarianism to a new and 'softer' authoritarianism. This soft authoritarianism constitutes the ideological system and political and developmental image which China is exporting especially to countries in Africa and South America.

Chinese soft power and the country's interaction at global and regional levels can be explained by a strong pragmatism that the Chinese employ in the face of new experiences encountered due to intensive modernisation. Ideological considerations or political dichotomies of the Cold War days are no longer valid. This pragmatism entails that China balances scepticism of all things Western with the realisation that much of this is useful – something that can be summarised in the Chinese expression 'Zhong ti xi yong': the core and fundamental principles of all learning will be Chinese, but it is both acceptable and desirable to learn practical and useful things from the West (Galtung 2009). These learning processes are already in place as a result of trade agreements, diplomacy, tourism, migration and cultural exchange and the expanding interaction with foreign societies and cultures represented by the growing number of Chinese working, studying and travelling abroad. These interactions have cultural and historical expressions which are distinctive but with structural similarities to corresponding development patterns such as Western modernisation. However, the Western past will not be China's future, and this is a future which is growing more and more attractive to the developing countries.

NOTES

1. Whether China has a non-confrontational diplomacy especially towards countries such as Vietnam, Japan, Taiwan, and so on is disputable.
2. In 2007, 93 percent of the USA's foreign trade deficit equalled the collective trade surplus of four countries, namely China, Japan, Germany and Saudi Arabia (Skarstein 2010).
3. Here the subject of rights illustrates questions regarding shared Asian values. The Bangkok Declaration sees rights as relational, being defined by, amongst other factors, generational status. Rights are not privileges which one has a natural, unconditional claim to, an aspect connected to the fact that the individual does not have an inherent worth in Chinese tradition.
4. http://www.chinahush.com/2009/10/31/shanghai-government-requests-residents-not-wearing-pajamas-in-public/.
5. I conducted 28 qualitative interviews in 2009 and 2010, where 15 were with students at East China Normal University and 13 were researchers at, or connected to, the Shanghai Academy of Social Science. The interviews were carried out semi-structured, flexible and open-ended by following an interview guide which helped structure the conversations. This means that informants were able to choose their own terms in explanations or replies to my questions. The interviews lasted between one and two hours. They were recorded, transcribed and made anonymous. The aim of these interviews has not been to end up with representative conclusions, but rather to outline the direction of the political processes connected to discipline, individualisation, liberalisation, and so on in contemporary China, the results of which remain unknown. Hence, the general significance of these empirical examples has an explanatory limit regarding the changing dynamics of Chinese politics in general, but can give some solid indications when seen in the context of correlated studies about social movements, internet-based protests, corruption, disciplinary campaigns, social unrest connected to the Olympics in Beijing and the EXPO in Shanghai, and so on (see amongst others Sæther 2006; Zhou 2006; Erbaugh 2008; Pang 2011).

REFERENCES

Bauman, Z. (2007), 'Forbrukersamfunn', in G.E. Schelderup and M.W. Knudsen (eds), *Forbrukersosiologi: makt, tegn og mening i forbrukersamfunnet*, Oslo: Cappelen Akademisk Forlag.

Beck, U. and E. Beck-Gernsheim (2002), *Individualization: Institutionalized Individualism and its Social and Political Consequences*, London: Sage.

Boas, T. and S. Kalathil (2003), *Open Networks, Closed Regimes: The Impact of the Internet on Authoritarian Rule*, Washington, DC: Carnegie Endowment for International Peace.

Dosch, J. (2010), 'China and Southeast Asia: a new regional order in the making?', in L. Dittmer and G. Yu (eds), *China, the Developing World, and the New Global Dynamic*, Boulder, CO: Lynne Rienner.

Eisenstadt, S.N. (2000), 'Multiple modernities', *Journal of the American Academy of Arts and Sciences*, **129** (1), 1–30.

Elias, N. (2000), *The Civilizing Process*, Oxford: Blackwell.

Erbaugh, M. (2008), 'China expands its courtesy: saying "hello" to strangers', *The Journal of Asian Studies*, **67**(2), 621–52.

Galtung, M. (2009), *Kina: Folket, Historien, Politikken, Kulturen*, Oslo: Aschehoug.

Goldsmith, J. and T. Wu (2006), *Who Controls the Internet? Illusions of a Borderless World*, Oxford: Oxford University Press.

Hansen, M.H. and S. Thøgersen (2008), *Kina – Individ Og Samfunn*, Oslo: Universitetsforlaget.

Honneth, A. (2004), 'Organized self-realization – some paradoxes of individualization', *European Journal of Social Theory*, **7**(4), 463–78.

Kristoffersen, H. (2010), *Det nye Kina: Kinesisk Handel, Kultur og Politikk*, Oslo: Universitetsforlaget.

Lagerkvist, J. (2006), *The Internet in China: Unlocking and Containing the Public Sphere*, Lund, Sweden: Department of East Asian Studies, Lund University

Leonard, M. (2008), *What Does China Think?*, London: Harper Collins

McGiffert, C. (ed.) (2009), *Chinese Soft Power and its Implication for the United States – Competition and Cooperation in the Development World*, Washington, DC: Centre for Strategic and International Studies.

Mertha, A.C. (2009), 'From "rustless screws" to "nail houses": the evolution of property rights in China', *Orbis*, **53**(2), 233–49.

Pang, C. (2011), *The Power of Cyber Communities Building Collective Life in China*, Oslo: University of Oslo.

Skarstein, R. (2010), 'Aksen USA/Kina og Ubalanser i Verdensøkonomien', in O. Madsen and S. Øyen (eds), *Markedets Fremtid*, Oslo: Cappelen Akademiske Forlag.

Saich, T. (2004), *Governance and Politics of China*, New York: Palgrave Macmillan.

Sæther, E. (2006), *The Polyphony of Critical Press Discourse in Chinese Media*, Oslo: Universitetsforlaget.

Tilly, C. (2004), *Social Movements, 1768–2004*, Boulder, CO: Paradigm Publishers.

Yan, Y. (2009), *The Individualization of Chinese Society*, London: London School of Economics.

Yang, G. (2009), *The Power of the Internet in China: Citizen Activism Online*, New York: Columbia University Press.

Yang, M. (1994), *Gifts, Favours, and Banquets: The Art of Social Relationships in China*, Ithaca, NY: Cornell University Press.

Zhou, Y. (2006), *Historicing Online Politics: Telegraphy, the Internet and Political Participation in China*, Stanford, CA: Stanford University Press.

16. The century belongs to all of us: East Asian regionalism and world society

Christopher M. Dent

1. INTRODUCTION

There remains much speculation concerning whether the 21st century will 'belong' to Asia. While there is value in considering Asia's future in the world system, ascribing 'ownership' of a future world epoch to any particular geopolitical power or construct may distract us from pursuing more crucial paths of scholarly enquiry. Given the escalating global-level challenges and problems that confront all humanity, it is more important to consider how may Asia, and particularly East Asia (the Asia continent's most geopolitically significant and coherent regional entity), contribute to resolving these challenges. I argue that they are best addressed by a formative world society, and that deepening regionalism in East Asia is in some way inter-constitutive to world society formation.

How the world's different nations, peoples and civilisations peacefully co-exist and co-operate with each other to deal with increasingly serious global-level challenges (for example environmental, poverty and energy related) may be thought of as prime meta-level issues of 21st century international relations. These challenges are best addressed by a collective worldwide response, and one that derives from a coherent association and unity of purpose between various forms of agency in the global system. The creation of different forms and structures of global governance represent an endeavour towards this end, but something deeper is required. As a general principle, it is when society as a whole takes ownership and responsibility for problems affecting all its members, even though the impact of these problems is asymmetric, that they are most successfully resolved. We should therefore work, at least in ideal terms, on the core premise that the 21st century belongs to us all rather than a certain geopolitical power or powers. This chapter argues that inherent to East Asia's deepening regionalism are particular forms of coherence – associative, integrational, organisational – that are also inherent to processes of world society formation. As such, regional community or society-building in East Asia may make potentially important contributions to the development of world society, and thereby concomitantly address global-level challenges.

2. THE 'OWNERSHIP' OF WORLD EPOCHS

The 'ownership' or 'co-ownership' of epochs in human civilisation has been a fixation for historians, other social scientists and futurists. We have in the past tended to define this in terms of empires (for example Roman, Mongolian, British) or dominant hub cultures (for example Egyptian, Mayan, Chinese), with the two often being synonymous with the other. Charting the rise and fall of great powers has derived from a similar scholarly interest (Kennedy 1988), focusing on structures and shifts in distributions of geopolitical power and influence. Long-wave theories of 'historic phase' development have adopted a somewhat different approach by highlighting more generalised economic, socio-cultural, political and technological forces emerging on a worldwide scale (Toffler 1980; Kondratiev 1984). Lines of this scholarly enquiry have in recent times increasingly converged with discourses on globalisation, and this in turn connects with debates over the 'domination' and 'ownership' of the emergent global system.

Returning to the historic context of 'great power' struggles, in the post-imperial era (that is, from the 1950s and 1960s onwards) opposing Cold War protagonists would still pejoratively refer to the other in imperial terms, and indeed both the United States and the Soviet Union possessed demonstrative features of quasi-imperial powers. After the demise of the Soviet Union in the early 1990s, the US appeared to be left standing in sole possession of such powers but by then the rules of the game had changed, from the geopolitical competition that defined the Cold War period to geoeconomic competition between the then dominant economic superpowers of the US, European Union and Japan. Accordingly, many scholars and analysts switched their attention to predicting which of these three 'triad' powers would come to dominate the 21st century (Thurow 1992; Albert 1993; Hart 1993).

The US's prospects of success were at this time by no means assured, although by the late 1990s they improved in light of East Asia's 1997/98 financial crisis, the disappointing economic performance of Europe's Single Market programme, the continued economic malaise of Japan, and America's economic renaissance enjoyed during the Clinton administration years. Subsequent predictions of the US's economic, socio-cultural and political supremacy into the early 21st century followed (Daalder and Lindsay 2003; Tremblay 2004). Yet these soon appeared premature after the evident 'imperial over-reach' revealed in its war against Iraq, the dynamic emergence of China as a challenging economic superpower, and the US's heavy dependence upon China, Japan and Middle East states to fund its burgeoning government deficit.

Furthermore, we may also speculate that (East) Asia's chances to 'dominate' the 21st century look reasonable, founded on China's ascendance, Japan's still formidable economic strengths and certain other regional-level dynamics and attributes. Indonesia and South Korea are also rising G20 powers, and Asia's global position is further augmented by India's own notable ascendance. However, there are inherent dangers in assigning this status to (East) Asia. While it is helpful to contemplate on the future nature and configurations of power, leadership and hegemony, what is most critically important to consider is how these best work in tackling serious global-level challenges facing all humanity.

3. THEORIES, CONCEPTS AND DEVELOPMENT OF WORLD SOCIETY

3.1 World Society in Context

The study of world society has been primarily based on a multidisciplinary fusion of international relations and sociological approaches. The general concept of 'society', deriving from the Latin word *societas*, may be defined as members of a group who voluntarily join forces to pursue goals that they are unable to achieve singularly (Martinelli 2005). The idea of an evolving 'world society' has gained increasing scholarly attention over recent years, and the now apparent rudiments of world society formation mark an historic stage in human civilisational development. As Martinelli (2005) observed, 'more and more people come to live in a single world system; a transnational civil society and an international public space are growing; a global communitarian culture and a cosmopolitan ethics are gaining ground' (p. 258). He further notes that the advent of world society has ultimately derived from expanding networks of social relations over time, 'a world association of peoples, nation-states, supranational unions, international organizations and transnational communities, who share a few core values of a cosmopolitan ethics and are integrated and regulated by a polyarchic form of democratic global governance' (p. 241). Shaw (1994) and other scholars equate world society with global society, synonymously representing 'a diverse social universe in which the unifying forces of modern production, markets, communications and cultural and political modernisation interact with many global, regional, national and local segmentations and differentiations' (Shaw 1994: 19). Jung (2001) contends, however, that whereas the evolution of a 'global society' represents simply a 'contingent historic process' (p. 451), 'world society' implies an ideal concept or construction of global integration. Thus, the development of *global* society (and globalisation more broadly), is more closely associated with modernity and modernisation, whereas *world* society derives more from idealist or revolutionary theoretical traditions.

Ideas concerning world society connect with various recent meta-level developments in international relations theory, such as the 'end of territoriality' (Ruggie 1993), 'retreat of the state' (Strange 1996), 'debordering the world of states' (Albert and Brock 2000), and globalisation generally. The makings of a world society also in some significant part derived from the long historic development of international society, or the 'society of states' as English School theorists of international relations alternatively refer to it. Watson (1992) charts the arrival of a 'European' international society in the early 19th century, what he refers to as the Concert of Europe's collective hegemony, and how this system formed the basis of a global-level international society through the latter 19th century and into the 20th century, culminating in the League of Nations.

From a geo-spatial perspective, different layers of society and social relations have always co-existed. The prevalence of local, national, international, regional and world societal forms are simultaneously possible but the development of one may be at the expense of another. The extent to which world society formation is at odds with local or national society (interests) depends on what kind of world society is being constructed. It is not the intent of this chapter to generally speculate on the future likely nature of any emergent world society. Considering the benefits of world society formation provides, though, a more useful analytical purpose when deliberating on its prospective relationship with regionalism and regional society formation. Firstly, worldwide problems are best addressed by a collective worldwide response, and one that derives from a coherent association and unity of purpose between various forms of agency in the international system. It is when society as a whole takes ownership and responsibility for problems affecting all members of that society – even if the impact of these problems is asymmetric – that they are most successfully resolved. In relation to causality and effect, addressing the various global-level (for example climate change, poverty alleviation, energy security) challenges currently facing all humanity itself contributes to the world society formation process by cultivating the politics of global-level responsibilities. Multilateral organisations and transnational civil society have been at the forefront of articulating these responsibilities, and moreover helping to create architectures of global governance and co-operation that in their own way lay stronger foundations on which world society may build. Secondly, world society formation – both as objective goal and process – marks the development of more harmonious relations amongst the world's peoples, and thus a *de facto* path towards conflict resolution and establishing a firmer basis for long-term peaceful co-existence on the planet.

3.2 Foundational Elements of World Society

According to Martinelli (2005), the foundational elements or empirical basis of world society can be generally viewed from the perspectives of cosmopolitan ethics, governance and transnational civil society. Martinelli offers a succinct summary of the key cosmopolitan ethics criteria that underpin the formation of world society:

- *Establishing and defining a basic set of common goals*: peace, human dignity, social justice, individual freedom, cultural pluralism, sustainable development.
- *A growing awareness of a common fate*: for example, our shared vulnerability to global environmental, social and political crises, for example poverty and unemployment, disease and pollution.
- *Worldwide sense of community*: specified in terms of *four basic types of consciousness*: the *anthropological* consciousness that recognizes unity in our diversity, the *ecological* consciousness that recognizes our singular human nature within the biosphere, the *civic* consciousness of our common responsibilities and solidarity, and the *dialogical* consciousness that refers both to the critical mind and to the need for mutual understanding;
- *Fostering a cultural attitude of contextual universalism*: that is, the fertile and non-destructive encounter of cultures and the according of mutual respect among different cultural outlooks (Robertson 1992; Beck 1997).
- *Significant level of cosmopolitan loyalty*: that may at times have to take precedence over national and other 'localised' obligations, for example where nation-state interests are in clear conflict with the global public good. This also entails a sense of common identity through which we are not indifferent to the suffering of others, and give the interests of others equal weight with our own (Nagel 1986).

- *Diffusion of the notion of multiple citizenships*: through which different overlapping identities (local, national regional and cosmopolitan) can define different sets of rights and responsibilities.

These are ideal types of cosmopolitan ethics criteria on which a strong world society would be constructed. Concerning governance, it should be noted initially how international law played a vital role in the early development of international society, encoding basic principles of humanitarianism into the behaviour of a 'civilised' society of states, helping foster the socialisation of states by that same process. As Armstrong (1999) observed, 'Humanitarian principles were written into the laws of war, and international law imposed increasing obligations on states to notify outbreaks of disease and take measures to deal with them . . . In the first half of the twentieth century the League of Nations saw a further extension of such institutionalized norms' (p. 549). He further notes that the creation of the United Nations Charter and multilateral environmental agreements such as the Kyoto Protocol represented further stages in this evolutionary process. The further advancement of international law may prove crucial to strengthening the governance structures of an emergent world society. There are in addition important organisational dimensions to consider. While there is the somewhat inevitable centralisation of management and control functions in the development of world systems, institutionalised co-operation and frameworks of 'global governance' that bring together elite decision-makers to work towards universal public goods can play a vital role in world society development. This involves the harmonisation or at least co-ordination or congruence of policies, the strengthening of supranational and international organisations and other forms of governance structure, the specification of rules for peaceful co-existence underwritten by shared principles of conduct and decision-making and the articulation of a co-operative ethos.

The evolution of global-level social relations and processes, creating transnational associative links amongst peoples across the planet, is a fundamental element to world society formation (Herkenrath 2007). The development of transnational civil society has primarily derived from the expansion of international collective movements, non-government organisations (NGOs), advocacy networks and epistemic communities. Many transnational NGOs champion the universal values or interests that unite all humanity, a growing awareness of our common fate as human beings, and the need for democratically accountable global governance structures and processes. Notwithstanding the advocacy of global harmony normally associated with transnational civil society, NGOs also occupy the extreme ends of social, ideological and religious spectrums and hence conflicts within transnational civil society arise here just as they do elsewhere in the world system. Thus, what kind of associative links between various disparate elements of transnational civil society are being forged is crucial to understanding their contribution to world society formation.

An emergent world society of sorts is currently apparent. However, judged in terms of the above criteria on cosmopolitan ethics, governance and transnational civil society, it has reached only a rudimentary level of development. As Martinelli (2005: 247) summarises:

> we live both in a single system and in a fragmented world. Globalization is marked by the tension between global economic and technological interdependence and social interconnectedness, on one hand, and cultural fragmentation and political division, on the other hand . . . the sentiment of a common human identity and some notion of world citizenship are still overwhelmed by national local, ethnic, religious separated and sometimes idiosyncratic identities.

3.3 Situating Concepts and Theories of World Society

Scholarship on world society has been generally situated in an inter-constitutive relationship with closely related concepts and theories. There are two general cases to consider, the first being in relation to world polity theory and world systems theory, and the second concerning ideas on the international system and international society.

World polity theory, world systems theory and world society

World polity theory primarily derives from 'Stanford School' scholars (Meyer et al. 1997) and focuses on the operations, structure and content of world culture and how this explains key aspects of global development. It emphasises the propagation of global cultural knowledge, principles and prescriptions that define, legitimise and shape the actions of state and non-state actors. This forms an important socio-political and socio-cultural basis for the formation of world society. World polity theorists saw world society as the medium through which 'global standards' of institutional, cultural and social practice were spread. However, the theory has been criticised for stressing the homogenising effects of globalisation and viewing global development as generally harmonious, and moreover for glossing over competition between multiple civilisational models (Western, East Asian, Islamic, and so on), persistent global inequalities and resistance to accepting global cultural principles such as women's equality (Boli 2007).

By way of contrast, original theorisation on world society tended to focus more on the 'social systemic' dimensions of world polity developments (Albert 2007). The first real holistic theory of world society was offered by Burton (1972), conceiving it in terms of ever denser 'cobwebs' of communicative relations amongst the world's social actors. He generally separated state and society when distinguishing between the system of states on the one hand, and world society on the other, and hence connections exists here with English School theory. A similar emphasis on communications was made by Luhmann (1995) who contended that the development of world society is founded essentially on the networked expansion of international communications systems in their various forms. Furthermore, world society is not primarily differentiated into 'segments' (for example nation-states or national societies) but rather into functional systems such as the political system, economic system, legal system, and so on. Meanwhile, Heintz (1982) postulated that world society was an overarching social system that had evolved from the expanding integrative development of various social systems around the world.

World systems theory also emphasises systemic integration but affords primacy to underlying economic and technological forces (Wallerstein 1978, 1979), emphasising how worldwide interaction networks have become gradually larger over time owing to developments in communication and transportation technologies. This is a long historic process that can be charted from the development of relatively small regionalised 'world systems' (for example the development of medieval Asian trading systems from 1000 to 1500) that expanded and merged to become planetary wide systems (Chase-Dunn and Hall 1997). In summarising relational aspects of the theory, Chase-Dunn (2007) noted that 'the modern world-system can be understood structurally as a stratification system composed of dominant core societies (themselves in competition with one another) and dependent peripheral and semi-peripheral regions' (p. 1306). These 'dependency' relationships are driven and determined by capitalist accumulation and geopolitics whereby states and firms – both managed by transnational capital class elites – compete for power and resources. This has close connections with neo-Marxist interpretations of world society as a structured transnationalised hierarchy of social classes based on identifiable strata: a world bourgeoisie, a world working class, a world peasantry, etc.

International system, international society and world society

Theorisation on world society formation has also been situated in a 'progressive development' context in relation to concepts of international system and international society. The World Society Research Group (2000) contended that an international system or systems gradually developed from deepening interactions and interdependence amongst peoples and nations. Based on such trends, international society then emerged, founded on the institutionalised collective regulation of behaviour between states through the establishment of collective norms and organisational coherence. World society hence represents the final progressive stage of this development, involving a greater diffusion of actors and greater differentiation of levels of action that is consistent with deepening trends of transnationalisation. Thus, world society is viewed here as being an extension or next evolutionary stage of international society based on the further development of transnationalising forces, and more specifically world society formation is founded on developments in both international society and transnational social relations (ibid.).

From a different analytical perspective, Buzan (2004) situates the concept of world society in English School thinking on international relations. To Buzan, the international system is viewed in a Hobbesian realist light as being about power politics amongst states where anarchy and inter-state rivalry prevail. The notion of international society – the flagship idea of the English School – is seen in a Grotian rationalist perspective, focusing on the institutionalisation of shared interests and identity amongst states. Here, the creation and maintenance of shared norms, rules and institutions lie at the core of international relations theory for English School scholars, and like (neo-)realist theory is based on an ontology of states. In contrast, world society can be viewed in generally Kantian idealist or revolutionist terms, transcending the states system as the analytical foci by considering individuals, non-state actors and ultimately the global demos as the basis of establishing global social identities and arrangements. Buzan's work presented a revisionary theoretical framework of English School thinking, also tackling the broader debate concerning state-centricity in international relations theory. Traditionally, the English School sought a middle road between the 'inter-national system' of realism and notions of 'world community' espoused by idealist thinkers (Brown 2001; Neumann 2001; Bellamy 2005). Core ideas on international society were founded on realist premises of nation-states being the primary actor where 'society' meant little more than an association of states whose mutual relationships are norm-governed (Bull 1977; Wight 1977). Furthermore, international society was viewed as a practical association or arrangement that allowed states to peacefully co-exist rather than embark on any synergistic project that aims to create anything bigger than the sum of its state-unit parts (Nardin 1983).

Building partly on the earlier work of Brown (2001), who acknowledged the importance of collective identity in the formation of world society, Buzan (2004) sought to incorporate constructivist thinking to English School theory, and in so doing take into account the greater density of inter-state and societal relations under the conditions of deepening globalisation. In applying the pluralism–solidarism debate concerning the nature and potentiality of international society (Falk 2005; Williams 2005), Buzan contended that pluralism defines 'second-order' societies of states with relatively low levels of shared norms, rules and institutions, and the primary concern of the group is establishing a framework for orderly co-existence and competition, with some attention to the collective management of common problems. Under the conditions of solidarism, international societies demonstrate a relatively high degree of shared norms, rules and institutions, and place a greater emphasis on co-operation, whether concerning the pursuit of joint gains, or the realisation of shared values. A solidarist international society thus errs towards the Kantian side of rationalism, and is hence more inclined to evolve into an ideal world society type.

4. EAST ASIAN REGIONALISM AND WORLD SOCIETY

4.1 Introduction

Regionalism may be considered as constituent to broader processes of internationalisation and globalisation. While some scholars argue that regional 'blocism' fragments the world system, the meta-elements of regionalism and globalisation are fundamentally similar, namely increasing levels of integration, connectivity and interdependence within a geo-spatial whole. Regionalism is also often a mediator between global and local responses to global challenges, and greater co-operation at the regional level can help resolve global-level challenges (Cooper et al. 2008; Herkenrath 2008). In basic terms, the pessimistic rival blocism view on the regionalism – world society relationship argues that competing regional blocs or groups pursue their own collective interests at the expense of others and with scant care for the global public good. Additionally, world society formation and other global projects are at risk of subjugation by regional powers (for example, the EU, China, Japan, Russia, India and Brazil) or other dominant actors (Nardin 1983). This is then essentially a realist perspective whereby region is a proxy for nation-state in an Orwellian anarchic inter-bloc world order. In contrast, the building bloc view contends that regionalism provides a foundation for world society development, helping condition both state and non-state actors to broader interactions in the world system, as well as cultivating international and transnational network linkages that make up the expanding global patchwork of such linkages.

Very little scholarly work has been undertaken on the regionalism–world society relationship. Munch (1996) provided an early study, commenting that, 'In the converging world society, we will have to get used to living in social units which do not have the same unity, stable identity or the associative, democratic and communicative substructure of the nation-states, but which nevertheless organize our actions' (p. 399). Using the EU as his empirical focus, he contended that regional collectives with a common identity are forged through three main processes: (i) outward demarcation and external struggles with third party powers; (ii) inner homogenisation processes; and (iii) inclusion, permitting wide participation and engagement in the collective unit and common identity project. Munch noted how European 'regional' identity-formation generally undermined national identity and helped define European interests more distinctly from non-European interests, thus pointing to the potential tensions arising between the interests of regions, nation-states and world society, and hence suggesting *rival blocist* outcomes.

According to Buzan (2004, 2005), most English School writers have mostly ignored the regional level of analysis when studying international society, or viewed it in negative 'rival blocism' terms concerning the development of global international society. However, Buzan viewed developments in regionalism increasingly in solidarist terms regarding international and world society formation. While acknowledging the problems of exclusivity arising from regionalist endeavours seeking to ascribe a political quality to regional cultural zones, such as 'Asian values', he asserts that 'sub-global' entities (for example regions) that exhibit solidarist features can provide the foundational basis of a stronger international and world society, thus complying with the building bloc argument. He identified East Asia, the EU and North America as the most salient sub-global interstate societies that are the more 'thickly developed' of all the global regions. In comparing these three, he notes that the EU is highly institutionalised and has programmatically pursued both social market and single market objectives. In comparison, NAFTA is less ambitious and organised primarily in accordance to neo-liberal rules. East Asia, meanwhile, 'has few institutions or formal rules and is largely organised by state-sanctioned private capital and a tiered system of development' (p. 209). He further noted that East Asia's international society is mostly 'coexistence' in character, arguing that the region possesses no overall shared culture beyond that already provided at the global level, and moreover exhibits strong adherence to nationalism and is far from constituting a security community. Buzan does concede, though, that there have been some moves towards greater co-operative solidarism in East Asia in recent years.

4.2 The 'Coherence' of East Asian Regionalism

East Asia and regionalism

East Asia is one of the world's most dynamic, diverse and important regions. Much of its contemporary significance derives from the dramatic economic transformation the region achieved in the second half of the 20th century. In 1960, East Asia accounted for only 4 percent of world gross domestic product (GDP) but by the mid-1990s this share had risen to around 25 percent. The region has become the new workshop of the world, the location of fast emerging markets, and a new financial power in the making. Japan had first spearheaded East Asia's economic rise up to the 1990s, and now China has become a major force behind the region's economic momentum. East Asia is also host to the world's highest concentration of newly industrialised economies, for example South Korea, Taiwan Singapore, Thailand and Malaysia. East Asia's economic advance was in many ways founded on the particular regional dynamics of shared developmentalist approaches to economic governance and the increasingly dense micro-level regionalisation of trade, investment and production linkages. Rising levels of functionally integrative economic interdependence within the region at the micro-level has been accompanied by greater endeavours of region-wide co-operation and integrative projects at the macro-level, that is involving whole countries. The formation of regional organisations and frameworks such as the Association of Southeast Asian Nations (ASEAN) and ASEAN Plus Three (APT) broadly derives from the need to manage regional interdependences as well as regional community-building in an emerging 'world of regions' (Katzenstein 2005).

Regionalism may be generally defined as the structures, processes and arrangements that are working towards greater coherence within a specific international region in terms of economic, political, security, socio-cultural and other kinds of linkages (Dent 2008). The key instrumental term in this definition is coherence, which itself concerns the uniting or unifying of different elements into new whole forms or entities. We may theorise that this coherence may take three generalized forms – associative, integrational and organisational – as outlined in Figure 16.1. The conceptual basis and underlying attributes of each form of coherence relates to its fundamental nature and characteristics, while principal unifiers relate to the prime forces or drivers (for example social, technological) in the formation of these different types of coherence.

Furthermore, regionalism is constituent to wider associative, integrational and organisational forces of coherence apparent within the world system, and can thus play a potentially important role in world society formation. Before we analyse the 'coherence interface' between regionalism

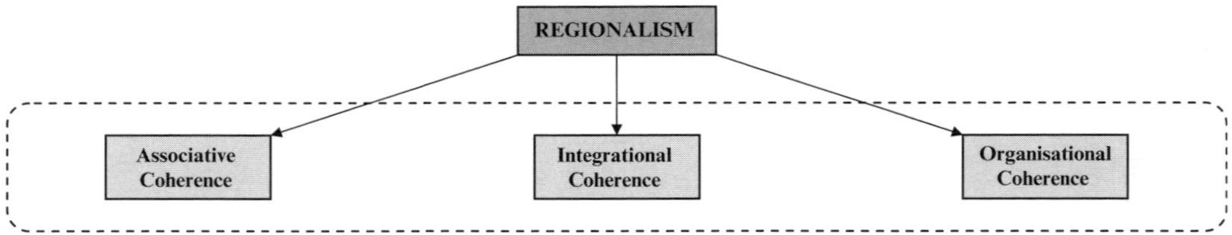

	Associative Coherence	Integrational Coherence	Organisational Coherence
Conceptual basis (and underlying attributes)	Relational (people, actor group and society-centred, informal [network] structures)	Technical (policy instrument-based, operationalised practice-oriented)	Systemic (governance-based, formalised structures)
Principal unifiers	Social, cultural	Technological, technocratic	Political, corporate
Main processes	Socialisation through economic, political, cultural and other forms of exchange Identification of common or inter-linked interests at the regional level Regional identity and community formation Issue-determined forms of association, and association through issue-linkage	Regionalisation of business and other civil sector technical activities Transborder infrastructure link-ups 'Passive integration' – commercial policy liberalisation and deregulation. 'Proactive integration' – policy cooperation, coordination, harmonisation (including on infrastructure)	Formation of regional organisations, frameworks, agreements and networked systems
Prime manifest examples (or empirical domain)	Region-wide social movements and networks of social relations that are common interest or issue based (e.g. social justice, commercial affairs) Shared region-wide experiences and phenomena, (e.g. popular culture, 'haze' pollution) Transnational business communities Inter-governmental policy networks/communities International migration networks	National economies become more integrated through the creation of transborder and regional economic spaces. Technical development of IPNs/RPNs, creation of region-wide business mechanisms and processes Deepening intra-regional economic relations that are becoming increasingly functionally integrative 'Natural' growth polygons, (e.g. SCSGT) Commercial liberalisation projects (e.g. AFTA, bilateral FTAs), economic cooperation measures (e.g. APEC's ecotech programmes), financial policy cooperation/ coordination (e.g. CMI, ABMI)	Governance of regionalised business systems, (e.g. of IPNs/RPNs) Regionalised governance of NGOs 'Governed' growth polygons, (e.g. GMS, IMSGT, TRADP) Regional organisations, (e.g. ASEAN, APEC, ADB) Regional frameworks, (e.g. APT, EAS)

Figure 16.1 Regionalism as coherence: main framework

and world society formation, we should first acknowledge that various obstacles have lain in the path of deepening East Asian regionalism. East Asia is probably the most diverse region in the world in terms of economic development asymmetry, mix of political regimes and socio-religious traditions and characteristics. Moreover, it is a region marked by historic animosities between rival nations, of where conflicts still persist between old and new states alike, and where nationalism remains a potent force in many countries of the region. Regional community-building in East Asia remains a difficult endeavour, and yet significant progress has been made. This is evident in terms of deepening region-wide economic exchange, cross-border infrastructural linkages, international policy co-operation and co-ordination (including regional organisation development), social movements, shared popular culture, and various socialisation processes occurring amongst the peoples and societies of East Asia. In overcoming numerous constraints of diversity and division, the various manifestations of East Asian regionalism has demonstrated the ability of the region's actors to positively interact and co-operate in the international system, thereby conditioning them to participation in wider forms of international and world society. In this sense, engagement in East Asia's emerging regional society may lead to a progressive engagement with world society. The following analyses of associative, integrational and organisational coherence consider both their respective progress in relation to East Asian regionalism and their connections with world society formation, with some comment on the prospective and inter-connected futures of both these aspects.

Associative coherence

This first form of coherence is essentially a relational concept, its principal unifiers being social and cultural in nature. Regionalism cannot effectively advance without the strengthening of associative links amongst people, groups and societies within the region concerned. Moreover, East Asia's regional community-building is grounded in various region-wide socialisation processes stemming from intensifying intra-regional economic, social, political, cultural and other forms of exchange. Government officials from different East Asian countries are meeting on an increasingly regular basis in regional and other international fora, building up inter-governmental policy networks and communities within the region. The expansion of international production network (IPN) activity and other forms of transnational business operations in East Asia are more closely networking companies together on a regional basis. A similar trend is apparent in East Asia's civil society sector as NGOs seek to develop stronger associative ties with each other across the region (Curley 2007). The growth of international labour migration is further deepening inter-societal exchanges within East Asia (Ito 2004), while the expansion of pan-regional social and cultural movements – especially developments in East Asian popular culture (for example Japanese cartoons and karaoke, Korean pop music, Star TV) – have also in their own way fortified associative links amongst the peoples of East Asia (Pempel 2005). Furthermore, the greater openness of East Asian countries to the popular culture influences of other East Asian countries have arguably made East Asians more open to global and other foreign forms of popular culture, albeit still largely Western dominated. East Asians have thus become more conducive to adopting particular forms and levels of cosmopolitan ethics underpinning world society formation, albeit to a still limited degree, yet positive movement in this direction is an observable aspect of East Asian regionalism.

While the associative coherence of East Asian regionalism has progressively strengthened over recent years, the aforementioned diversities and divisions amongst the region's states and people remains a considerable hindrance. If East Asia's peoples are unlikely to develop a stronger sense of shared norms and values at the regional level, then their propensity for adherence to a broader world of cosmopolitan ethics would appear low. In specific reference to Martinelli's (2005) criteria here, East Asia's regional organisations and frameworks (for example ASEAN and APT) have made some progress, especially since the 1997/98 financial crisis, on establishing and defining a basic set of common goals, as detailed under 'organisational coherence'. There is also a growing awareness of a common fate arising out of new security sector concerns – the most important being energy, food and environment – and these transnational issues are being more seriously addressed through sub-regional and regional level co-operation. For example, in January 2007 at the second East Asia Summit (EAS) meeting, leaders of the group's 16 member states signed a Declaration on Energy Security, committing them to reduce the region's dependence on conventional fuels, explore options for stockpiling oil and developing renewable energy capacity, and improving energy efficiency. A biennial Pacific Energy Summit process was initiated in 2009, bringing together government, business and civil society leaders to discuss regional energy security matters.

More generally, the associative coherence of East Asian regionalism has also derived from the identification of common or inter-linked interests amongst region's actors, for example on matters of commercial practice, cultural behaviour, environmental concerns, political ideology, socio-religious belief, and so on. Similarly, associative links have been in some cases largely issue-determined, with actor-based networks forming around particular region-wide issues, such as those related to matters of humanitarian missions (for example the 2004 Asian tsunami disaster), social justice, environment, consumer affairs, and so on. These regional-level interests and issues are invariably linked to global-level forms of association (regional networks as part of global networked agency) and global-level challenges, and is illustrative of how we may think generally of regional coherence as being embedded in global coherence. For example, transnational environmental concerns, such as Southeast Asia's forest fire haze problem and transborder acid rain zones, have raised awareness in East Asia of global ecological issues. The extent to which this has engendered a stronger ecological and civic basis of worldwide sense of community in East Asia is, though, debatable. Moreover, the deep vein of nationalism running through many East Asian states combined with the social, cultural and religious diversity of the region pose notable challenges in the region's contribution to world society formation with respect to fostering a cultural attitude of contextual universalism and establishing a significant level of cosmopolitan loyalty. The World Society Research Group (2000) noted, for example, how at the 1993 Vienna Human Rights Conference, ASEAN spoke critically of what they perceived as a particularist Western philosophical tradition concerning human rights, contrasting this with 'Asian values' informed perspectives on the issue. This is just one of many instances of Asian and other sources of resistance against Western-style universalism that have arisen.

Notwithstanding these constraints, East Asians, like other peoples around the world, are capable of accepting notions of multiple citizenships, as individuals maintaining multi-layered identities, for instance as simultaneously Shanghaiese, Chinese, East Asian and world citizen. This can, however, depend simultaneously on the social and geographic mobility of the individuals concerned, and most East Asians still move within relatively small socio-geographic localities, thus reducing their scope for engendering wider associative links on a regional and wider international basis.

Integrational coherence

This second coherence type is essentially a technical-related concept that considers the mechanisms and modalities by which integrative links are being forged within a region (Figure 16.1). The principal unifiers of integrational coherence are essentially technological and technocratic, and its underlying attributes are policy instrument-based and operationalised practice-oriented. Hence, the technical practices of both firms and governments are particularly relevant, such as the expansion of IPN operations and how transportation and communications technologies are forging regional infrastructure networks. From a geographic perspective, this can be understood in both networked and zonal terms concerning various patterns of integrated activities and how these have enhanced region-scale economic and social mobility. Integrational coherence thus provides an important practical means for facilitating associative coherence by enabling the expansion of intra-regional contacts in East Asia. Close connections exist with world systems theory as particular emphasis is afforded to systemic integration and the primacy of underlying economic and technological forces. We noted earlier the idea of how the 'modern' world system was in one way constructed through the integration of regionalised systems of commerce, for example the European and the Asian many centuries ago.

East Asia's regional infrastructure development is amongst the densest zones of such development in the world (see Figure 16.2), yet has been embedded in, and has also contributed to the expansion of global infrastructure networks. The same applies to the development of East Asia's regionalised IPNs that are invariably integral to global production networks (Figure 16.3). These developments have cultivated transnational social relations both inside East Asia and with the region's social relations with the rest of the world through higher facilitated levels of commerce, tourism, migration and other modes of social interaction. Moreover, they further illustrate the important role played by 'world cities' – in East Asia and elsewhere – as key hub centres on which the network development of regionalisation and a rudimentary world society have been concomitantly based (Knight and Gappert 1989; Smith 2004; Dent 2008). The importance of integrational coherence is consistent with the emphasis early world society theorists such as Burton (1972) and Luhmann (1995) placed on the networked expansion of communications generally, and the inter-constituent links between integrational and associative coherence are clearly evident here.

From a more economistic and policy-oriented perspective, the passive integration (for example trade liberalisation) and proactive integration (for example policy co-operation, co-ordination and harmonisation measures) technical programmes have strengthened the macro-level integrational coherence of East Asian regionalism by binding together the region's firms and national economies into more functionally integrative relationships. Passive integration measures are so called because they essentially involve the removal or reduction of barriers impeding economic exchange between countries. They do not entail the formation of common, congruent or co-ordinated technical policy elements amongst international or regional partners as such, unlike proactive integration measures. East Asia's recent proliferation of free trade agreements (FTAs) or economic partnership agreements (EPAs) tend to fall into the passive integration category,

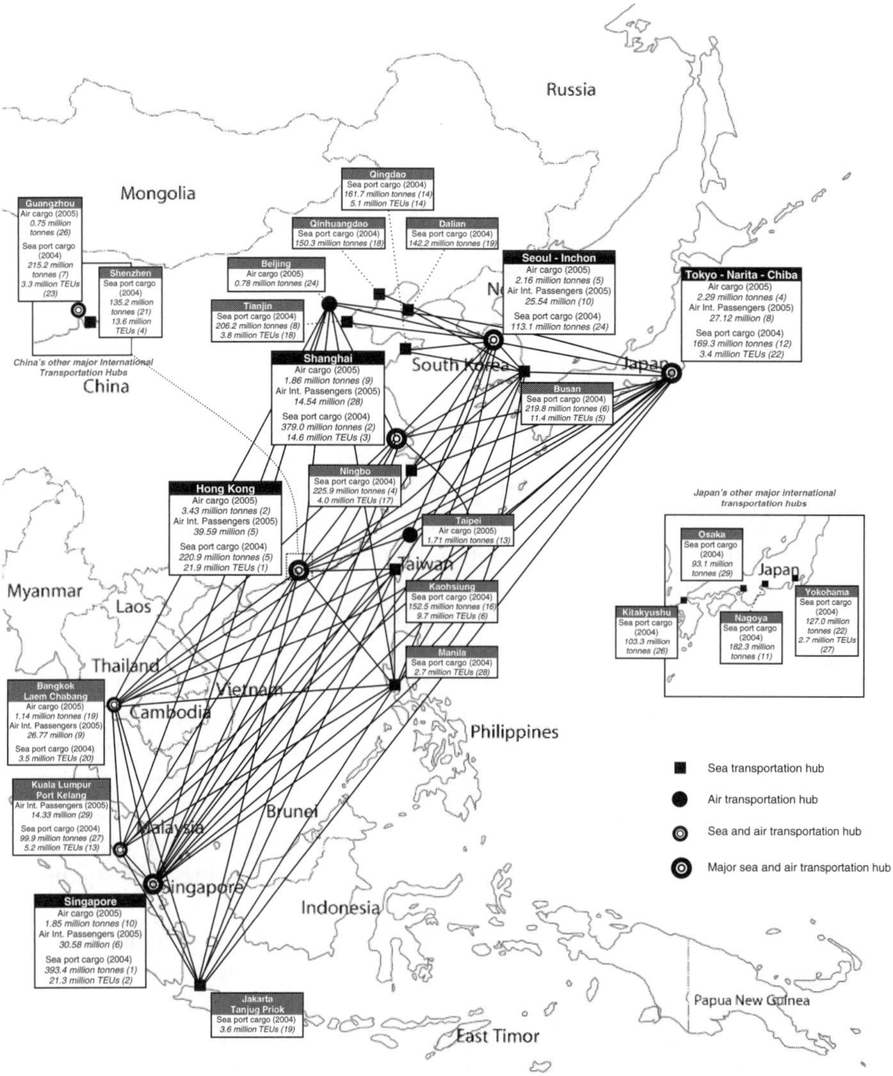

Notes: Numbers in brackets relate to world ranking for that transportation volume. Only those East Asian air and sea transportation hubs (that is, airports and sea ports) that were ranked in the world top 30 have been included. Port names have been included where these are not the same as the city hub to which they are linked, for example, Kuala Lumpur and Port Kelang. TEUs (twenty-foot equivalent units) relate to container capacity.

Sources: Airports Council International, American Association of Port Authorities.

Figure 16.2 East Asia's main regional transportation hubs and corridors

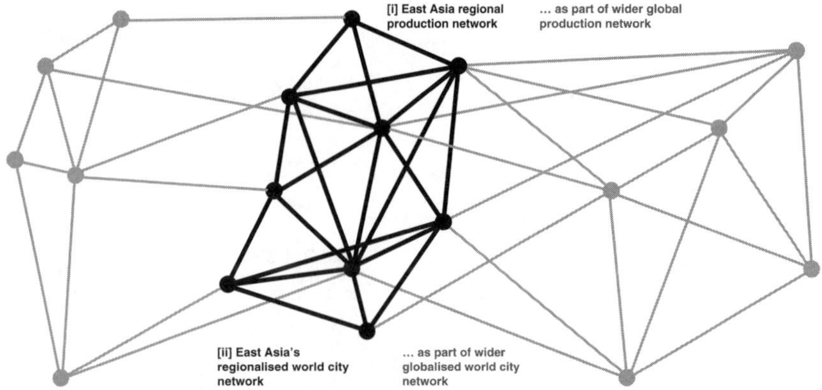

Figure 16.3 Regional networks embedded in global networks

while programmes such as APT's Chiang Mai Initiative Multilateralised (a US$120 billion regional system of currency swap agreements amongst APT member states) and Asian Bond Market Initiative (a region-wide plan to foster bond market development, also devised to strengthen regional financial governance in East Asia) of a proactive integration nature. The deeper commitments made by East Asian governments to passive and proactive integration have conditioned the region's state and non-state actors generally to interaction within the global economy, and the policy-related demands of global-multilateral economic institution membership. For example, China would not have been able to play a leading advocacy role on behalf of developing countries worldwide within the World Trade Organisation if it had not first embarked on a course of passive and proactive integration, and connections exist here with organisational coherence as we later discuss.

The integrational coherence of East Asian regionalism remains weak, though, in a number of areas, most significantly concerning the pronounced 'development divide' that persists between relatively well-developed core zones of the region and much less-developed periphery zones. East Asia's most advanced economic development is concentrated along a pan-regional development corridor a few hundred miles wide ranging from Japan and northeast China down through to Singapore in Southeast Asia, as revealed by the density pattern of regional infrastructure networks links in Figure 16.2. Those parts of East Asia that lie outside this main development corridor (for example deep interior provinces in China, eastern Indonesia, Myanmar, Mongolia) have limited engagement with the region's integrational dynamics. East Asia's development divide is thus apparent at both the macro-level (that is, whole countries) and the micro-level where capital or world cities dominate their home country's participation in regional trade, investment and other forms of economic exchange. With further relevance to world system theory, dependency relationships between East Asia's core and periphery economic and social development zones expose certain divisions and fragmentation in East Asia's regional society. Such a constraint on regional community-building also poses a corresponding challenge to East Asia's contribution to world society formation. As world systems theorists argue, stable regional and world societies are difficult to achieve and maintain when pronounced dependency relationships persist.

Organisational coherence

This third and last coherence type may be generally conceptualised in systemic terms, and is primarily concerned with how regionalism – and thereby its different aspects of associative and integrational coherence – may take some kind of organisational form. Its underlying attributes are governance-based, while political (that is government or state) and corporate (that is private or civil sector, either acting separately or with the state) actions are the principal unifiers of organisational coherence. Regional organisations and frameworks of which East Asian countries are members (for example ASEAN, APT, EAS) are more obvious examples, as are the region-wide governance structures created by NGOs such as Greenpeace, and the governance-related and systemic development of regionalised IPNs. East Asia is also host to a growing number of regional-level associations (for example Asian Network of Major Cities), regional NGO networks (for example Southeast Asia Rivers Network, Rivers Watch East and Southeast Asia) and regionally organised, multi-sector (that is public, private, civil) consultative mechanisms (for example East Asian Business Council and Asian Bellagio Group).

On the one hand, regional organisations and frameworks, more than any other manifestation of regionalism, define the exclusivity of regional formations and thus regions as defined separate entities in the international system, a point stressed by the 'rival blocism' argument. On the other hand, the very notion of the East Asia region – and thus which nations and peoples are legitimate members of it – is contested and in flux. The debate over whether Australia, New Zealand and India qualified for EAS membership is a case in point. Moreover, as Figure 16.4 shows, East Asian countries are party to a wide range of regional-overlapping organisations and frameworks that extend into the wider Asia continent and Asia-Pacific trans-region. There are thus extra dimensions to this aspect of East Asian regionalism's organisational coherence that are non-exclusive in a geo-spatially defined sense, and where extended and multiple

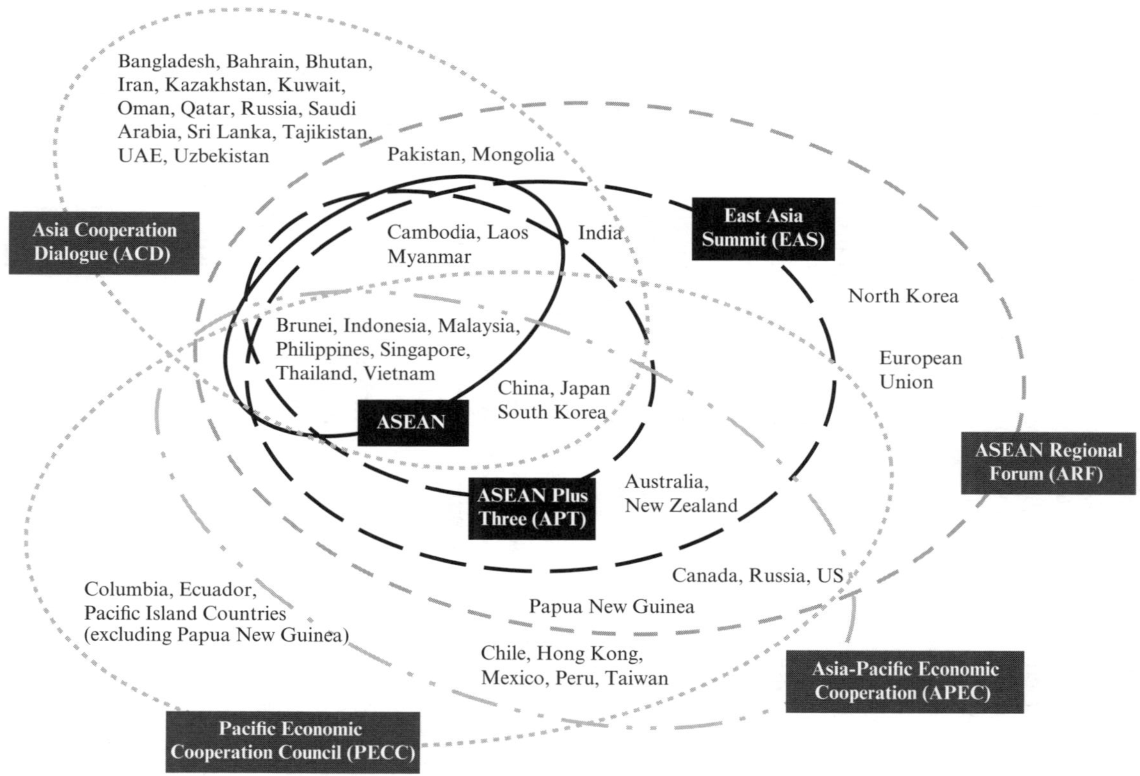

Figure 16.4 Main regional organisations and frameworks involving East Asia

memberships of region-based arrangements or 'neighbourhoods' have become the norm. Hence, and in connection with associative coherence, a number of East Asian countries may simultaneously identify themselves as being 'East Asian', 'Asian', 'Asia-Pacific', or constituent to some other international society grouping that cuts across many regions, for example G8, OECD, G20, Cairns Group.

The deepening participation of East Asian nations in regional organisations and frameworks is, then, creating overlapping 'society of states' arrangements in and around the region. While some may be seen in competition with each other in a 'contested regionalism' or 'rival blocist' sense (for example the 'East Asian' APT versus the 'Asia-Pacific' APEC), other arrangements are at least in principle supposed to work in tandem with one another, most significantly ASEAN, APT and EAS. These three arrangements have between them made steady progress at establishing rules of co-operative and integrative engagement between nation-states with long histories of adversarial relations. Notwithstanding the discord and animosity that persist between many East Asian countries, regional organisations and frameworks have helped delineate shared interests, norms and practical measures towards resolving mutual problems and challenges facing East Asian regional society, as previously alluded to in the associative coherence section. An important example of this has been the APT's work on strengthening various forms of regional financial governance after the 1997/98 East Asian financial crisis. Another is the ASEAN Charter, signed by Southeast Asian countries in November 2007 that aims to codify shared norms and rules of conduct for creating stronger economic, social-cultural and security communities in the region. These regional organisations and frameworks have afforded greater attention to addressing the region's development divide (for example the Initiative for ASEAN Integration), albeit it in a somewhat limited way to date.

East Asian states' participation in regional frameworks and organisations may be viewed in 'building blocist' terms if one argues it constitutes stronger exercises of international society practice, and that solidarist advances in international society may be considered evolutionary progress towards world society formation. Furthermore, ASEAN, APT, EAS and so on should look to develop their multilateral utility by helping construct and strengthen different forms of global governance (Dent 2004). However, these aspects of organisational coherence will continue to be generally weak while East Asia's regional organisations remain under-institutionalised. This particularly relates to regional institutions charged with overseeing various common regional policy-making processes and structures. In comparison to Europe, it will be some time before East Asian countries prove ready to pool their sovereignty to the levels required to create regional institutions such as the EU's European Commission and European Central Bank. East Asia also lacks a region-specific legal framework, although deeper participation in regional organisations and frameworks may induce or condition greater East Asian nation-state compliance to international law, depending on how those regional organisations and frameworks themselves develop, as well as their relationships with different forms of global governance.

5. CONCLUSION

Speculating on whether the 21st century will 'belong' to Asia or any other geo-political power or construct is an interesting and useful scholarly exercise to undertake. Yet an even more important question to ask is how East Asia will contribute to the future development of world society. This is premised on the argument that deepening global-level challenges (for example environmental, poverty and energy related) are best addressed by a collective worldwide response based on a coherent association and unity of purpose between various forms of agency in the international system. This is the essence of world society, where its constituent members collectively take ownership and responsibility for problems affecting all members of the global demos, no matter how asymmetric the impact of those problems.

We should thus think more in terms of the 21st century belonging to us all, and how East Asia can play a significant constructive role in world society formation. The further development of East Asian regionalism is highly relevant here because of the scope to exploit an inter-constitutive relationship that exists between regionalism and world society formation. This has been explored from the conceptual perspectives of associative, integrational and organisational coherence. Assessing the extent, levels and qualitative progress in the different forms of coherence to East Asian regionalism can be difficult to quantify, and moreover the interpretation of outcomes is contested and open to debate. The same applies to the extent of the 'coherence interface' between East Asian society and world formation, and the degree to which regionalising trends in East Asia are making solidarist contributions to the development of world society. We can, however, make informed observational analyses of current trends in these areas from which some form of reasoned assessment and speculation can be made on this issue.

Both the opportunities and constraints of East Asia's deepening regionalism to fostering the future development of world society were noted, as were connections with parallel or linked theories. For example, there exist close inter-linkages regarding integrational coherence between East Asian regionalism and world system development. In addition, recent macro-level developments in the organisational coherence of East Asian regionalism – especially concerning regional organisations and frameworks – have strengthened international society arrangements in the region. It was generally argued that various aspects of East Asian regionalism are embedded within or constituent to broader worldwide processes of associative, integrational and organisational coherence, making it difficult at times to disaggregate the regional from the global, be these of an economic (for example trade, investment and finance generally), socio-cultural (for example rise of middle class consumerism and mass popular culture), socio-political (for example regional and global NGO network formation) or other nature. This is an essential aspect of the regionalism–world society relationship. Ultimately, the prospects for East Asia contributing positively to world society formation and addressing the increasingly serious global-level problems that confront all humanity depends primarily on what kind of East Asia regionalism develops in the future. That which connects the regional with globally aligning forms of association, governance, co-operation and responsibility as the 21st century unfolds offer the most promising prospects for achieving this.

REFERENCES

Albert, M. (2007), 'World society theory', in R. Robertson and J.A. Scholte (eds), *Encyclopaedia of Globalisation*, London: Routledge.

Albert, M. and L. Brock (2000), 'Debordering the world of states: new spaces in international relations', in M. Albert, L. Brock and K.D. Wolf (eds), *Civilising World Politics: Society and Community Beyond the State*, London: Rowan and Littlefield.

Armstrong, D. (1999), 'Law, Justice and the Idea of a World Society', *International Affairs*, **75**(3), 547–61.

Beck, U. (1997), *What is Globalisation?*, Frankfurt, Germany: Suhrkamp.

Bellamy, A. (2005), 'Conclusion: whither international society', in A.J. Bellamy (ed.), *International Society and its Critics*, Oxford: Oxford University Press.

Boli, J. (2007), 'World polity theory', in R. Robertson and J.A. Scholte (eds), *Encyclopaedia of Globalisation*, London: Routledge.

Brown, C. (2001), 'World society and the English School: an international society perspective on world society', *European Journal of International Relations*, **7**(4), 423–41.

Bull, H. (1977), *The Anarchical Society*, London: Macmillan.

Burton, J. (1972), *World Society*, Cambridge: Cambridge University Press.

Buzan, B. (2004), *From International to World Society? English School Theory and the Social Structure of Globalisation*, Cambridge: Cambridge University Press.

Buzan, B. (2005), 'International political economy and globalisation', in A.J. Bellamy (ed.), *International Society and its Critics*, Oxford: Oxford University Press.
Chase-Dunn, C. (2007), 'World-systems theory', in R. Robertson and J.A. Scholte (eds), *Encyclopaedia of Globalisation*, London: Routledge.
Chase-Dunn, C. and T.D. Hall (1997), *Rise and Demise: Comparing World Systems*, Boulder, CO: Westview.
Cooper, A.F., C.W. Hughes and de P. Lombaerde (eds) (2008), *Regionalisation and Global Governance: The Taming of Globalisation*, London: Routledge.
Curley, M.G. (2007), 'The Role of civil society in East Asian region building', in M.G. Curley and N. Thomas (eds), *Advancing East Asian Regionalism*, London: Routledge.
Daalder, I.H. and J.M. Lindsay (2003), *America Unbound: The Bush Revolution in Foreign Policy*, Washington, DC: Brookings Institution.
Dent, C.M. (2004), 'The Asia–Europe meeting (ASEM) and inter-regionalism: towards a theory of multilateral utility', *Asian Survey*, **44**(2), 213–36.
Dent, C.M. (2008), *East Asian Regionalism*, London: Routledge.
Falk, R. (2005), '(Re)imagining the governance of globalisation', in A.J. Bellamy (ed.), *International Society and its Critics*, Oxford: Oxford University Press.
Heintz, P. (1982), *Die Weltgesellschaft im Spiegel von Ereignissen*, Diessenhofen, Switzerland: Ruegger.
Herkenrath, M. (ed.) (2007), *Civil Society – Local and Regional Responses to Global Challenges*, Münster, Germany: Lit Verlag.
Herkenrath, M. (ed.) (2008), *The Regional and Local Shaping of World Society*, Zurich, Switzerland: World Society Foundation.
Ito, S. (2004), 'The issues and prospects of international migration in East Asia', *The Japanese Economy*, **32**(2), 113–38.
Jung, D. (2001), 'The political sociology of world society', *European Journal of International Relations*, **7**(4), 443–74.
Katzenstein, P.J. (2005), *A World of Regions: Asia and Europe in the American Imperium*, Ithaca, NY: Cornell University Press.
Kennedy, P. (1988), *The Rise and Fall of the Great Powers: Economic Change and Military Conflict from 1500 to 2000*, London: Fontana.
Kondratiev, N.D. (1984), *The Long Wave Cycle*, New York: Richardson and Snyder.
Knight, R.V. and G. Gappert, (eds) (1983), *Cities in a Global Society*, London: Sage.
Luhmann, N. (1995), *Social Systems*, Stanford, CA: Stanford University Press.
Martinelli, A. (2005), 'From world system to world society', *Journal of World Systems Research*, **11**(2), 240–60.
Meyer, J.W., J. Boli, G.M. Thomas and F.O. Ramirez (1997), 'World society and the nation-state', *American Journal of Sociology*, **103**(1), 144–81.
Munch, R. (1996), 'Between nation-state, regionalism and world society: the European integration process', *Journal of Common Market Studies*, **34**(3), 379–401.
Nagel, T. (1986), *The View from Nowhere*, Oxford: Oxford University Press.
Nardin, T. (1983), *Law, Morality, and the Relations of States*, Princeton, NJ: Princeton University Press.
Neumann, I.B. (2001), 'The English School and the practices of world society', *Review of International Studies*, **27**, 503–7.

Pempel, T.J. (2005), 'Introduction: emerging webs of regional connectedness', in T.J. Pempel (ed.), *Remapping East Asia: The Construction of a Region*, Ithaca, NY: Cornell University Press.
Robertson, R. (1992), *Globalisation, Social Theory and Global Culture*, London: Sage.
Ruggie, J.G. (1993), 'Territoriality and beyond: problematising modernity in international relations', *International Organisation*, **47**(1), 139–74.
Shaw, M. (1994), *Global Society and International Relations*, London: Polity Press.
Smith, D.A. (2004), 'Global cities in East Asia: empirical and conceptual analysis', *International Social Science Journal*, **56**(3), 399–412.
Strange, S. (1996), *The Retreat of the State: The Diffusion of Power in the World Economy*, Cambridge: Cambridge University Press.
Toffler, A. (1980), *The Third Wave*, New York: Bantam Books.
Tremblay, R. (2004), *The New American Empire*, West Conshohocken, PA: Infinity.
Wallerstein, I. (1978), 'World system analysis: theoretical and interpretative issues', in B.B. Kaplan (ed.), *Social Change in the Capitalist World Economy*, Beverly Hills, CA: Sage.
Wallerstein, I. (1979), *The Capitalist World Economy*, Cambridge: Cambridge University Press.
Watson, A. (1992), *The Evolution of International Society: A Comparative Historical Analysis*, London: Routledge.
Wight, M. (1977), *Systems of States*, Leicester: Leicester University Press.
Williams, J. (2005), 'Pluralism, solidarism and the emergence of world society in English School theory', *International Relations*, **19**, 19–38.
World Society Research Group (2000), 'Introduction: world society', in M. Albert, L. Brock and K.D. Wolf (eds), *Civilising World Politics: Society and Community Beyond the State*, London: Rowan and Littlefield.

Index